THE EXCELLENT AND PLEASANT WORKE

COLLECTANEA RERUM MEMORABILIUM

THE EXCELLENT AND PLEASANT WORKE

COLLECTANEA RERUM MEMORABILIUM

OF

GAIUS JULIUS SOLINUS

TRANSLATED FROM THE LATIN

(1587)

BY

ARTHUR GOLDING

A FACSIMILE REPRODUCTION
WITH AN INTRODUCTION

BY

GEORGE KISH
University of Michigan

Gainesville, Florida
SCHOLARS' FACSIMILES & REPRINTS
1955

Scholars' Facsimiles & Reprints
118 N.W 26th Street
Gainesville, Florida

Harry R. Warfel, General Editor

REPRODUCED FROM A COPY IN,
AND WITH THE PERMISSION OF,
THE WILLIAM L. CLEMENTS LIBRARY
of the University of Michigan

L. C. Card Number 55-10771

PRINTED IN THE U.S.A.
LETTERPRESS BY WAYSIDE PRESS
LITHOPRINTING BY EDWARDS BROTHERS
BINDING BY UNIVERSAL-DIXIE BINDERY

"habent sua fata libelli . . ."

INTRODUCTION

Caius Julius Solinus' *Collectanea Rerum Memorabilium* is a description of the lands and peoples, of the products and marvels, and of the world known to third-century Romans. The book enjoyed unabated popularity for over a thousand years. Solinus' word was taken for unchallenged truth by the great bishop Isidore of Seville, when he wrote his encyclopedic *Etymologiae* in the seventh century. Solinus' statements are mirrored with equal faith in the great world maps of the schoolmen of the late Middle Ages and in the Hereford and Ebstorf maps of the thirteenth century. His tales, be they ever so tall, appealed to the imagination of the men of the Dark Ages, and the book was still of enough interest to warrant reprinting both in the original Latin and in translations into the languages spoken in sixteenth-century Europe.

Yet if "books have their fate," surely this one does not deserve the place of honor it held for so long. It is a strange hotchpotch of a few facts and scores of fictitious statements. It is an inferior compilation, not only by the standards of our time but even by comparison with the works of Greek and Roman writers who had preceded the author by centuries. Still, it would be misleading to judge Solinus' book as we would the geographies of Herodotus or Strabo. This work was written in a time of stress. It is an image of the fabulous and unattainable, destined to appeal to men whose own world offered so little to distract the imagination.

Caius Julius Solinus, nicknamed Polyhistor, "he who tells of many things," was a Roman citizen. Nothing is known about the man beyond his name and the book attributed to him in over one hundred and fifty manuscript copies still extant from the ninth and tenth centuries of the Christian era. It seems certain that he lived and wrote in Italy during the third century A.D. His omission of any reference to Christianity and his use of the name Byzantium for Constantinople give evidence that he was active during the middle years of the third century. Perhaps, in the words of the Introduction to Golding's translation, "he left other monuments also of his wit, which either by force of time are perished, or else perchance lie hid in some blind corner among moths." But this collection is the only one known to have survived.

The third century was an era of domestic strife and foreign invasions in the Roman Empire. It was a time of clashes between rival emperors, who were raised on the shields of the armies they commanded, only to vanish within a brief span of time into oblivion. The Empire was threatened by the Barbarians from without, by civil war from within. The peace and prosperity of the age of the Antonines that Gibbon nostalgically called "the golden age of mankind" had long since vanished. In the words of H. A. L. Fisher: "Gradually, the towns shrank in size, and being walled to meet the hazards of the third century, lost something of the abundance and expansiveness of their earlier life; . . . long before the Roman Empire went down, its cities had adopted the medieval livery of fear."

The third century was a time of decline. In the words of Saint Cyprian, there were not enough farmers to till the fields, not enough sailors to man the ships, not enough soldiers to guard the Empire. Inflation was undermining the economy of the Roman Empire, while civil and foreign wars drained its best resources. And with this decline in the material resources went a decline of the arts and letters. The world had shrunk since the days of Herodotus, eight hundred years before. Essentially, it consisted of the lands surrounding the Mediterranean and the Black Sea; northern and western Europe; Africa north of the Sahara; and of glimpses of Central Asia, China, India, and Ceylon.

Solinus, who is considered to be a true representative of his time, certainly cuts a very inferior figure to the great masters of Latin style who had gone before him. He is the first to admit his shortcomings; he says in his Epistle Dedicatorie, "For what can we call properly our own, since the diligence of men in old times had been such that nothing had remained untouched unto our days?" This melancholy confession is borne out by a careful examination of the sources upon which Solinus drew for his work. Nearly nine-tenths of the material contained in it is copied from Pliny the Elder's great *Natural History*. The rest comes from a variety of sources, none of which is outstanding in quality.

The emphasis throughout the book is on the marvelous, the unusual, the unbelievable. But the marvels described by Solinus caught the imagination of his contemporaries and of his successors. Mommsen, in his magnificent critical edition of the book, has painstakingly counted the number of statements found in the works of later authors and obviously derived from Solinus. The citations run into the hundreds. It is indeed safe to say that no other book of geography had remained popular as long as Solinus'. He is the authority quoted by the schoolmen for centuries after Europeans possessed first-hand information on the countries he wrote about.

Solinus had access to information of all kinds. Some of it is remarkably accurate, such as the description of suttee, the burning of widows in India, or the story of the pearls of Ceylon. Other items are frankly fabulous: the men with one eye, the men with one foot, the basilisk, the men and beasts existing on air alone. No effort was spared to make the recital complete, for, as Solinus says, "Surely it is not expedient to omit any thing, wherein the providence of nature is to be seen."

Arthur Golding (1536?-1605?), the author of this—the only English—translation of Solinus' *Collectanea,* was a distinguished man of letters of the sixteenth century. He is assumed to have been a native of London, and there is a tradition, as yet unsubstantiated, that he was educated at Queens College, Cambridge. His reputation is solidly established on his translations of important classical works and of some of the theological writings of John Calvin. Besides the *Commentaries* of Caesar and the *Metamorphoses* of Ovid, he had also made an English version of the works of Pomponius Mela, a Roman geographer and one of Solinus' sources of information. His "industrious toyle" met with the approval of his contemporaries, who spoke with praise of "the thondryng of his verse." Doubtless Golding translated *Collectanea,* though thirteen hundred years old, because the book most likely was still in use in some schoolrooms of Elizabethan England, to be learned by rote as it had been for centuries before.

Solinus has not fared well at the hands of later critics. There is unanimous agreement about the inferior quality of his writing, the absence of any critical evaluation in his work, the lackluster character of his Latin style. Yet he himself defends his work and pleads his own cause in these words: "Sundry things that have been reported of the Hyperboreans had been but a fable if the things that have come from thence unto us had been believed rashly. But seeing the best authors and such as are of sufficient credit do agree in one constant report, no man needs to fear any falsehood." We could do worse than believe him. In fact, we owe him a debt of thanks for preserving intact some of the legends and fables that have always shone out of man's reach, in the light of the distant stars.

George Kish

University of Michigan

BIBLIOGRAPHY

The best critical edition is Theodor Mommsen, *C. Iulii Solini Collectanea Rerum Memorabilium* (Berlin, 1895). For biographical data see Ch. Diehl, "Iulius Solinus" in *Pauly-Wissowa Realencyclopaedie der classischen Altertumswissenschaft,* Revised edition, Vol. X, col. 823 et seq. A geographical evaluation is in C. Raymond Beazley, *The Dawn of Modern Geography,* Vol. I, pp. 246-273 (London, 1897); and in George H. T. Kimble, *Geography, in the Middle Ages,* pp. 5-6 (London, 1938). For an account of the third century see Maurice Besnier, "L'Empire Romain de l'Avenement des Séveres au Concile de Nicée," *Histoire Ancienne,* 3e partie; *Histoire Romaine,* Tome IV, 1ere partie (Paris, 1937).

The excellent and pleasant worke of Iulius Solinus Polyhistor.

(∴)

Contayning the noble actions of humaine creatures, the secretes & prouidence of nature, the description of Countries, the maners of the people: with many meruailous things and strange antiquities, seruing for the benefitt and recreation of all sorts of persons.

Translated out of Latin into English, by Arthur Golding. Gent.

At London

Printed by I. Charlewoode for Thomas Hacket. 1587.

THE LIFE OF SOLINVS, VVRITTEN BY IOHN *CAMERTES.*

THere is no certaintie left in writing by them that are skilfull, in what time *Iulius Solinus* florished. Which thing I beleeue to haue happened, because the monuments of such as writ after him, perished almost vniuersally, at such time as the barbarous nations made hauock of all thinges. I maruell that the cōpiler of the Supplement of Chronicles (in all other respects a base wrighter) hath reported that this *Solinus* florished in the time of *Augustus Cæsar*, to whom he surmiseth him to haue dedicated hys Polyhistor. For it is euident that in this worke, *Solinus* maketh mention of the Emperor *Vespasians* dooings. Furthermore hee speaketh of *Suetonius Paulinus*, whō *Plinie* saw, as he witnesseth himselfe. Besides this, *Solinus* hath drawn almost all his matter out of *Plinies* fountaines, and yet neuerthelesse in wrighting these thinges, he desireth his freende in the beginning of his worke, to beare wyth hys simplicitie. But forasmuch as he no where maketh mention of *Plinie*, (by whom he was furthered) I coniecture that *Solinus* wrate this work while *Plinie* was yet aliue. And therevppon (by likelihoode) it comes to passe, that hee made no mention of hys author at that time liuing. By like reason it might fall out, that *Plinie* no where maketh mention of *Dioscorides* a famous wrighter of the same time that he was, when notwithstanding it is apparant, that *Plinie* borowed many thinges out of him into his work. The same fault also might bee imputed to *Dioscorides* (for it might bee founde in *Ammon* which of them purloyned from other) if hee suppressing the name of *Plinie*, haue filched so manie thinges out of him. They that haue written moste precisely of the liues and manners of *Xenophon* and *Plato*, and sundry other things of thẽ, report that in al the nũbers of Volumes which eche of thẽ wrate, neyther *Plato* made once mention of the name of *Xenophon*, nor *Xenophon* of the name of *Plato*.

Beleeue me such is Enuies kind, that Readers very seeld.
To wryters in their present times deserued thanks do yeeld.
For Enuy feedeth on the quick: but when that men be dead,
The sting of Enuie stints, and hath no poison more to shead.

VVhich saying of *Naso* is very true. VVhat may be sayd of *Macrobius*, who diuers times taketh whole leaues out of *Gellius*? Or of *Placidus*, who boroweth of *Seruius*? or of *Acron*, who stea-

leth

leth from *Porphyrio?* VVhat shall wee say of sixe hundred others, who in long treatyses, suppressing the names of them from whom they borowed them, haue word for word attributed all thinges to themselues: No man doubteth but that *Aulus Gellius* the very Diamond of the Latin tongue) profited greatly by reading *Liuie*, and yet hee will not in any wise that *Liuie* the prince of Latin Historiographers should be partaker of hys Nyghts. Yet am I not of the opinion of sum men, which thinke that *Solinus* made no mention of *Plinie*, in hope that *Plinies* works should vtterly haue perished, & so his collections onely haue remained, and in processe of time no man shoulde haue bin able to discouer his filching, as *Florus* and *Iustine* are thought to haue trauelled to the like end & purpose. Wolde God there were none other cause then this of the losse of so many good Authors. Then (to passe ouer the Greekes by the way) the monuments of *Cato, Varro, Nigidius, Salust, Hyginius, Celsus, Ennius, Furius, Varius, Actius, Neuius*, and *Pacuuius*, all noble Authors, (which nowe are perished, to the great hinderaunce of Students) shoulde haue remained vnto this day. But howsoeuer the case standeth, *Solinus* courteously confesseth, that whatsoeuer he hath comprehended in hys Polyhistor, proceedeth out of most allowed Authors: and he chalengeth nothing for his owne, in as much as (sayth hee) the diligence of men in olde time hath beene such, that nothing hath continued vntouched to our dayes. And againe he sayth plainly, that hee leaueth the auouching of the trueth of thinges, to such Authors as hee hath followed in this worke. Neither is it to be vpbraided to *Solinus* as a shame, that hee hath euery where followed *Plinie*, more then *Virgill* is to be found fault with for translating into his worke the verses of the auncient Poets, & specially of *Homer*. For it is no small commendation to counterfet singulerly a singuler Author.

That *Solinus* was a Romaine, it is to be coniectured both by his phrase of wryting, and also for that commonly when occasion serueth to speake of the Romaines, hee is wont in most places to call them our men, or my countrymen. Not onely the latter wryters, (as *Sipontinus*, *Perottus*, *Domitius*, *Calderinus*, *Angelus Politianus*, *Hermolaus Barbarus*, *Ianus Parrhasius*, and diuers others such like, whom not without cause a man might account among the auncient wryters.) But *Seruius* also in his seconde booke vpon *Virgills* Husbandry, and *Priscian*, two of the sixe notable Gramarians, haue cited the authoritie of *Solinus* by name. Also the interpreter of *Dennis*, (whither it were *Priscian* or *Rhemninus*) hath oftentimes put whole sentences of *Solinussis* in his verses. If I be not deceiued, all that which *Macrobius* reciteth of the diuision of the yeere, and of the odde dayes, are *Solinussis*. Moreouer, the Doctors of the Church, *Ierom*, *Ambrose*, and *Austen*, and other Doctors also, haue many times borowed sentences worde for worde out of *Solinus*.

There

The life of Solinus.

There are some that terme *Solinus* by the name of *Plinies* Ape, in like manner as *Iulius Capitolinus*, *Plinius Cæcilius*, and *Sidonius Apollinaris* reporte, that *Titian* was called the Ape of the Orators, and *Arulen* the Ape of the Stoiks. But these men consider not, that such are wont to be called Apes, as eyther repeate thinges written by others altogether in the same order without alteration, or els such as counterfet, not the Authors but their shaddowes. But *Solinus* hath so folowed *Plinies* phrase, that (vnder correction bee it spoken) there may scarce any other be found, that hath approched neerer to the maiestie of *Plinies* style. He intitled his Booke (as is found in certaine olde Coppies) to his freend *Autius*, to whom also hee deliuered it to be corrected. Some hold opinion, that he left other monuments also of hys wytte, which eyther by force of time are perished, or els perchaunce lie hid in some blind corner among Mothes. Finis.

¶ C. Iulius Solinus ſendeth hartie commendations to his freende Autius.

FOraſmuch as certaine perſons rather of too much eagerneſſe then of good will, haue haſted to ſnatch vp this little peece of vvorke that I was in hande withall, and haue published it beeing yet vnpolliſhed, before the matter that I had begunne, could be fully finiſhed: & nowe alſo do blaze abroade in corrupted copies, the things that are diſallowed, as though they had beene well allowed: ſlyghtly ouerpaſſing ſuch thinges as by further aduiſe haue beene added for the increaſe of knowledge: Leaſt paraduenture ſuch a rude and vnperfect hochpotch should be brought vnto your handes as a booke by mee well ouerlooked: I haue ſent you this worke in ſuch ſort, as you may knowe it to be by myne owne aduiſe ſet in order: First, for that the proceſſe of the whole diſcourſe was to be referred to your diſcretion: and ſecondlie to the intent that the ilfauoredneſſe of that ruſtie publication might by the true edition bee abolished. The title of this worke therefore shall be Polyhiſtor. For it is my minde that the title which I had purpoſed vppon at the beginning, (that is to ſay, A collection of thinges woorthy remembraunce) should bee abolished with the reſt of thoſe thinges that I haue diſallowed. Wherefore when you shall compare this Epiſtle with the Epiſtle which is in the beginning of the other Copie, you shall vnderſtande that I haue made the ſame account of you, as of him to vvhō I haue dedicated the whole ſubſtaunce of my trauell.

Farewell.

The

THE EPISTLE DEDICATORIE of the Author written to the *same Autius.*

INasmuch as I vnderstande, that both in fauourable perusing the dooings of other men, and also in knowledge of the lyberall Sciences, you excell alothers, wherof I my self also haue had so good experience, so as I cannot seeme to haue presumed vnaduisedly vpon your courtesie, any further then becommeth me: I thought to dedicate the web of this my little worke specially vnto you, as at whose hand I hoped eyther for your learninges sake to bee the sooner allowed, or for your courtesies sake to be the easier borne withall. The booke is framed to a breefenesse, and (as farre as reason woulde suffer) so moderatlye abridged, that there is not in it, eyther to lauash a-

boundaunce, or to nigardly skantnesse. And if you consider it aduisedly, you shall finde it rather leuened with knowledge, then vernished with eloquence. For I confesse my selfe to haue studied earnestly certaine choyse Bookes, to the intent to digresse further of frõ thinges knowne, and to make longer tariance in things more strange. Recitall of places occupyeth the most part of this worke, as whereunto the whole matter is somewhat inclined of it selfe. And heereof I minded in such wyse to entreate, as I might set out the platts of the famous Lands, & the notable Bayes of the Sea, euery one in theyr order, keeping the accustomed distinstion of the world.

Also I haue interlaced many thinges some what differing (but not disagreeing) from the matter, to the intent that (if nothing els, yet at least wyse) the varietie it selfe myght ease the wearines of the Readers. Heerewythall I haue expressed the natures of men and other lyuing things. And not a few things are added concerning straunge Trees and Stones: cõcerning the shapes of farborne people: and concerning the diuersities of customes of vnknown nations. Moreouer, there are diuers thinges worthy to be intreated of, which to passe ouer, I thought had beene a poynt of negligence, inasmuch as they be auouched by the authority of most allowed wryters, which thing inespecially I would your wysedome shoulde vnderstand. For what can wee callenge properly for our owne, sith the dilygence of menne in olde tyme hath beene such, that nothyng hath remayned vntouched

vnto

vnto our dayes. VVherefore I beseech you waygh not the credite of this woorke that I put foorth, in the ballance of thys present tyme. For I ensuing the print of the olde stampe, thought good rather to take my choyse of all the olde opinions, then to alter them. Therefore if any of these thynges shall sound otherwyse to your understanding, then I wysh they shold: I pray you beare wyth my vnskylfulnes, and let those Authors which I haue followed stande to the auouching of the trueth. And euen as they that drawe the Images of men, setting all the rest aside, doo first and formost proportion out the head, & meddle not with portraying out the other limbes before they haue taken theyr begynning (as yee woulde say) at the very topcastle of shape and proportion: So wyll I also take my begynning at the heade of the world, (that is to weete) the Cittie of Rome. *And although the best learned Authors haue left nothyng that may bee spoken a newe to the prayse thereof, and that therefore it be almost a superfluous matter to trace the pathe, that hath beene troden ouer in so many Chronicles. yet neuertheles, because it shal not be altogether ouer slipped, I wyll set forth the Originall thereof wyth as much faythfulnesse as may be.*

Farewell.

CAP. I.

The first Chapter of C. Iulius Solinus Polyhistor, entreateth of the first foundation of the Citty of Rome.

Opinions concerning the name of Rome.

THere are some which wold haue it seeme, that ẏ name of Rome was gyuen first of all by *Euander*: who finding there a Towne built before by the yong men of Latium which they called Valentia, kept the signification of the firste name, & called it in Greeke Rhome, which is the same that Valentia is in Latin. And forasmuch as the Arcadians planted thēselues there vppon the highest top of an Hill, it came to passe ẏ euer after the Latines termed the strongest places of Citties by the name of Arces. *Heraclides* is of opiniō, ẏ after the taking of Troy certain Achiues came by the Riuer Tyber, & arriued in the place where Rome is now: and that afterward by perswasion of one *Rome* a noble Lady, (who was prisoner among them and at that time in their companie,) they did set fire one their ships, setled thēselues to abide, reared the wals, & called the Towne Rome, after the name of the Ladie. *Agathocles* wryteth, that it was not this *Rome* the prisoner as is aforesaid, but the daughter of *Ascanius*, and grandchilde to *Aeneas*, that was the cause of this foresaide name of thys Cittie. There is also registred a peculiar name of Rome: but it is not lawful to be published, forasmuch as it is enacted among other secretes of our Ceremo-

Valentia.

nies, that it should not be blazed abrode, to the intent that the reuerence giuen to the inacted secrecie, might abolish the knowledge thereof. And *Valerius Soranus* (because he durst be so bold as to disclose it contrary to the Law) was put to death in recompence of his ouerliberall talke. Among our auncientest Religions, we worship the Chappell of Angerona, to whom wée doo sacrifice before the * twelfth day of the Calends of Januarie, which Goddesse (as the Gouernour of silence) hath her Image there with mouth closed, and lyppes sealed fast together. As concerning the times of the building of the Cittie, it hath raysed doubtfull questions, inasmuch as certayne things were builded there long before the time of *Romulus*. For *Hercules* (according to the vowe that hee had made for the punishing of *Cacus*, and the recouerie of his Oxen,) dedicated an Altar to his Father *Iupiter*, whom he surnamed ẏ finder. This *Cacus* inhabited a place named Salines whereas is now the Gate called Trigemina. Who (as *Cœlius* reporteth) béeing sent to ward by *Tarchon* the Tyrrhenian (to whom he came of Ambassade from King *Marsias*, accompanied with *Megales* the Phrygian) brake out of prison, and returning from whence he came, raysed a greater puissaunce, and subdued all the Country about the Riuer Vulturnus & Campane. Wherewith béeing not content, as he attempted the conquest of those thinges that were come in possession of ẏ Arcadians, he was vanquished by *Hercules*, who by chaunce was there at the same time. And the Sabines receyuing *Megales* again, were taught by him the art of Byrdspelling. *Hercules* also hauing learned of *Nicostrate* the mother of *Euander* (who for her skill in prophesying, was also called Carmentis) that he should become immortall, erected an Altar to hys owne maiestie, which among our Byshops is had in

* That is about the 19. day of December.

The time of the buildinge of Rome.

Hercules. Cacus.

Tarchon.

Marsias.

Megales a Phrygian the firste founder of the arte of Birdspelling among the Sabines.

Nicostrate couñted one of the nine Sybilles.

very

very great reuerence. Morcouer he made the consept, within the which he taught the Potits, howe they shoulde solemnize his rites and ceremonies in offering Oxen. *Hercules* Chappell is in the Oxe-market, wherein are remayning the monuments of hys banquet and maiestie, euen vnto this day. For such a gyft is giuen it from Heauen, that neither dogs nor flyes can enter into the place. For at such time as hee was offering the inwards of his sacrifice, it is sayd that he cursed the God *Myagrus*, and left his Clubbe in the Porche, at the smell whereof dogges ran away, and so it continueth to this howre. The Church also which is called the Treasory of *Saturne*, was builded by hys companions in the honor of *Saturne*, whō they had learned to haue béene an inhabiter of that Country. Furthermore they named the Hill where now is ẏ Capitoll, Saturnes Hyll. Of the Castle also which they builded, they named the Gate Saturnes Gate, which afterward was called Pandangate. At the foote of the Hill Capitoline, was the dwelling of *Carmentis*, and there is nowe the Chappell of Carmentis, wherof the Gate of Carmentis taketh his name. As for ẏ Pallace it is not to be doubted but that the Arcadians were founders thereof, who also before that time builded the Towne Palanteum, which the Aborigens inhabited a whyle, but afterward (for the noysomnesse of the fenne and marrys which the Tyber running by it had made) left it vp and remoued to Rhæatee. There are that thinke thys Hill tooke hys name of the bleating of shéepe by chaunging of Letters, or of *Pale* the Goddesse of Shéepeheardes, or (as *Silenus* prooueth) of *Pallas* the daughter of *Hyperboreus*, whom *Hercules* deflowred on that Hyll. But howsoeuer these thyngs agrée: it is manifest that the glorye of the Romaine name did chéefely spring out of that * luckye foretoken: specially séeing that the account of the yéeres

Hercules Chappell, and the institution of hys Ceremonies.

Myagrus the God of Flyes.

The Treasorie of Saturne.

The dwelling of Nicostrate.

Wherof the Romane Pallace tooke that name.

* That is to say of Romulus.

bringeth good reason to ground the trueth vppon. For (as *Varro* a most exquisite Author affirmeth) *Romulus* the Sonne of *Mars* and *Rhea Siluia*, or (as divers other suppose) of *Mars* and *Ilia*, builded Rome. And at the first Rome was called square, because it was platted out by line and levell. It beginneth at the Groue that is in the flore of *Apollo*, and endeth at the vpper brew of *Cacus* staiers, where as was ẏ cotage of *Faustulus*. And there dwelled *Romulus* that luckely layde the foundation of the walles in the 18. yeere of his age the * eleuenth Calends of May betweene two & three of the clock, as *Lucius Tarutius* the famous Mathematick hath left in wryting. *Iupiter* beeing at that time in Pisces, *Saturne*, *Mars*, *Venus*, & *Mercurie* in Scorpio: the Sunne in Taurus: and the Moone in Lybra. And it was euer after kept for a custome, that no sacrifice should be slayne by men on theyr byrth dayes, to the intent that that day should be pure from bloodshed. The signification whereof (suen holde opinion) was taken of the deliueraunce of *Ilia*. The said *Romulus* raigned thirty and seauen yeeres. Hee ledde the first Tryumph that euer was. And first he triumphed ouer the Ceninenses, and spoyled *Acron* theyr King, whose Armour he first dedicated to *Iupiter Feretrius*, and hung it vp in hys Temple, terming it by ẏ name of a Rich spoile. Secondly he triumphed ouer the Antenuates; and lastly ouer the Vients. Finally at ẏ Fen of Caprea he vanished away, the * Nones of July.

The time of the building of Rome by Romulus, the 19 of April.

The first Tryumph.

* The second day of July,

Now will I shew in what places the other Kinges dwelt. *Tatius* dwelt in the Towre where as nowe is the Temple of *Iuno Moneta*: who in the fift yeere after his comming into the Cittie, beeing murthered by the Laurents, departed out of this life, the 27 Olimpiad. *Numa* dwelt first on Quirins Hyll, and afterward by *Vestaas* Church, in the Court, which yet styll beareth

Tatius king of the Sabynes.

Numa Pompilius the second K. of the Romaines

beareth the same name. Hee raigned 43. yeeres, and is buried vnder Ianiculum. *Tullus Hostilius* dwelt in Velia, where afterward was made the Temple of Houshold Gods. He raigned two and thirty yeeres, and dyed in the thirty-fiue Olympiade. *Ancus Martius* dwelt in the vpper ende of the holy streete, wher now is the Temple of the Gods called *Lares*. Hee raigned thirty and foure yeeres, and dyed the 41. Olympiade. *Tarquine* the elder, dwelt at the Gate Mugonia, aboue the New streete, and raigned seauen and thirty yeres. *Seruius Tullius* dwelt in the Exquilies aboue Olbyes Hyll, and raigned forty and two yeeres. *Tarquine* the proude dwelt in the Exquilies also, vpon Mount Pullus, by the Beechie Lake, and raigned twentie & fiue yeeres. *Cincius* thinketh that Rome was builded in the twelfth Olympiad. *Fabius victor* thinketh it was builded in the eyght. *Nepos* and *Lactatius* approuing the opinions of *Eratosthenes* and *Apollodorus*) suppose it was builded in the second yeere of the seuenth Olympiad. *Pomponius Atticus*, and *Marcus Tullius Cicero*, hold opinion, that it was builded ẏ third yeere of the first Olympiad. Therefore by conferring our times with the Greekes, wee finde that Rome was builded in the beginning of the seauenth Olympiad, the foure hundred and three and thirty yeere after the taking of Troy. For the gaming of Olympus (which *Hercules* made in ẏ honor of *Pelops* hys great Grandfather by the mothers side,) beeing left of, was by *Iphiclus* (one of hys posteritie) renued after the destruction of Troy, the foure hundred and eyght yeere. Whereupon it commeth to passe, that the first Olympiad is reckoned from *Iphiclus*. So letting passe sixe Olimpiads betweene *Iphiclus* & the building of Rome, of which euery Olympiad conteyneth foure yeeres, seeing that Rome was builded in the beginning of the

Tullus Hostilius

Ancus Martius

Tarquine the Elder.

Seruius Tullius.

Tarquine the proude.

Opynions of the time of the building of Rome.

An Olimpiad and what it conteyneth.

seauenth Olimpiad, it must néedes fall out that there were iust foure hundred thirty and thrée yéeres betwéene the destruction of Troy, and the foundation of Rome. To the proofe of this argument maketh, that when *Caius Pompeius Gallus*, and *Quintus Veranius* were Consuls, it was the eyght hundred and first yere from the building of the Cittie: which time of theyr Consulshipp was registred in the common Recordes, to be the two hundreth and seuenth Olimpiad. Nowe multiplie two hundred and sixe Olimpiads by foure, and they shall amount to eyght hundred and twentye foure yéeres, to the which must bee added ỹ first yeere of the seauenth Olimpiad, to make vp full twenty and fiue aboue eyght hundred. Out of the which summe, abate twenty and foure yeeres for the sixe Olimpiads that were behind: and the remnant shall appeare to be eyght hundred and one yéeres. Wherefore séeing that the beginning of the two hundred and seauen Olimpiad is accounted for the eyght hundreth and firste yéere of the building of the Cittie, it is to bee beléeued that Rome was builded the first yéere of the seauenth Olimpiad. The which was gouerned by Kinges two hundred and one and forty yéeres. The estate of the Tennement was erected the thrée hundred and second yéere. The first Punick warre was begun the foure hundred fourescore and ninth yéere. The second Punick war, the fiue hundred and thirty fiue yéere. The third Punick warre, the sixe hundred and foure. The warre of the Confederats, the sixe hundred thréescore and second yéere. Vnto the yéere that *Hircius* and *Pansa* were Consuls, there had passed seauen hundred and tenne yéeres. In the time of whose Consulship, *Caesar Augustus* was created Consull in the eyghteenth yéere of his age. Who so behaued himselfe in the entrye of his raigne, that through hys circumspectnesse

Of the sundry gouernments in Rome.

Cæsar Augustus.

nesse, the Empyre of Rome was not onely in quiet, but also safe and free from all danger. The which time was almost alone to be found, wherein warres for the most part had longest discontinuance, and witts chiefly florished. Undoubtedly to the intent that during thys vacation time, when warres ceased, the exercises of vertue should not growe out of vse.

CAP. II.

Of the diuision of the yeere, and of the odde dayes added in the Leape-yeeres.

ABout thys tyme was the orderly course of the yeere perceiued, which from the beginning of the worlde hadde beene deepely hidden in darknesse. For before *Augustus Cæsar*, men reckoned the yeere diuerslie and vncertainely. The Ægiptians determined it in foure monethes. The Arcadians in three. The Acarnanians in sixe. The Lauinians of Italy in thirteene: and this their yeere was reported to be of three hundred threescore and fourteene dayes. The Romaines at the firste, accounted ten monethes for a yeere, beginning at March. In so much that in the firste day thereof, they kindled fire on the Altars of *Vesta*, they shifted theyr olde Baye Garlandes for Greene, the Senate and people chose newe Officers, the Matrons serued theyr seruaunts at the Table, in like sort as the Masters did at the feaste of

Saturne: the Matrons to the intent through this courtesie to prouoke thē to ẏ more obedience, the Maisters as it were, to rewarde them in respect of theyr paynes taken: specially seeing this moneth is the first, and chiefe of all the rest, which may wel be proued, in that the fift moneth from it was called *Quintilis*, & when the full number was fulfilled, December did close vp the whole circuit within the three hundred and foure day. For at that time thys number of dayes accomplished the yeere, so that sixe monethes were of thirty dayes a peece, and the other foure had thirty and one a peece. But forasmuch as that account before the comming of *Numa* differed from the course of the Moone, they supplyed the yeere to the computation of the Moone, by putting thereto one and fiftye dayes. To the intent therfore to make vp full twelue monethes, they tooke from eche of the sayd sixe monethes one day, and put them to these one and fiftye, and so made iust fifty and seauen, the which were deuided into two monethes, whereof the one contained twentie and nine dayes, the other twenty and eyght. So the yeere began to haue three hundred fiftye & fiue dayes. Afterward, when they perceiued the yéere to be vnaduisedly determined within the foresayd daies, forasmuch as it appeared that the Sunne finished not hys ful course in the Zodiack before ẏ three hundreth threescore and fift day, wyth the ouerplus welnere of a quarter of a day: they added that quarter and tenne dayes, to the intent the yéere should consist of ful thrée hundred threescore and fiue dayes, and the fourth part of a day. Whereunto they were the rather induced for obseruing the odde number, which (according to the doctrine of *Pythagoras*) ought to be preferred in all thinges.

And heerevpon it commeth to passe, that January for

for hys odde dayes is dedicated to the Gods supernal, and February for hys euen dayes as vnlucky is allotted to the Gods infernall. Therefore when as thys order of account seemed alowable to the whole world, for the exacter keeping of the sayd quarter, it was of diuers Nations diuersly added, and yet it could neuer be brought to passe, to fal out euen with the time. The Greekes abated out of euery yeere eleuen dayes, and the fourth part of a day: which beeing eyght tymes multiplyed, they reserued to the ninth yeere, to the intent that the number of nine beeing gathered into one grosse summe, might be deuided into 3. monethes of thirty dayes a peece. The which being restored againe the ninth yeere, made foure hundred forty and foure dayes, which they called odde or superfluous dayes. The Romaines liked well of this reckoning at the first. But afterward mislyking it in respect of the euen number, they neglected it, and within short space forgot it, committing the order of the addition to the Priestes: who to pleasure the tolegatherers in theyr accounts, did after theyr owne fancy shorten or lengthen the yeere as they lysted.

Whyle thinges stoode in this case, and that the manner of adding was sometime too short, and sometime too long, or els dissembled and let slip altogether: it happened oftentimes that the monethes which had beene woont to passe in Winter, fell one whyle in Sommertime, and another while in the fal of ẏ leafe. *Caius Cæsar* therefore to the intent to set a stay in this variablenesse, did cutte of all this turmoyling of the tymes. And that the error foreslypped myght be reduced to some certaine staiednesse: he added twenty and one dayes and sixe houres at a time, by meanes wherof the monethes being drawn backe to theyr accustomed places, might from thenceforth kéepe theyr Or-dinarie and appointed seasons. That onely yéere therfore had thrée hundred and foure and forty daies, and all the rest afterward had thrée hondred thréescore and fiue daies, and sixe howres. This notwithstanding, then also was a default committed by Priestes. For whereas order was taken that they shoulde euerye foure yeere adde one daie, which ought to haue beene done at the ende of the fourth yéere, before the fifte yéere began, they reckoned it in the beginning of the fourth yéere, and not in the ende. By meanes wherof, in thirtie and sixe yéeres, whereas nine daies had béen sufficient, twelue daies were reckoned. The which béeing espied, *Augustus* reformed in this wise. Hee commaunded that twelue yéeres should passe without leape, to the intent ẏ those thrée daies aboue the nine, which were superfluously added, might by this means be recompensed. Uppon which discipline was afterward grounded the order of all times. Notwithstanding, albeit that for these and many other thinges, we may thinke our selues beholding to the raigne of *Augustus*, who was almost péerelesse in his gouernment: yet there are to be found so manie mis-fortunes in his life, that a manne can not easily discerne whither hee were more miserable or happy. First, for that in his sute to his Uncle for the Lieuetenantship of the horsmen, *Lepidus* the Tribune was preferred before him, not without a certaine foyle of his first attempts. Secondlie, for that he was greatlie anoied by the authoritie of *Antony* ioyned with him in the office of the Thréemen, and with the battell at Philippo. Thirdly for the hatred that hee raised against himselfe for proclayming the Noblemen Traytors: The disheriting of *Agrippa*, (borne after the decease of his Father) whom he had adopted before to be his Sonne, and the great

The mis-fortunes of the Emperour Augustus.

great repentance he tooke thereof afterward, for the desire he had unto him. His shipwrackes in Sicill: his shamefull lurking in a Caue there: the often mutinies of his Souldiours against him: the thought hee tooke in the siedge of Perusium: the detecting of hys * Daughters adoutrie, and of the intent shee had to murther him: and (as shamefull a matter as ye other) the infamie of his Neece, blamed for the death of her Sonnes: the greefe of his solitarinesse for the losse of his Children, which was not a corzie alone: The pestilence yt raigned in the Cittie. The famine through all Italie, in the time of his warres in Illirick: the narrowe shifts that he was driuen to for want of Souldiours: the crazednes of his body which was alwaies sicklie: the spightfull discention of *Nero* hys Wyues Sonne: the unfaithfull imaginations of his wife and her Sonne *Tiberius*: and manie other thinges of the same sort.

* Her name was Iulia.

Notwithstanding, as though the World hadde bewailed this mans ende, the euils hanging ouer mens heades, were shewed before by tokens nothing doubtfull. For one *Fausta* a woman of the meaner sorte, brought forth at one burthen foure Twinnes, two Sonnes, and as manie Daughters: prognosticatinge by her monstrous fruitfulnesse, the great calamitie that was to come. Howbeit that *Trogus* the wryter of Histories affirmeth that seauen are borne together at one burthen in Ægypt: which thing in that Country is not so great a wonder, forasmuch as the Ryuer Nilus with his fruitfull water, maketh plentifull, not onelie the soile of the grounde, but also mens bodyes. Wee reade that *Cneus Pompeius* did shewe openly in the Theater at Rome, one *Eutichis* a woman of Asia, with her twentie Children, which she was certainlie knowne to haue beene deliuered of at three burthens

Foretokens of the death of Augustus.

Monstruous fruitfulnesse of Women.

Twentie Childrẽ at three child beddes.

burthens onelie. And therefore I thinke it expedient to treate in thys place concerning the generation of Man.

CAP. III.

Of Man and of his byrth: of men of wonderfull strength: and of the stone Alectorius, *or the Cockstone.*

FOr inasmuch as we are minded to make a note of thinges woorthy to be touched, concerning lyuing creatures, as yͤ Countries of eche of them seuerally shal put vs in remembraunce. Reason would we should begin chiefly at that creature which nature hath preferred before al others in iudgement of vnderstanding, and capacitie of wisedome. Of Women, some bee barren for euer: othersome by change of Husbandes become fruitfull. Many beare but one Childe: and diuers bring forth eyther onely Males, or onelie Females. After fiftie yéeres the fruitfulnesse of them all is at a point: but Men begette Children vntill they be fourescore, like as King *Masinissa* begat his Sonne * *Metymathnus*, when he was of the age of fourescore and sixe yéeres. *Cato* when he was full fourescore yéere old and vpward, begat the Grandfather of *Cato* that killed himselfe at Vtica, vpon the Daughter of his Client *Salonius*. Thys is also found to be of a truth, that when two are conceiued

He was also called Methymnus.

ceiued one somewhat after another, the Woman goeth out her full time of them both: like as hath beene séene in *Hercules* and his brother *Iphiclus*, who béeing carryed both in one burthen, had notwithstanding like distaunce of time betwéene their birthes, as there was distance betwéene their begetting. And likewise in a wench called *Proconesia*, who committing aduoutry with two sundry men, was deliuered of a payre of Twinnes eche of them resembling his Father. This *Iphiclus* begat *Iolaus*, who entering the Iland Sardinia and there alluring vnto concord the wauering minds of the inhabitants, builded Olbia and other Greeke Townes. They which after his name were called Iolenses, reared a Temple ouer his Tombe, because he folowing the vertues of his Uncle, hadde deliuered Sardinia from manie euilles. The tenth day after cōception will by some paine put the Mothers in remēbraunce that they be with Child. For from that tyme forward, their heads shall begin to bée disquieted, and their sight shal waxe dimme. Also the appetite of their stomack shall abate, and they shall beginne to loathe meate. It is agréed vpon among all men, that of the whole flesh, the first part that is formed is the harte, and that it increaseth vnto the thréescore and fift day, and afterwarde diminisheth againe: and that of gristles are made the backbones: and therefore it putteth them in daunger of death if eyther of bothe those partes be hurt. Doubtlesse if it be a Malechild that is in fashioning, the Women that beare them are better coloured, and their deliueraunce is more spéedy, and finally it beginneth to stirre at the fortie day. The Female stirreth not before the fourescore and tenth daie, and the conception thereof dyeth ẏ countenaunce of the Mother with a pale colour, and also hindereth the legges with a faint slownesse in going. In bothe

The byrth of Hercules and Iphiclus.

Of the conception of Man.

kindes, when the heare beginneth to growe, then is the greater disease, and the paine is more breeme in the full of the Moone, wᶜ time also is alwaies noysome to thē when they are borne. When a Woman wyth Child eateth meates that are ouersalt, the Child shalbe borne without nayles. At such time as the byrth beeing fully rype approcheth to the instant of deliuerraunce, it greatlie auaileth the Woman that laboreth to hold her breath, for asmuch as yawning dooth wyth deadlie delay prolong the deliuery. It is againste nature for the byrth to come foorth with his feete forward: and therefore as Children hardly borne, they are called in Latine, *Agrippæ*. Such as are so borne, are for the moste parte vnfortunate and short liued. Onely in one Man, namely *Marcus Agrippa*, it was a token of good lucke: howbeit not altogether so missfortunelesse but that hee suffered more aduersitie then prosperity. For with miserable paine of his feete, and the open aduoutry of hys wife, and certaine other marks of ill luck, hee did abye ẏ foretoken of his awke byrth. There is also an vnfortunate manner of byrth in the Female kinde, like as was seene by *Cornelia* the Mother of the *Gracchusses*, who made satisfaction for her monstrous byrth, wyth the vnluckye ende of her Children. Againe the byrthe is the more luckie where the Mother dyes of it: as was seene by the first *Scipio Affricanus*, who after ẏ death of his Mother, because hee was ript out of her wombe, was the firste of the Romaines that was called *Cæsar*. Of Twynnes, if the one remaine still and ẏ other perrish by beeing borne before his time, hee that is borne at hys full tyme is called *Vopiscus*.

Of such as are borne wyth theyr feete forwarde.

The first Cæsar among the Romaines.

Some are borne wyth teeth, as *Cneus Papirius*, *Carbo*, and *Marcus Curius*, who for the same cause was surnamed the toothed. Some insteede of teeth haue

the

the rome supplied with one whole bone. After which manner *Prusias* King of Bythinia had a Sonne. The teeth differ in number according to the difference of the kind. For in men are moe, and in women are fewer of those teeth which are called dogteeth. Unto such as haue two double teeth growing vp vppon the right side of theyr mouth, it behighteth the fauour of Fortune. And vnto such as haue them on the left side, it betokeneth the contrary.

The firste voyce of Children after they bee borne is wayling. For the declaration of myrth is delayed to the forteth daie. Wee knowe of none that laughed the same howre he was borne, but onely one: that is to weete, *Zoroastres*, who became moste skilfull and cunning in all good artes. But *Crassus*, the Graundfather of him that was slayne in the battell againste the Parthians, because he neuer laughed, was surnamed * Agelastos. Among other great thinges ŷ were in *Socrates*, this is worthy to bee noted, that hee continued alwayes in one manner of countenaunce, euen when hee was troubled with aduersitie. *Heraclitus* and doggysh *Diogenes* did neuer abate one whitte of theyr stiffe stomackes, but treading vnder foote the stormes of all casualties, continued vnchaungable in one purpose, against all greefes and miseries. It is Registred among other examples, that *Pomponius* the Poet, such a one as hadde beene Consull, did neuer rasp.

Zoroastres king of the Bactrians.

Crassus.

* That is to saye laughterlesse.

Socrates.

Heraclitus and Diogines.

It is verye well knowne, that *Antonia* the Wyfe of *Drusus* didde neuer spette. Wee haue heard of dyuers that haue beene borne wyth whole boanes not hollow wythin, and that such are wont neither to sweat nor to be a thirst: of the which sort *Ligdamus* of Syracuse is reported to be one: who in the thyrtie and three Olimpiad caried away the firste Garlond of vic-

Examples of singuler stregth.

* Running leaping, buffeting, wrestling and throwing of the Sledge.

tory in the * fiue exercises of actiuitie, from ẏ gaming of Olympus, and his bones were founde to haue no maroe in them. It is most certaine that the greatest substaunce of strength commeth of the sinewes: and that the thicker they bee, so much the more dooth the strength increase. *Varro* in his Register of monstruous strength, noted that there was one *Tritanus* a Swordplayer a Samnite borne, that had sinewes both right out, and crosse ouerthwart, and that not only the bulke of his breast, but also his handes and his armes, were as it were lattised with sinewes: who foyled all his aduersaries with a fillippe, and almost with carelesse encounters: And that the Son of the same Man a Souldiour of *Cneus Pompeius*, beeing borne in the same sort, did set so light by an enemie that did challenge him, that beeing himselfe vnarmed, he ouercame him, and taking him prisoner, carried him with one of his fingers into his Captaines Pauilion. *Milo* also of Croton is reported to haue donne all thinges aboue the reache of Mans power. Of whō this is left in wryting, that with the stroke of his bare fist, hee felled an Oxe starke dead, and eate him vpp himselfe alone the same day that he killed him, without ouercharging his stomack. Hereof there is no doubt. For vppon hys Image is an inscription in witnesse of the facte, wyth these wordes. Hee died a conquerer in all attempts. There is a stone called * Alectorius, of the bignes of a Beane, like vnto Christall, founde in the bellies of Cockes, meete (as is reported) for them that goe to battell. Moreouer, *Milo* florished in the time of *Tarquine* the Elder.

* The Cockstone.

CAP.

Iulius Solinus Polyhistor.

CAP. IIII.

Of the likenesse of shape and fauour: of the tallnesse of certaine personages: of the measure of a Man: and of the reuerence of the deade.

NOw who so bendeth hys minde to consider the causes of likenesses, shall perceiue the wonderfull disposition of the workmanshippe of nature. For somtime such likenesses belong to some stocke, and descende from issue to issue, into the succession: like as diuers times young Children beare sometime Molles, sometime scarres, and sometime any other marks of theyr auncestors. As among the Lepids, of whom thrée of the same line (but not successiuelie one after another) are found to haue béene borne after one sorte, with a * filme ouer theyr eye. As in the famous Poet of Byzance, who hauing a Mother that was the bastarde of an Æthiopian, although there were nothing in her resembling her Father, yet did he degenerate againe into the likenesse of the Æthiopian that was his Grandfather. But this is the lesse wonder, if wee consider those thinges that haue béene séene betwixt mére straungers. One *Artemon* a man of the baser sort in Syria, did so resemble King *Antiochus* in face, that afterwarde the Kinges wyfe *Laodice*, by shewing this rascall fellowe, kept

* A seely how.

Of straungers that resembled one another.

 close

close the death of her Husbande so long, untill such a one was ordeyned successor of the Kingdome as shee listed to appoynt. There was such likenesse to all respects in personage and making, betwéene *Cneus Pompeius*, and *Caius Vibius* a man of meane byrth, that the Romaines called *Vibius* by the name of *Pompey*, and *Pompey* by the name of *Vibius*.

Rubrius the Stage-player did so fully expresse the Orator *Lucius Plancus*, that ẏ people called him *Plancus* also. *Mirmillo* a Neateheарde, and *Cassius Seuerus* the Orator did so resemble one another, that if they were séene together at any time, they coulde not be discerned which was which, unlesse there were a difference in theyr apparell. *Marcus Messala Censorius*, and *Menogenes* a fellowe of the verye rascallest sort, were so like, that euery Man thought *Messala* to bée none other then *Menogenes*, nor *Menogenes* anie other than *Messala*.

A Fysherman of Sicill was likened to the Proconsull Sura (besides other things,) euen in the drawing or wringing of his mouth also. So fully dyd they agrée, in the same impediment of spéeche, and slowe bryngyng foorth of theyr wordes, through the defaulte of nature. Sometime also it hath béene a wonder to sée the undiscernable likenesse of countenaunces, not onely in straungers, but also euen in such as haue béene brought together from the furthest partes of the whole worlde. For where as one *Thoranius* solde unto *Antony* bearing at that time the office of Triumuir, for thrée hundred Sestercies, two Boyes of excellent beautie for Twynnes, of which he had gotten the one in Fraunce and the other in Asia,) so resembling eche other in all poynts, that they might haue béene taken bothe for one, if theyr spéech hadde not bewrayed them: and that therefore *Antonie* was displeased

pleased, thinking hymselfe to haue béene deluded, because they were not Twynnes indéed. *Thoranius* pleasantlie auouched, that that thing was chiefely to be estéemed, which the Chapman founde fault wyth. For it had béene no wonder to haue had two Twyns like: But this was it which could by no meanes be prysed according to the value, that béeing of two diuers Coũtryes so farre distaunt, they were borne more like one another then any Twinnes. With which aunswere *Antonie* was so appeased, that euer after hee woulde tell men, he had not any one thing of all hys possessions, that he did sette more store by.

Of the talenes and goodly personages of men in olde time.

Nowe if wée shall moue question concerning the personages of menne, it will manifestly appeare, that antiquitie hath vaunted no lyes at all of it selfe: but that the offspring of our time béeing corrupted by succession growing out of kinde, hath through ỷ decrease of them that are nowe borne, lost the comlinesse of the auncient beautie. Therefore although dyuers doo conclude, that no man can excéede the stature of seauen foote, because that *Hercules* was no hygher then so: yet notwithstanding, it was founde in the time of ỷ Romaines vnder the Emperour *Augustus*, that *Pusio* and *Secundilla* were tenne foote high and more: the corses of whom, are yet to bee séene in the Charnelhouse of the Salusts.

Pusio and Secundilla.

Afterward, in the raigne of *Claudius*, there was one named *Gabbara* brought out of Araby, that was nyne foote and as many inches hygh. But almoste a thousande yeeres before *Augustus*, there was no such personage séene, neither after ỷ time of *Claudius*. For what is he in our dayes ỷ is not borne lesser then his Parents? As for the hugenes of menne in olde time, the Reliques of *Orestes* doo testifie. Whose bones béeing founde of the Lacedemonians at Tegæa by the

Gabbara

Orestes.

information of the Oracle the fiftie and eyght Olympiad, wee are assured were full seauen cubites long. Also there are wrytings Registred in remembraunce of thinges doone in auncient time, which auouch the assurednesse of the trueth, wherein it is specified, that in the Candian warre, at such time as ẏ Riuers more outragiously flowing than freshe waters are wont, had broken vp the ground there, after the fall of ẏ sayd waters, among many clifts of the grounde, there was found a body of thrée and thirty cubits. For desire to sée the which, *Lucius Flaccus* the Lieuetenant and *Metellus* himselfe also, béeing wonderfully amazed at the straungenesse thereof, went thither, and beheld the wonder wyth theyr eyes, which they thought a Fable to heare reported. I may not let passe the Son of *Euthymines* of Salymis, who grewe thrée cubits high in thrée yéeres. But he was slow of gate, dull wytted, boystrous of voyce, too sone rype, and immediatly beset with many diseases: so as hee recompensed hys ouerhasty growth with vnmeasurable punishment of sicknesse.

A dead body of monstrous bignesse.

An ouerswift growth.

The manner of measuring agréeth two wayes. For looke how much a man is betwéene the endes of his two longest fingers stretching hys armes out. so longe is hee betwéene the sole of hys foote and the crowne of his head: and therefore the naturall Philosophers déeme man to bee a little Worlde. Unto the ryght side is ascribed the handsomer mouing, and vnto the lefte side the greater firmenesse. And therefore the one is more apt to dauncing and other exercises of lyghtnesse, and the other better able to beare burthens.

The manner of measuring a Manne.

Nature hath decréed a kinde of reuerence to bee obserued euen of bodyes disceased: so that if at anie time it happen the carkasses of such as are kylled, to

Naturall reuerence in bodyes disceased

to bée borne vppe wyth the waues, Mennes bodyes fléete with their faces vpwarde, and Womens with theyr faces downewarde.

CAP. V.

Of swiftnes: of sight: of the valiantnesse of certaine Romaines: and of the excellency of Cæsar the Dictator.

Of Swiftnes.

Ladas.

Polymestor.

Phylippides.

Antistius and Philonides.

BVt to the intent we may passe to the title of swiftnesse: the pricke and prise in that behalfe, obtayned one *Ladas*, who ranne in such wyse vpon the loose dust, that the sande houered still vp, and he left no printe of his fooetsteppes behinde him. *Polymestor* a Boy of Miletum béeing sette by his Mother to féede Goates, ranne after a Hare in sporte and caught it. For the which déede within a while after the owner of the hearde brought him to ye gaming in the forty and sixe Olimpiad, (as *Bocchus* reporteth) and there in the race he gained the Garland. *Phylippides* ranne one thousand, two hundred and fortye furlongs from Athens to Lacedæmon in two dayes. *Antistius* a Lacedæmonian and *Philonides* the Lackies of great *Alexander*, iournied a thousande and two hundred furlongs from Sycion to Elis, in one day. The same yéere that *Fonteius* and *Vipsanus* were Consuls, a Boy in Italy of eyght yéeres olde, went 45. myles betwéene noone and night.

Quickſighted-nes. Strabo.

135

The quickeſt of ſight was one *Strabo*, whom *Varro* auoucheth to haue ouerlooked a hundred thirty & fiue miles, and that hee was wont exactlie to viewe from the watch Towre of Lyliby in Sicill, ŷ Punicke fleete ſetting out of the Hauen of Carthage, and to reporte the iuſt number of their Shippes. *Cicero* maketh report, that the Ilias of *Homer* was ſo finely written in Velame, that it might be cloſed in a Nutſhell *Callicrates* carued Ants of Iuory ſo finely, that ſome of thē could not be diſcerned from other Ants. *Apollonides* declareth that in Scythia there is a race of Women called *Bythies*, which haue two balles in eche eye, and doo kill folke with their ſight, if they happen to caſt an angry looke vppon anie body. Such there bee alſo in Sardinia.

Callicrates.

A race of ſtrange Women.

Valiantnes. Lucius Sicinius.

That *Lucius Sicinius* the toothed excelled in valiantneſſe among the Romaines, the number of hys titles doo declare. This man was one of the Protectors of the cominalty, not much after the dryuing out of the Kinges, when *Spurius Tarpeius*, and *Aulus Thermus* were Conſuls. Hee beeing vanquiſher in eyght challenges hand to hande, hadde fiue and fortie ſcarres in the forepart of his bodye, and on hys backe part not one He tooke ſpoyle of his enemie foure and thirtie times. In horſetrappers, pure ſpeares, Bracelets and Crownes, hee earned three hundred & twelue rewards. Hee followed nyne Grandcaptaynes in tryumphe that had conquered by his meanes. Next after him *Marcus Sergius* ſeruing twice in the warres, in the firſt time receiued thirty and three wounds on the forepart of his body, and in the ſecond loſt his ryght hande, and therefore made him a hande of yron. And whereas almoſt none of both his handes were able to doo him any ſeruice in fight, yet notwithſtanding hee fought foure times in one day, and gotte the victorie with

Marcus Sergius, the Father of Catiline.

with his left hand,hauing had two Horses slayne vnder him. Béeing twise taken prisoner by *Hanniball*,he scaped awaie,when by the space of twentie monethes in which he had béene prisoner,he had at no time béen without Giues and Fetters. In all the sharpest battels which the Romaines tasted of in those dayes, he béeing honoured with warlike rewards, brought Ciuill Crownes from Thrasymenus,Trebia,and Pauy, At the battell of Canuas also, (out of the which it was counted a poynt of valiantnesse to escape wyth lyfe) he onelie receiued a Crowne. Happie doubtlesse had hée béene in so manie aduauncements of honor, if *Catiline* his next heyre by lineall descent, had not defaced his so renowmed praises with the hatefulnesse of hys cursed name.

As much as *Sicinius* or *Sergius* excelled among the Souldiours,so much among the Captaines (or rather among all men) excelled *Cæsar* the Dictator. Vnder his conducte were slaine eleuen hundred , fourescore and two thousand enemies. For he would not haue it noted howe manie hee ouerthrewe in the ciuill wars. He fought in piched fielde two and fiftie times, alonely surmounting. *Marcus Marcellus*,who in like sorte had fought nine and thirtie times. Besides this, no man wrote more swiftly,nor no man read more spéedilie. Moreouer,hee is reported to haue indited foure Letters at once. He was of so good a nature,that such as he subdued by battell,he more ouercame them with gentlenesse.

C. Iulius Cæsar.

CAP. VI.

VVho were notable for memorie: who loste theyr speech by mischaunce, or gotte it by chaunce, who florished in eloquence: of the prayse of manners, of godlinesse, of chastity, and who hath beene iudged happy.

Cyrus King of Persia.

CYrus was notable for the good gifte of memorie, who in the most populous armie whereof hee was Captaine, coulde call euerie seuerall personne by his name.

Lucius Scipio.

The same thing did *Lucius Scipio* amōg the people of Rome. But wee may beleeue that bothe *Scipio* and *Cyrus* were furthered by custome.

Cyneas.

Cyneas the Ambassador of *Pyrrhus*, the next day after he was entered into Rome, saluted both the Knights and also the Senators by their propper names.

Methridates.

Methridates King of Pontus ministred iustice without an interpreter, to two and twenty Nations that were vnder his dominion.

Memorie made by Arte.

It is manifest that memorie may be made by arte, like as in the Philosopher *Metrodorus* that was in the time of doggyshe *Diogenes*: who furthered himselfe so much by dailie practise, and beating with himselfe, that he kept in remembraunce what many men spake at once, not only in order of sence, but also in order of wordes. Notwithwithſtanding it hath béene often ſéene, that nothing may eaſiler be periſhed by feare, by falling, by chance, or by ſickneſſe. We haue founde that he that was but ſtriken with a ſtone, forgot to reade. Surely *Meſſala Coruinus* after a diſeaſe that hee had endured, was ſo ſtriken with forgetfulneſſe, that he remembred not his owne name, and yet otherwiſe his wit was freſhe enough. Feare aſtonieth ẏ memorie. And again feare is an enforcement of ſpéeche, the which it not onelie ſharpeneth, but alſo extorteth although there were none before. Surely when *Cyrus* in the eyght and fiftie Olympiad entred by aſſault into Sardis, a Towne of Aſia, where *Cræſus* at that time lay hidden, *Athis* the Kinges Sonne (who vnto that inſtaunt hadde alwaies béene dumbe,) burſt out into ſpéech by force of feare. For it is reported, that he cryed out: *Cyrus* ſpare my Father, and learne to know (at leaſt wiſe by our caſualties) that thou art a Man.

The periſhing and loſſe of memorie.

Meſſala Coruinus.

Feare.

Athis the Sonne of king Cræſus.

Nowe remaineth to intreate of manners, the excellentnes whereof appeared moſte in two men *Cato* the founder of the ſtocke of the Portians was a verye good Senator, a very good Orator, and a verie good Captaine. Neuertheleſſe, for diuers quarrelles picked vnto him of malice, he was endited and arrayned fortie and foure times, but yet was alwaies quitted. The praiſe of *Scipio Aemilianus* is yet greater: who beſides the vertues for which *Cato* was renowmed, ſurmounted alſo in loue towards the common weale. *Scipio Naſica* was iudged to bee the beſt man then lyuing, not onely by the voice of the commons, but alſo by the othe of the whole Senate, inaſmuch as none coulde bee founde worthier then he, to be put in truſte with a miſterie of chiefe Religion, when the Oracle gaue warning to fetch into the Cittie the holy Ceremonies of the mother of the Gods from Peſsinus.

Excellency of manners.
Cato.

Scipio Æmilianus.

Scipio Naſica

Eloquence or learning.

Many among the Romaines florished in eloquence, but this gift was not heritable at any time, sauing to the house of the Curios, in the which, three were Orators successiuelie one after another. Surely thys was counted a great thing in those dayes, when eloquence was had in chiefe estimation both of God and manne. For at that time *Apollo* bewrayed the murthers of the Poet *Archilocus*, and the deede of the felons was detected by God.

The singuler estimation of learning in those dayes.

Archilocus the Poet.

Sophocles the Tragedy wryter.

And at such time as *Lysander* King of Lacedæmon besieged Athens (where ẏ body of *Sophocles* the Tragedie wryter laye vnburied) *Bacchus* sundry times warned the Captaine in his sleepe, to suffer hys darling to be buried, and neuer ceased calling vppon him, vntyll *Lysander* hauing knowledge who it was that was departed, and what the God demaunded, tooke truce with the Athenians, vntill so worthy a corse might be buried accordinglie. *Castor* and Pollux standing wythout the dore in the sight of all men, called P*indarus* the Harper out of a place where he was making merrie, (which was at the point to fall) to the intent he should not perrish with the rest. Whereby it came to passe, that hee onelie escaped the daunger that hunge ouer their heads. Next vnto the Gods is *Cneus Pompeius* to be reconed: who when he should enter into the house of *Possidonius*, the notablest professor of wysedome in those dayes, forbadde his Mace-bearer to strike ẏ dore as the custome was: and so holding downe his sheaf, albeit hee hadde at that time dispatched the warre agaynste *Methridates*, and was Conqueror of ẏ East, yet of his owne free wyll he gaue place to the Gate of Learning. The firste *Scipio Affricanus* commaunded that the Image of *Quintus Ennius* shoulde be sette vppon his Tombe. *Cato* that slewe himselfe at Vtica, brought vnto Rome two Phylosophers, one when he

Pindarus the Harper.

Possidonius the Philosopher.

Quintus Ennius.

was Marshall of the Hoste, and another when he was Ambassador in Cyprus: alledging that in so dooing, he had greatlie benifited the Senate and people of Rome albeit that hys great Grandfather had oftentimes decreede, ÿ al Greekes should be utterly driuen out of the Citty. *Dennis* ÿ Tyran of Sicill sent a Shyppe decked wyth Garlonds to meete *plato*, and hee himselfe in a Charyot drawne with foure White steedes, entertained him honorably at his first comming to lande. Perfect wisedome was adiudged onely to *Socrates* by the Oracle of *Apollo*. Plato. Socrates.

The proofe of godlinesse and naturall affection toward the parents shined in the familie of the *Metels*. But it was found moste euident in a poore childbearing Woman. This Woman who was of lowe degree, and therefore not altogether so famous, beeing with much adoe (and after much serching oftentimes of the Gaolers, leaste shee shoulde haue carryed any meate in with her) suffered to goe to her father, (who was condemned to the punishment of perpetuall prysonne) was founde to feede him with the milke of her breasts: which thing consecrated bothe the deede and the place. For the Father which was condemned to death, beeing gyuen unto his daughter, was reserued in remembraunce of so woorthy a deede, and the place beeing dedicated to the power that wrought the deede, was made a Chappell, and entitled the Chappell of godlines. The ship that brought the holy misteries out of Phrygia, in following ÿ hearelace of *Claudia*, gaue unto her the preheminence of chastitie. But *Sulpitia* the daughter of *Paterculus* and wyfe of *Marcus Fulnius Flaccus*, was by the verdite of all the Ladyes in Rome aduisedlie chosen out of a hundred of the vertuousest of them, to dedicate the Image of *Venus* according as ÿ bokes of *Sybill* gaue warning to be done. Godlinesse. A poore childbearing woman. Chastitie. Claudia. Sulpitia,

Happynes.

As touching the title of happinesse, hee is not yet found that may rightly be iudged happy. For *Cornelius Sylla* was happie rather in name then in deede.

Cornelius Sylla

Aglaus.

Surelie *Cortina* iudged onelie *Aglaus* to be blessed: who beeing owner of a poore peece of ground in ẏ narrowest nooke of all Arcadie, was neuer founde to haue passed out of the boundes of his naturall soyle.

CAP. VII.

Of Italy and the prayse therof: and of many peculiar thinges that are founde therein.

AS concerninge Man I haue saide sufficient. Now to the intent we may returne to our determined purpose, our stile is to be directed to the recital of places: and chiefelie and principally to Italy, ẏ beautie whereof we haue alreadie touched lightly in the Cittie of Rome. But Italie hath beene written of so throughlie by all menne, and specially by *Marcus Cato*, that there cannot bee found that thing which the diligence of former Authors hath not preuented, for the Country is so excellent, as it ministreth matter of praise aboundantly, while the notablest writers consider the healthfulnesse of ẏ places, the temperatenesse of the ayre, the fruitfulnes of the soyle, the open prospects of the Hills, the coole shadowes of the woods, the vnhurtful lowe grounds, the plentifull increase of Vines and Oliues, the Sheepes

courses,

courses, the pasture groundes, so manye Riuers, so great Lakes, places that beare flowers twice a yeere, together with the Mountaine Vesuuius, casting vppe a breath of flaming fire as if it had a soule, the Bathes with their springes of warme water, the continuall beautifying of the Land with newe Citties, so goodlie a sight of auncient Townes, which first ẏ Aborigens, Arunks, Pelasgians, Arcadians, Sicilians, and lastlie the inhabiters of all parts of Greece, and aboue all others, the victorious Romaines haue builded. Besides this, it hath shoares full of Hauens, and coastes with large Bayes and harbouring places, meete for trafficke from all places of the world. Neuerthelesse, least it may seeme altogether vntouched of our part, I think it not vnconuenient to busie my wittes about those thinges that haue beene least beaten, and slightly to trauell through those thinges ẏ haue beene but lightly touched and tasted by others. For who knoweth not that Ianiculū was either named or builded by *Ianus*? Or that Latium was called so, & Saturnia of *Saturne*? Or that Ardea was builded by *Danaee*? Polydee by the companions of *Hercules*? Pompeios in Campane by *Hercules* himselfe, because that after his victory in Spayne hee draue his Oxen with a pompe that way? Or that the stonie fieldes in Lombardy tooke theyr names of that, that *Iupiter* fighting against ẏ Gyants, is supposed to haue rayned downe stones thither? Or that the Region Ionica tooke his name of *Ionee* the daughter of *Naulochus*, whom *Hercules* is reported to haue slaine, because he malepartlie stopped ẏ waies against him? Or that Alcippe was builded by *Marsias*, king of the Lidians, which beeing afterward swallowed with an Earthquake, was dissolued into the Lake Fucinus? Or that the Temple of *Iuno* of *Argos* was founded by *Iason*: Pisæ by *Pelops*; the *Dawnians*

The founders of the cheefe Cities and places in Italie.

by *Cleolaus* the Sonne of *Minos*: the Iapigians by *Iapix* the Sonne of *Dædalus*: the Tyrrhenians by *Tyrrhenus* King of Lydia: Cora by *Dardanus*: Argilla by the *Pelasgians*, who also brought Letters first into Latium: Phalisca by *Halesus* the Argiue: the Phalerians by *Phalerius* the Argiue: Fescininum also by the Argiues: the Hauen of Parthenium by the *Phocenses*: Tybur (as *Cato* witnesseth) by *Catillus* the Arcadian the Admirall of *Euanders* fleete: or (as *Sextius* saith) by the youth of *Argos*? For *Catillus* the Sonne of *Amphiaraus*, after the monstrous destruction of his Father at Thebæ, beeing sent by his Grandfather *Oecleus* with all his issue or ceremonies into Italy, begot there three Sonnes: *Tyburtus*, *Cora*, and *Catillus*, who dryuing out of the Towne the Sicanes of Sicill ẏ auncient inhabiters thereof, called the Cittie after the name of the elder brother *Tyburt*. Anon after was the Temple of *Minerua* builded by *Vlisses*, among the Brutians.

Who brought Letters first into the shyre where Rome is.

The Ilande of Ligæa tooke his name of the bodie of the Meremaid *Ligæa* cast a land there. Parthenopee was so called of the Meremaide *Parthenopees* Tombe: which towne it pleased *Augustus* afterward to call Naples. Prenestee (as *Zenodotus* reporteth) tooke his name of *Pranest* the Nephewe of *Vlisses*, and Sonne of *Latinus*: or (as the bookes of ẏ Prenestines make mention) of *Cæculus* whom the Sisters of the Digitians found by the fatall fires, as the bruite goeth. It is knowne that Petilia was founded by *Philoctete*, Arpos and Beneuent by *Diomed*, Padua by *Antenor*, Metapont by the *Pylians*, Scyllace by the Athenians, Sybaris by the Troyzenians, and by *Sagaris* the sonne of *Aiax*, of Locres. Salentum by the Lycians, Ancon by the Sicilians, Gabye by *Galace* and *Bius* of Sicill, brothers: Tarent by the posteritie of *Hercules*, the

Iland

Ilande Tensa by the Ionians , rest by the Dorians, Croton by *Myscell* and *Archia*, Rhegium by the Chalcidians, Cawlon and Terin, by the Crotonians, Locros by the Naritians. Heret by the Greekes, in the honour of *Iuno* whom they call *Hera*, Aritia by *Archilocus* the Sicilian, whereof the name (as liketh *Cassius Hermina*) is deriued.

In thys place *Orestes* by admonishment of the Oracle hallowed the Image of *Diana* of Scythia which he had fetched from Taurica, before hee went with it to Argos. The Zanclenses builded Metawre, and the Locrines builded that Metapont which is now called Vibo. *Bocchus* saith plainelie, that the Vmbrians are the auncient of-spring of the Galles. *Marcus Antonius* affirmeth that they were called Vmbrians in Greeke, because that in the time of the generall destructiõ that was by water, they escaped the daunger thereof. *Licinius* is of the opinion, that the originall of Messapia (which was giuen by *Messapus* a Gréeke) was afterwarde turned into the name of Calabrie, which in the first beginning *Peucerius* the Brother of *Oenotrius* had named Peuceria.

The like agreement also is among Authors, that Palynure tooke that name of *Palynure* the Pylotte of *Aeneas* his Shyppe, and Misene of hys Trumpetor *Misene*, and the Iland Leucosie of his Systers daughter *Leucosia*.

It is fully agréed vppon among all menne, that Caiet tooke that name of *Caieta*: *Aeneassis* Nurce, and Lauine of his wyfe *Lauinia*, which Towne was builded the fourth yéere after the destruction of Troy, as *Cussonius* auoucheth. Neither must it be omitted that *Aeneas* arryuing on the coast of Italy the second sommer after that Troy was taken (as *Hemina* reporteth) wyth no moe then 600. in hys companie, piched hys

The time of the comming of Æneas into Italy

Campe in the fieldes of *Laurent*, and there while hee was dedicating the Image that he had brought wyth him out of *Sicill*, vnto his Mother *Venus* by the name of *Aphroditee*, he receiued the Image of *Pallas* of *Diomed*, and anon after receiuing fiue hundred Acres of ground of King *Latinus*, hee raigned thrée yéeres in equall authoritie with him. After whose decease, when he had raigned two yéeres, he went to the Riuer *Numicius* and was neuer séene more.

The seauenth yéere after, was giuen to him the name of Father *Indiges*. Afterward were builded, by *Ascanius*, *Alba longa*, *Fidenee*, and *Antium*: by the *Tyrians*, *Nola*: and by the *Eubæans*, *Cumes*. There is the Chappell of the same *Sybill* which in the fift Olympiade was present at the *Romaine* enterprises, whose booke our Bishops resorted to for Counsell, vntill the time of *Cornelius Sylla*: for then was it together with the Capitoll consumed with fire. As for her two former bookes, shee hadde burned them with her owne handes, because *Tarquine* the proude did offer her a more niggardly price then she had sette them at. Her Tombe remaineth yet in *Sicill*. *Bocchus* auoucheth that *Sybell* of *Delphos* prophesied before the battel of *Troy*, and he declareth that *Homer* did put many of her verses into his worke.

Sybill of Cumes

Sybill of Delphos.

After her, within fewe yéeres space, followed *Heriphylee* of *Ærythra*, who was also called *Sybill* for the affinity she had with ye other in the same kind of knowledge: who among other great thinges, warned the *Lesbians* that they should loose the dominion of ye Sea, many yéeres before the thing came to passe. So ye very order of the time prooueth, that *Sybill* of *Cumes* was third after this. *Italy* therefore (wherein sometime the auncient Country of *Latium* stretched from the mouth of *Tyber*, vnto the Ryuer *Lyris*) ryseth whole together

Sybill of Ærithra.

The description of Italie.

together from the sides of the Alpes and reached to the toppe of the Promonorie or headlonde of Rhegium, and the Seacoast of the Brutians, where it shooteth Southward into the Sea. Procéeding from thence, it rayseth it selfe by little and little at the backe of the Mountaine Appenine, lying in length betwéene the Tuscane Sea and the Adriatish Sea, that is to saye, betwéene the vpper Sea and the neather Sea, like an Oken leafe, that is to say, larger in length than in breadth. When it commeth to the furthest, it deuideth into two hornes: whereof the one butteth vppon the Ionish Sea, and the other vppon the Sea of Sicill. Betwéene which two heades it receiueth not ẏ winding Sea in with one whole and maine shoare, but shooting foorth as it were sundrie tongues, it admitteth the Sea disseuered by the heads running forth in to the déepe.

There (to the intent we may note thinges heere and there by the way) are the Towres of Tarent, the Countrye Scyllæa with the Towne Scylleum, and the Riuer Crathis the mother of Scylla as antiquitie hath fabled: the Forrests of Rhegium, the Valies of Pesta: the Meremaids Rocks, the most delectable coast of Campane, the playnes of Phlegra, the house of *Circæ*: the Iland of Tarracine, sometime enuironed with the wauing Sea, but nowe by continuance of time landed vppe to the firme grounde, hauing cleane contrarie fortune to the Rhegines, whom the Sea by thrusting it selfe betwixt, hath violently dissenered frō the Sicilians. Also there is Formy inhabited somtime by the Lestrigones, and many other thinges entreated of at large by pregnant wittes, the which I thought more for mine ease to passe ouer, then not to set them out at the full. But the length of Italy, which runneth from Augusta Pretoria through the Cittie and Capua — The length of Italy.

vnto the Towne of Rhegium, amounteth to a thousand and twenty miles. The breadth of it where it is broadest, is foure hundred and ten myles: and where it is narrowest, a hundred and fixe and thirtie miles, sauing at the Hauen which is called *Hanniballes* Campe, for there it exceedeth not fortie miles. The hart of the Realme is in the fieldes of Rheatee (as *Varro* testifieth.) The compasse of the whole circuite together, is two thousand, foure hundred, fourescore and tenne miles. In the which circuit ouer againste the Coast of *Locres*, is finished the first Coast of Europe. For the seconde beginning at the heade of Laciuium, endeth at the Cliffs of * Acroceraunia. Furthermore Italie is renowmed with the Riuer Po, which Mount Vesulus one of the toppes of the Alpes, powreth out of hys bosome from a spring that is to be seene in the borders of * Ligurie: from whence Po issueth, and sinking into the ground, ryseth againe in the fieldes of Vibo, not inferior to any Ryuer in fame, and it is called of the Greekes, *Eridanus*. It swelleth in the beginning of the dogge dayes, at such time as ẏ snowes and hoarefrosts of the former Winter begin to melt: and so beeing increased with ẏ surplusage of waters, it carrieth thirtie Ryuers with him into the Adriatish Sea.

The breadth of Italie.

The whole circuit of Italy

* Now called mount Cimera.

The Ryuer Po.

* Nowe called Lombardy.

Among other thinges woorthy of remembraunce, this is famous and notably talked of in euery Mans mouth, that there are certaine housholds in the Countryes of the *Phalisks*, (which they call Hirpes.) These make yeerely sacrifice to *Apollo* at the Mountaine *Soractee*, and in performing thereof, doo in honor of the diuine seruice friske and dawnce vppe and downe vpon the burning wood without harme, the fire sparing them. Which religious and deuout kinde of ministration the Senate rewarding honourably, priuiledged the

A certaine kindred priuiledged from hurt of fire.

the Hirpes from all taxes, and from all kind of seruice for euer. That the Nation of the Marsyes can not bee hurt by serpents, it is no maruell. For they fetch their pedegrée from the Sonne of *Circee*, and of the power descended to them from their auncestors, they vnderstand that venemous thinges ought to stande in awe of them, and therefore they despise poysons. *C. Cælius* saith, that *Oetas* had thrée daughters: *Augitia*, *Medea*, and *Circee*, and that *Circee* possessed the Hilles called Circes Hilles, there practising to make sundry shapes and fashions through her sorceries and charmes. And that *Augitia* occupyed the Country about Fucinum, and there (after practising the wholesome sciences of Léechecraft against maladies and diseases) when shée forewent this life, was reputed for a Goddesse. And that *Medea* was buried by *Iason* at Buthrote, and her Sonne raigned among the Marsyes. But although that Italy haue this customable defence: yet is not altogether frée from Serpents. Finally, the inhabiters chased the Serpents from Amycle which the Amycleans of Greece had builded before.

A people vnable to be hurt by Serpents.

Circe, Augitia, and Medea the daughters of Oetas King of Colchos.

There is great store of a kinde of Vyper whose byting is incurable. They be somewhat shorter then the reste of Vipers that are founde in other places of the world, and therefore while they bee not regarded, they hurt the sooner. Calabrie swarmeth with Snakes that liue bothe by water & by land, called Chersydres: and it bréedeth the Boa, which is a kinde of Snake reported to grow to an vnmeasurable bignesse. First, it seeketh after Heardes of mylche Kyne, and what Cowe soeuer yeeldeth most milke, her dugs dooth hée draw. And batling with continuall sucking of her, in processe of tyme hee so stuffeth out hymselfe wyth ouerglutting hym tyll hee bée readie to burste, that at the last no power is able to withstande hys hugenesse.

A horrible kind of Viper.

A wonderfull kind of Snake.

So that in fine rauening vp the lyuing creatures, hee maketh the Countries waste where he keepeth. And in the raigne of *Claudius* there was séene a whole Chylde in the mawe of a Boa that was kylled in the filde which nowe is called Vaticane.

Wolues. Italy hath Wolues which are vnlike the Wolues of other Countryes, and therefore if they sée a Manne before a Man sée them, he becommeth dumbe, and beeing preuented with theyr hurtfull sight, although hee haue desire to crie out, yet hath he no vse of voice to doo it withall. I passe ouer manie thinges willingly concerning Wolues. This is moste certainly tryed, that in this beastes tayle is a very fine hare, that hath the power of loue in it, the which hee is willing to loose, and therefore casteth it away when he feareth to bee caught, for it hath no vertue vnlesse it be pulled from him while he is aliue. Wolues goe to sault not aboue twelue dayes in all the whole yéere. In time of famine they féede themselues with earth. But those that are called Hartwolues, although after long fasting when they haue hardly founde fleshe, they fall to eating it: yet if they happen to cast theyr eye vpon anie thing by chaunce, they forget what they are in dooing, and forsake theyr present aboundance, gadde to séeke newe reléefe wherewith to fill theyr bellyes. In thys kind of beastes is also rekoned the Lynxes, whose Urine such as haue narrowly searched the natures of stones, doo vphold to congeale into the hardnesse of a precious stone. Which thing that the Linxes themselues doo well perceiue, is proued by thys tryall: that as soone as the water is passed from them, by and by they couer it ouer (as much as they can) with heapes of sande: verily of spight (as *Theophrastus* auoucheth) least such matter issuing from them shoulde turne to our vse. This stone hath the colours of Amber. It draweth

Hartwolues.

Lynxes.
The stone Lyncurion.

it draweth vnto it thinges that bee néere at hande, it qualifieth the gréefe of the raynes : it remedieth the kinges euill, and in Gréeke it is called * Lyncurion.

* That is to say, Lynxpisse.

Dumb Grashoppers.

Grashoppers are dumbe among the Rhegines, and not elswhere, which silence of them is wonderfull: and good cause why, séeing the Grashoppers of ẏ Locrines theyr next neighbors, cry louder then all others. *Granius* reporteth the cause thereof to bee this: that when they made a yelling about *Hercules* as he rested there, he commaunded them to cease their chyrping, wherevpon beginning to holde theyr peace, they continued mute from thenceforth to thys day. The * Lygusticke Sea bringeth foorth shrubbes, which so soone as they be in the déepes of the water, are lushe and almost like a grystle to touch. But assoone as they come aboue the water, by and by degenerating from theyr naturall sappe, they become stones. And not onely the qualitie, but also the colour of them is turned, for straight way they looke Redde as Scarelette. The braunches of them are such as we sée on Trées, for the most part halfe a foote long, but seldome to bee found of a foote long. Of them are carued many prety things to were about folkes. For (as *Zoroastres* sayth) thys substaunce hath a certaine singuler power, and therefore whatsoeuer is made thereof, is counted among those thinges that are wholesome. Other folke call it Corall, and *Metrodorus* nameth it Gorgia. The same man affyrmeth also that it withstandeth whirlwinds and thunder and lightning. There is a precious stone dygged vp in a part of Lucanie, so pleasant to behold, that it casteth a Saffron colour vpon the starres dimmed inwardly and glimmering vnder a myste. The same stone is called a Syrtite because it was founde first vpon the Seacoast of the Syrts. There is also the Veientane stone, so named of ẏ place wher it is found,

* The Sea of Genoa.

Corall.

The Syrtite or sandstone.

The Veiétane Stone.

the colour whereof béeing blacke, for the more beautie of varietie, is enterlaced distinctly with white lynes, and whitish strakes. * The Ilande which faceth the coast of Puell, is renowmed with the Tombe & Temple of *Diomed*, and alonely nourisheth *Diomeds* birds. For this kind of Foule is no where els in al ÿ worlde but there. And that thing alone might séeme woorthy to bée recorded, though there were not other thinges beside not méete to bee omitted. They are in fashion almost like a Coote, of colour whyte, with fierie eyes, and toothed bylles. They flie in flocks, and not without order in theyr setting forth. They haue two Captaines, that rule theyr flight: of whom the one flyeth before, and the other behinde: the formost as a guyde to direct them certainly which way to flie, the hindermost as an ouerséar to haste forward them that lagge behinde, with continuall calling vpon them. And this is the order that they keepe in theyr fléeting. When bréeding time is at hande, they digge pits with their billes: and then bending wickers ouer them after the manner of Hardles, they close in that which they haue made hollow vnderneath.

* This Ilande is nowe called S. Maryes of Trinitie.

Diomedes birds

The wonderfull nature of them.

And least they might bee vncouered if paraduenture the windes should blowe awaie theyr woodden roofes, they coope this watling ouer with the earthe which they hadde throwne out when they digged the pittes. So they build theyr nestes with two entryes, and that not at a venture: insomuch that they caste their entries in and out, according to ÿ quarters of the heauen. The dore that they goe out at to their féeding, openeth into the East: and that which receiueth them home againe, is towarde the West. To the intent the light may both hast them when they make tariaunce, and also not faile them to return home by. When they will purge their paunches, they mount aloft against the wind, to the intent it may carrie their odoure the further from them. They discerne a straunger from a man of the Country. For if he be a Greeke, they approche unto him, and as far as may bee understanded, doo fawne gentlie uppon him as their Countriman. But if he be of anie other Nation, they flye upon him and assault him. They frequent the holy Church euery day after this maner. They wash their feathers in the water, & when they haue wet their wings throughlie, they come flocking al on a deaw, & so shaking the moisture uppon the Church, doo purge it. Then they rouse their feathers, & afterwarde, as hauing doone their deuotion, depart again. Hereuppon it is reported ẏ *Diomedes* cōpanions were turned into birds. Certainely before ẏ comming of ẏ Ætolian Captaine, they were not called *Diomedes* birds, but euer since they haue had that name.

The running forth of Italy through the Liburnians (which are a people that came out of Asia,) extendeth to the foote of Dalmatia, and Dalmatia unto the borders of Illyrick, in which coast ẏ Dardanians haue their dwelling, a people descended of the line of Troy, but growne wilde and sauage, and degenerated into barbarous manners. On the otherside it extendeth by the marches of Lombardie unto the Prouince of Narbone, in which the Phocenses (beeing in olde time chased out of theyr Countrey by the comming of the Persians,) builded the Cittie of Marsills in ẏ fiue and fortieth Olympiad.

Dalmatia and Illyrick are novv one countrey, and are called Sclauoni.

The founding of the Citty of Marsilles.

Caius Marius in the tyme of the warre against the Cymbrians, did let in ẏ Sea in Channels made wyth mans hand, & mittigated the dangerous sayling of the riuer Rhone, which falling down frō the Alps rusheth first through Swicerland carying with him a nūber of

The description of the Ryuer of Rhone.

waters that meete him by the way, and afterward by his continuall encrease becommeth more troublesome then the very Sea wherinto it falleth, vnlesse it bee when the Sea is raised with the wyndes. Rhone is rough euen in calme wether, and therefore they account him among the greatest Ryuers of Europe. In the same place also florished *Sexties* bathes, sometime the Consulles winter garrison, and afterward garnished with walles: the feruent heate whereof beeing breathed out, is vanished awaie by continuaunce of time, and it is not nowe according to the auncient report thereof. If we haue a mind to the Greekes, it is best to looke to the Seacoast of Tarent, from whence, (that is to saie from the Promontorie or Headlonde which they call * Acra Iapigia) is the shortest cutt for such as wil sayle to Achaya-ward.

Saint Mary of Leke.

CAP. VIII.

Of certaine base Iles of the Tyrrhene *Sea, which lye against* Italy *: Of Corsica, and of the stone Catochites.*

FRom hence our style is to bee directed another waie, and other lands call vs to treate of their matters, & it were a long péece of worke to goe leysurelie along the Seacoast to all the Ilandes that face the Promontories of Italy, although for that they bee scattered in most delectable out-

outnookes, and set by nature as it were to the shewe, they were not to be omitted. But how farre should I steppe aside, if delaying the chiefe thinges, I should of a certaine slothfulnesse treate of *Pandataria, or of *Prochita, or *Ilba plentifull of yron, or *Capraria, which the Greekes call Ægila, or *Planasia so called of the leuelnesse of the Sea, or of *Vlisses* straying: or *Doue-Ilande, the mother of the byrdes that beare that name, or Ithacesia, which is reported to haue been the watch-towre of *Vlisses*, or *Anaria named of *Homer* Iuarimee, and other no lesse fruitfull then these. Among which, manie hauing somewhat more largely treated of Corsica in wryting, haue moste exquisitlie comprised it to the full, and nothing is omitted which were not superfluous to be touched againe. As howe the Ligurians sent first inhabiters thither: how towns were there builded. How *Marius* and *Sylla* sent people a newe to refresh it: and howe it is beaten vpon with the Saltwater of the *Lygustick sea. But let all this geere passe. Neuerthelesse the Country of Corsica, (which is a peculiar thing to that land) doth onely bring forth the stone which they call Catochites, most worthie to be spoken of. It is bigger thē the rest, that are ordeined to decking, and it is not so much a Iewell as a common stone. If a man lay his handes vppon it, it holdeth them downe, so fastening it selfe vnto seuerall substances, that it cleaueth to the thinges that it is touched of. For there is in it I cannot tell what, a kinde of clammy glew and gummishnesse. I haue heard say, that *Democritus* the Abderite didde oftentimes vse to boast of this stone, to proue the hid power of nature, in the contentions that he hadde against the wyzardes.

* Palmaria or Palmarosa.
* Procida
* Elba.
* Caprara.
* Pianosa.
* Ischia.
* The sea of Genoa,
The Catochite

Iulius Solinus Polyhistor.

CAP. IX.

Of the Ile Sardinia *: of the* Shonnsunne *: of the hearbe* Sardonia *: and of the wonderfull power of waters.*

S*Ardinia* which we reade of in *Timæus*, by the name of Sandaliotes, and in *Chrysippus* by the name of Ichnusa, is sufficiently knowen in what Sea it lyeth, and who were firste inhabiters thereof. Wherefore it is to no purpose to tell howe *Sardus* was begotten of *Hercules*, and *Norax* of *Mercurie*: and howe the one comming from Lybye, and the other from as far as Tartesus in Spaine into these quarters: the Lande tooke his name of Sardus, & the Towne of Nora toke his name of *Norax*. Or howe anon after, *Aristæus* reigning ouer them, vnited the people of bothe the races together into the next Cittie Caralis which himselfe had builded, and knitt the two sundry Nations which hetherto had béene disseuered, together into one order of lyuing: in such sorte as the strangnesse thereof made them not disdaine to become hys Subiects. This *Aristæus* also begatte *Iolaus*, who inhabited the Countrie thereabouts. Furthermore, wée wyll passe ouer both the Ilians and Locrines.

Sardinia is without Serpents. But looke what noysomnesse Serpents bring to other places, the same noysomnesse bringeth the Shonsunne to the Countrey of Sardinia. It is a verie little Worme and like to a

The Shonsunne

Spyder

Spyder in shape, and it is called a *Shonsunne* because it shunneth the daie light. It lyeth moste in Syluer Mynes, for the soile of that Land is rich of Siluer. It creepeth priuily, and casteth the plague vppon such as sitte vpon it vnwares. To the furtheraunce of thys mischiefe cometh also the Hearbe *Sardonia*, which groweth much more plentifully the needeth, in groues where springes runne. If it be eaten, it drawweth together the sinewes, and wryeth the mouth, so yͤ such as thereby drawe vnto death, doo die with resemblance of laughter. Contrariwise, all the waters of that Ile, doo serue to diuers commodities. The standing pooles are full of fish. The Winters rayne is kept to releeue the Sommers drowght, and the Men of *Sardinia* haue much aduauntage of raynie water. For they gather it and keepe it in store, that it may doo them ease when the springes faile them which serued them for theyr meate & drinke. In some places doo bubble vp warme and holesome springes, which serue for cures in knitting of broken bones, or expulsing yͤ poysonne sheaded by the *Shonsunnes*, or in dryuing away diseases of the eyes. But those that remedy yͤ eyes, haue power also to discouer theeues. For whosoeuer denyeth the theft wyth an oath, washeth his eyes with thys water. If hys oath bee true, his sight becommeth the clearer: if he forsware himselfe, the fact is detected by blindnesse: and he is driuen to confesse hys faulte in darknesse, with the losse of hys eyes.

The Hearbe Sardonia.

The wholesomnesse and commoditie of the waters of Sardinia.

A water that discouereth theft.

Iulius Solinus Polyhistor.

CAP. X.

Of Sicill, and the Land Pelorias, *and the nature of the waters there: of the Mountaine* Ætna, *and many other wonders of that Ile: and of the seauen Iles called* Vulcanes *Iles.*

AND if wee haue respecte to the order of the times or of the places: after *Sardinia*, the matters of Sicill doo call vs next.

First, because that bothe those Iles beeing broughte in subiection to the Romains, were made Prouinces both at one time. For *Marcus Valerius* was made Gouernour of Sardinia, and *C. Flaminius* Pretor of Sicill all in one yeere: and secondly for that immediatly after you are out of the straights of Sicill, the Sea beareth the name of the Sardine Sea. Sicill therefore, (which thing is firste and formost to bee marked) by reason of his heads shooting forth, is platted three cornered. (a) Pachynnus lookes toward, (b) Peloponnesus and the South coast. (c) Pelorus beholdeth Italy, butting Westward vppon it. (d) Lylibye shooteth towarde Affrick. Among which, the Countrey about Pelorus is commended, for the temprature of ẏ soyle, inasmuch as it neyther wassheth away into durt through ouermuch moysture, nor crumbleth into dust through ouermuch drynesse. Where it goeth further

The Plat of Cicilye.
(a) Capo passaro
(b) Morea
(c) The heade of the fare.
(d) Capo Boey.

further into the maine land-warde, and enlargeth in wydenesse, it hath thrée Lakes. Of the one, that it is well stored with fish I count no great wonder. But the next vnto it, for that in the thicke groues among the shadowy shrubbes of young trées, it nourisheth wilde beastes, and admitteth hunters by drye pathes wherein they may haue accesse a foote by land, seruing to bothe vses of hunting & fishing, is numbred among the notable thinges. The third is proued to bee holie by an Altar standing in the mids, which deuideth the shallowes from the deepes. All the waie that leadeth vnto it, the water is but midde legge déepe. Whatsoeuer is beyonde, may neither be gaged nor touched. If it be: he that attempteth it is punished for his labour and looke howe much of himselfe he putteth into the water, so much he goeth about to destroy. They say that a certaine man threw a line as farre as he coulde into the déepes, and ÿ as to recouer it againe he thrust his arme into the water to the intent to haue ÿ more strength to pull, his hand became rotten. The coaste of Polorias is peopled with inhabitants of Tauromium, which Men in old time called Naxus. The towne of * Messana is sette directly oueragainst Rhegium of Italy; vnto the which Rhegium the Greekes gaue that name, by reason of the breaking of that place.

A Lake that serues both for hunting and fishing.

A straunge Lake.

* Messana.

Pachinnum is moste plentifull of Tunnyes and al other Sea fish, and therefore there is alwaies great fishing. The beautie of the Headlond of Lyliby, is the Towne Lylyby with the Tombe of Sybill. Long before the siedge of Troy, King *Sicanus* arryuing in the Ile with an Hoste of Spanyards, named it Sicanie. Afterwarde *Siculus* the Sonne of *Neptune* called it Sicill. Into this land resorted many of the *Corinthyans*, *Argiues*, *Ilians*, *Dorians*, and Men of Candy. Among whom also the * Master of all Carpenters & Masons

The first inhabiters of Sicill.

* Archimedes.

hath the chiefe Cittie, Syracuse, in which euen in winter season when fayre wether is hidden, the Sunne shyneth euery day. Moreouer the Fountaine Arechusa is in this Cittie. The highest hylles in it, are Ætna and Eryx * Ætna is hallowed vnto *Vulcane*, and Eryx, vnto *Venus*. In the toppe of Ætna are two chinkes which are named Cuppes, at which the vapor bursteth out, with a great roaring going before, which runneth rumbling a long while together in the bowels of the earth, through the burning brakes of hollow holes within. Neither do the flakes of fire rise out, vntill such time as the roaring & rumbling wythin haue gone before. This is a great wonder. And it is no lesse wonder that in that burning heate, nature is so stubborne, that it bringeth foorth snowe mingled wyth the fire: and that although it boyle in outragious heate, yet the toppe of it is whyte with snowe, as if it were continuall winter.

* Mount Gibell and the wonderfulnesse thereof.

There is therefore an inuincible force in bothe, so that neyther the heate is abated by the colde, nor the colde asswaged by the heate. There are also two hyls: Buckhyll and *Neptunes* hyll. Uppon *Neptunes* is a watchtowre that looketh into the Tuskane and Adriatish Seas. Buckhyll taketh hys name of the store of redde and fallowe Déere that walke vp and down there in heards.

Whatsoeuer Sicill bringeth forth, whither it bee by the nature of the soyle, or by the deuice of Man, it is next those thinges that are iudged to be the best: sauing that in the fruits of the earth, there is none comparable to the fruite of * Centuripe. Heere was the Commedy inuented: heere came the sporting of Iesters firste vppon the Stage: heere was the house of Archimedes, who accordynge to the Scyence of Astronomie, was the fyrste inuenter of Engynes.

* Cantorby.

Héere

Héere was that *Lais* that hadde rather choose her Countrey then bee knowne of her Countrey. The great Caues vnder the grounde beare witnesse of the race of the Cyclops. The place wherein the *Lestrygons* dwelt, beareth theyr name still. Of that Countrey was *Ceres* the Ladie of tillage and husbandry. In the selfe same place is the fielde of * Ænna continuallie full of Flowres, and freshe like the spring euerye day of the yeere, by which there is a hole sunken into the grounde, whereat *Dis* the Father of Hell hadde frée passage into the worlde (as fame goeth) when hee rauished *Proserpine*.

* That place is now called Anna.

Betwéene * Catina and * Syracuse is contention for the memoriall of the two famous Brethren, whose names eche part chalengeth seuerallie to themselues. If we giue eare to the *Catinenses*, it was *Anapias* and *Amphinomus*. If we credite that which the *Siracusans* would willingly haue, we must thinke they were *Aemanthius* and *Crito*. Neuerthelesse, the cause of ye déede procéeded from the Countrie of Catina. Into which at such time as the fire of Ætna had burst out, two young men taking vppe theyr Parents, carryed them out through the flames vnhurt of the fire. They yt came after, didde so reuerence the memorie of these younge men, that the place where they were buried, was named the field of the godly.

* Catanea.
* Saragoza.

A notable example of loue toward the Parents.

As touching Arethusa and Alpheus, it is true vnto thys day, that the fountaine & the Ryuer méete both in one channell. In the Riuer is the greatest store of wonders. If any man that is not of chast & cleane life take of ye water of ye fountaine *Diana*, which runneth by Camerine, the liquor of the wine, and the liquor of the water will not ioyne in one substance. Among the Segestans, the Ryuer Herbesus séething vp suddainlye in the mids of the streame, becommeth excéeding hote.

The Fountaine Arethusa and the Riuer Alpheus.

The Well of Diana.

Herbesus.

Acis.
Hymerus.

Acis, for all that it issueth out of the Mountaine Æt-na, yet can no Riuer be colder then it is. Hymerus is altered with the Coast of the ayre. For while it runneth Northward it is bytter: but when it turneth into the South it is swéete. There is not more strangenesse in the Waters then in the Saltmynes. If yee throwe the Salt of Arigent into the fire, it melteth in burning: and if ye put water to it, it cracketh as if it were burned.

Saltmynes.
* Gergent.

Æna beareth salt of a purple colour. In Pachynnus it is founde so shéere, that yée may sée through it. The other Saltmynes that are néere eyther to Arigent or Centuripe serue in stéede of quarries. For out of them they haue Images to the likenesse of men or Gods. In the places where the whote waters are, is an Ilande that groweth full of Réedes verye méete to make pypes of all manner of sortes: whither they be Precentories whose vse is to play before the shrynes of the Gods: or Vasks, which excéede the Precentories in number of holes: or maydenpipes, which haue that name of their cléere sounde: or Gingrynes, wᶜ though they be shorter, yet haue they a shriler sound: or Miluines which haue sharpest sounde of all: or Lydians which they call also Turaries: or *Corinthyans*, or *Aegiptians*, or any others, howe diuerslie soeuer they bee named by Musicians, according to the diuers and sundrie vses which they serue for. In the Country Halesine there is a Fountaine, at all times quiet & calme, when no noyse is made, which riseth vpp if a Shalme be plaid vpon, leaping at the sound, and swelling ouer his brimmes as though he were in loue with ẏ swéetnesse of the Musicke. The Poole of Gelon with hys stinking sauour, dryueth away such as come nigh. Also there are two springes, whereof if a barraine Woman taste the one, she shall become fruitfull: and if a

A dauncing Fountaine.

A stincking Poole

child-

childbearing Woman taste of the other, shee becommeth barrain. The Poole of the Petrenses is hurtfull to serpents, but wholsome to men. In the Lake of Arigent swimmeth an Oyle aboue. This fatnes throgh the continuall wauing of the Reedes, cleaueth to the toppes of them: out of the sedgie heare whereof is gathered a medicinable oyntment against the diseases of great Cattell. Not farre from thence is *Vulcans* Hyll, vpon which when men doo sacrifice, they lay Vynesticks vppon the Alters, without putting fire thereto when they cast on the offalles.

Vulcans Hyll, See howe the deuill can worke false miracles.

If the God like well of it, (for that is the tryall of the sacrifice) the sticks (bee they neuer so greene) doo take fire alone, and the God to whome the sacrifice is made, causeth it to burne without kindling. And as they are making mery, the flame playeth with them, and scoping out in wreathed flakes among them sindgeth not any man whom it toucheth. but sheweth it selfe to be none other thing then the Image of fire, declaring that the vowe is rightfully performed In the same field of Arigent, doo burste out quagmyres of mudde. And as ÿ vaines of Fountaines serue to make Riuers, so in this part of Sicill the soile neuer faileth, and earth with continuall vtterance casteth out earth. Sicill yeelded first the stone * Achates, founde in the banks of the Ryuer Achates, which was of no small price as long as it was found no where els. For the vaines imprinted in it do portrait such natural shapes therein, that when it is of the best making, it representeth the likenesse of many thinges. For which consideration the Ring of King *Pyrrhus* that made war against the Romaines, was not meanely spoken of, the stone whereof was an Agate, wherein were to bee seene the nine Muses, euerie one with theyr seuerall cognisaunces, and *Apollo* with hys viall in hys hand,

* The Agate.

The Ring of king Pyrrhus.

 not

not engrauen by arte, but growne by Nature. But nowe it is founde in diuers other places. Candy yéeldeth a kind of them which they call Corallagats, because they are like Corall. It is powdered with drops glistering like Golde, and it resisteth Scorpions. Inde yéeldeth of them expressing the proportions of Forrests and Beastes: the sight whereof comforteth the eyes. And béeing receiued into the mouth, it stauncheth thyrst. There are also of them which béeing burned doo cast a sent like Myrrhe. The Achate is ful of redde spots like bloode. But those that are most setts by, haue the cléerenesse of Glasse as the Achate of Cyprus. For those that looke like ware, (because there is aboundance of them) are as little estéemed as ỹ stones in the stréetes.

Coralagats.

The circuit of all thys whole Ile, is thrée thousand furlonges about. In the narrowest Sea of Sicill, are the Iles Hephestiæ, fiue and twenty myles distant from Italy. The *Italians* cal them *Vulcans* Iles. For these by reason of the whole nature of their soile, do eyther borrow fire of the Mountaine Ætna, or els minister fire vnto it by priuie intercourse vnder the grounde. Héere was appointed the dwelling place of the God of fire. They are in number seauen. Lypara tooke that name of King *Lyparus*, who gouerned it before *Aeolus*. Another they called * Hiera. The same is chéefely halowed vnto *Vulcane*, and burneth moste in the night time wyth an excéeding hygh hyll. The thirde named * Strongyle which was the Pallace of *Aeolus*, standeth toward the Sunne rysing. It is least couered, and it differeth somewhat from the reste in cléerenesse of flames. Héerevppon it commeth to passe that chiefely by the smoake thereof, the inhabiters vnderstand before, what windes are like to blowe three daies after. And this is the cause why *Aeolus* was beléeued

The whole circuit of Sicilie.

Vulcans Iles.

* Maretam

* Strombolie.

leeued to be the God of wyndes. The rest, Didymee, * Ericusa, * Phænicusa, and Euonimon, because they be like the other, we haue as good as spoken of them already.

* Alicur.
* Fælicaria.

CAP. XI.

Of the thyrd Coast of Europe: of the Countryes and places of Greece: of many thinges worthy to be recounted in them: and of the Nature of Partriches.

THe third Coast of Europe beginneth at the Mountaines of * Ceraunii, and endeth at Hellespont. In this coast among the *Molossians* (where as is the Temple of *Iupiter* of *Dodon*) is the Mountaine Tomarus, renowmed for ẏ hundred Fountaines ẏ are about the foote of it, as *Theopompus* reporteth. In * Epyre is a holy wel, cold aboue all other waters, and of approued contrarietie. For if yee dippe a burning brand therein, it quencheth it: and if you hold it a good way of without any fire on it, of it owne nature it kindleth it. Dodon (as *Maro* sayth) is hallowed vnto *Iupiter*. Delphos is renowmed with the Riuer Cephisus, the Fountaine Castalie, & the mountain Parnasus. Acarnania hawnteth of Aracynth. This Country is deuided frō Ætolia wyth the Mountaine Pindus, which breedeth Acelous a ryuer anciently renowmed among the chiefe Riuers of

* Cimera of Albany.

* Albanye.
A well of strang nature.

Dodon.
Delphos.

The situation of Acarnania.

and not vnworthely, considering that among the little stones that lye glistring in his bancks, there is founde the * Galactite, which béeing it selfe blacke, if it bee chafed yéeldeth a whyte iuyce that tasteth like Milke. Béeing tyde about a woman that gyueth sucke, it maketh her breasts full of milke: béeing tyde to a Chyld, it causeth more aboundant swallowing of spettle, and béeing receiued into the mouth it melteth, but therewithall it perisheth the gyft of memory. Thys stone is founde in Nylus and Achelous, and not in any third place. Néere vnto the Towne of Patræ, is a place called Scioessa shadowed with the couert of nine Hylls, and not renowmed for any other cause, then that the beames of the Sunne come almoste neuer there. In * Laconia is an issue out of the earth, called Tænarus.

* The Galactite or Milkstone.

Scioessa

* The Country about Lacedemon.

Tænarus is also the Headlonde against Affricke, where as is the Chappell of *Arion* of Methymna, who was brought thither by a *Dolphin*, as hys Image of brasse witnesseth there portrayted out liuely, according as the chaunce happened, and as the thing was doone indéede. Moreouer, ẏ very time expressed there, namelie the twenty and nine Olympiad (in which the same *Arion* is recorded victor at the gaming in Sicill) auoucheth the selfe same thing to haue béene doone.

The storie of Arion the Musician, that was brought thether through the Sea vppon a Dolphins backe.

There is also a Towne called Tænaron of noble antiquitie. Furthermore there are certaine Citties, and among them Leutræ, somewhat famous by reason of the shamefull ende that the *Lacedemonians* made there of late: and Amyclæ brought to destruction in olde time through theyr owne silence: and * Sparta renowmed with the Temple of *Castor* and *Pollux*, and also with the tytles of Otryas a manne of greate fame: And Theramnee from whence first sprang the worshipping of *Diana*: and Pitane which *Archesilaus* the

* Called also Lacedemon, and now called Mizithra.

the Stoicke (who was borne there) did bring to lyght by the desert of his wysedome: And Anthea and Cardamilee, where was sometime ÿ Cittie Thyre, which now is but the name of a place, where was fought a notable battell betwéene the Lacedemonians and the Argyues, the seauentéenth yéere of the raigne of Romulus. For the Mountaine Taygeta and the Ryuer Eurotas are better knowne then that they néede to bée written of. Inachus a Ryuer of Achaia cutteth through all the Country of Argoly, which tooke his name of *Inachus* the first founder of the nobility of Argos. The beautie of Epidaurus is the Chappell of Æsculapius, where sicke and diseased personnes lodging, are informed by dreames of remedyes for their maladies. It is sufficient to put you in remembraunce, that there is in Arcady a towne called Pallanteũ, which by meanes of *Euander* the Arcadian, gaue the name to our Pallace.

Taygeta. Inachus.

Epidaurus nowe called Rhagusia and Dubronik

In Arcady are the Mountaines Cyllen, Lycæus, and Menalus renowmed with the Gods that were misered in them, among which, Erymanthus is not obscure. Also among the Rivers is Erymanthus springing out of the Hill Erymanthus, and the famous Ladon. Héereabouts the encounters of *Hercules* are apparant. *Varro* affirmeth that there is a * Fountaine in Arcady which killeth as manie as drinke of it. In this part of the world we finde this thing not vnworthy to be mentioned concerning byrds, that whereas in other places Mauisses be yellowe as golde, about Cyllen they are as whyte as milke. Neyther is the stone to be despised which Arcady sendeth. The name thereof is Asbest. It is of the colour of yron: and béeing sette on fire, it cannot be quenched. Into the Baye of Megara shooteth the Isthmos which is renowmed with gamings kept there euery fift yéere, & wyth the

Arcady.

* This Fountaine was named Phineus.

White Mauisses.

The stone called Asbest.

The gamings of Isthmos.

Temple of *Neptune*. The said gamings (as is reported) were instituted in resemblance of the fiue coastes of * Peloponnesus which are beaten vpon wyth fiue sundrie Seas. On the Northside with the Ionian sea, on the West with the Sicilian Sea, on ẏ Southweste with the Ægean Sea, on the Northeast with the Myrtoan Sea, and on the South with the Candian Sea. This pastime béeing put downe by the Tyrant *Cypselus*, was by the Corinthians restored to the former solemnitie, in the fortie and nine Olimpiad. But the name of Peloponnesus declareth that *Pelops* was king of that Countrey. The platforme of it, is like ẏ leafe of a Plane trée with Créekes and nookes, and it maketh a diuorce betwéene the Ionian Sea, and the Aegæan Sea, disseuering the one shore from the other, with a slender balke not aboue foure myles broade, which for the narrownesse thereof men call Isthmos. From hence beginneth Hellas, which properlye they would haue to bée the true Greece. That Countrey which is nowe called Attick, was in former time called, Actee. Therein is the Cittie Athens, néere wher to adioyneth Scyrons Rocke, extending sixe myles in length, so named in honour of *Theseus* his victorie, and in remembraunce of the notable punishment of *Scyron*. From this Rocke *Ino* casting her selfe headlonge into the déepe, increased the number of the Goddes of the Sea. But we will not so slightlie passe ouer the Mountaines of Attick. There are Icary, Brilesse, Lycabet, and Ægialus. But Hymet doth most worthelie beare the bell among them all, because that béeing verie full of flowres, the Honny thereof excelleth ẏ Honnie of all other places, not onely of forraigne Lands, but also of the same Countrey, in pleasaunt sauor and taste.

They wonder at the Fountaine Callyrhoee, & yet they

* Now called Morea.

The description of Peloponnesus.

The true Greece.

Athens nowe called Satines.

Mount Hymet.

The Fountaine Callyrhoe.

they make not therefore the leſſe account of another Fountayne called Crunesſos. The place of iudgment among ẏ Athenians is called Ariopagus. The plaine of Marathon was made famous by ẏ report of a moſt bloody battell foughten there. Manie Iles lye ouer against the maine Lande of Attick, but Salamis, Sunium, Cos, and Ceos which (as *Varro* witneſſeth) yéelded the firſt Garments of fine ſpynning ẏ were made of wooll for the decking of Women) are almoſte ſuburbes to the Cittie. Bæotia is renowmed with Thebæ, which Cittie was builded by *Amphion*. Not that he drew ſtones together with the ſound of his Harpe, (for it cannot ſéeme likely that anie ſuch thing ſhould be done) but for that with the ſwéetneſſe of his eloquence, he allured menne that dwelt in Rocks (who were altogether ſauage and vnnurtured,) to become obedient to ciuil order and diſcipline. This Citty glorieth in the Godds that were borne within her wals, as they affirme which with holy verſes doo ſet out the commendations of *Hercules* and *Bacchus*. At Thebæ is the Groue Helicon, the Forreſt Cytheron, the Riuer Iſmenius, and the Fountaines Arethuſa, Oedipus, Pſamatee, and Dircee: but before all others Aganippe and * Hippocrenee, which becauſe *Cadmus* the firſt inuenter of Letters founde out as he rode about to ſearche what manner of Country he was come vnto, the Poets ranne vpon the brydle of liberty, publiſhing in theyr writinges, bothe that the one of them was raiſed by the ſtamping of a winged Horſes hoofe, and that the other béeing taſted of, did endue mennes mindes with eloquence: and alſo that the winged Horſes hoofe was opened, and that the waters there of béeing dronke, inſpired folke wyth learning.

This battell was betweene the Perſians and Athenians.

Bæotia. Thebæ nowe called Thiua,

Helicon

* Horſewell

The Ilande * Eubea by ſhooting his ſide againſt the Coaſte of the maine Lande, dooth make the

* Negropont.

 Hauen

The Hauen of Aulis.

Hauen of Aulis, renowmed in all ages for remembe-raunce of the confederacie of Gréece. The Bæotians are the same people that were the Lelegs, through whose Country runneth the Riuer Cephisus & falleth into the Sea. In this land is the Bay of Oxus, the Towne of Larissa, and Delphiramne also, wherein is the Chappell of Amphiaraus, and the Image of *Diana*, which the Caruar *Phidias* did make. *Varro* supposeth that there are two Riuers in Bæotia, though of nature vnlike, yet nothing differing in wonderfulnesse. If shéepe drinke of the one, theyr fléeces change into a Russet colour. If they drinke of the other: as manie of their fléeces as were of a browne coloure, become whyte. He addeth moreouer that there is a pitte to be séene, that killeth as manie as drinke of it.

Two wonderfull Ryuers,

Where as Partriches in all other places are frée like as the rest of birds be, in Bæotia they are not frée: neither are they at liberty to flye where they list, but but haue boundes in the verie ayre, which they dare not passe. Insomuch that they neuer goe beyond theyr appointed limits, nor neuer flie ouer into ÿ Marches of Athens. This is peculiar to the Partriches of Bæotia. For such things as are common to all other Partriches, we will treate of generally héereafter. Partriches are slie in trimming and fencing their nestes. For they hedge in their haunts with pricking shrubs, and sharpe sprigges, to the intent such beastes as are noysome vnto them may bee kept off with the sharpnesse of the thornes. Vnder their Egges they lay dust: and they come and goe priuily, least theyr often haunting should bewray the place. Many times ÿ Hennes remoue the egges out of the way, to deceiue ÿ Cocks, who trouble them out of all measure with theyr continuall flickering about them. There is fighting among the Cocks for the Hens: and it is thought that those

The Partriches of Bæotia

The nature of Partriches in generall.

those which are ouercome, do abide the other to tread them as if they were Hennes. They are so ranke of nature, that if the winde do but blow from ẏ Cocks, the Hennes become with egge, euen wyth the verye sent of them. And if anie manne come neere the place where they sitte, the Hennes springing forth do offer themselues of their owne accorde to the commers, and feygning some default in their feete or their winges, (as though they might be by and by caught) they coũterfet a slowe pace before them. By which subtiltye they eg forth such as they meete, and mocke them vntill they haue tolled them and drawne them a greate way of from theyr neste. Neyther are their yong ones lesse carefull for theyr parte, howe to saue themselues. For when they perceiue that they are seene, they caste themselues vpon their backes, and take vp cloddes in theyr feete, with the couert whereof they hyde themselues so subtillie, that they escape euen when they are founde.

CAP. XII.

Of Thessaly *&* Magnesia, *and of the Townes therin: of the Riuer* Peneus*: of the plesantnes of* Tempee*: of the heyght of the Mountaine* Olimpus*: and of him that stroke out King* Philips *eye.*

T*Hessaly* is the same country ẏ beareth ẏ name of Æmonia, which *Homer* calleth Argos Pelasgicũ, where *Hellen* was borne, of whom the Kinges were called *Hellens*. At the backe heereof stretcheth Pieria toward Macedonie: which béeing cōquered, came in subiection to the *Macedons*. Manie Townes and many Ryuers are there. Of Townes the notablest are Phthia, Larissa, Thessalia, & Thebæ. Of Ryuers, the notablest is Peneus, which running downe by Ossa and Olimpus, by meanes of the Hyls bowing gently on bothe sides with wooddy bottoms, maketh the Thessalian Tempee: and swéeping thence wyth broader streames through Macedonie & Magnesia, falleth into the Gulfe of Thermy. Unto Thessalie belong the playnes of Pharsaly, wherein were the thundring stormes of the * ciuill wars. And to the intent we goe not altogether to knowne hyls: let them buzie themselues about Othrys & Pindus, which séeke for the originall of the Lapythes: or about Ossa which delight to linger in the Fables of the Centaures. As for Pelion, the mariage feast of *Peleus* and *Thetis* haue brought it so much to knowledge, that it may be a maruell howe it should be kept in huggermugger. For the thinges that are to bee séene in Olympus, do declare that *Homer* did not celebrate it throgh vnaduised rashnesse. For it ryseth so bigge, with so hygh a toppe, that the dwellers by do call the knappe of it heauen. Ther is on the top of it an Altar dedicated to *Iupiter*, where vpon if any part of the inwards be layd, they are neyther blowne a sunder wyth blastes of the wynde, nor washed away with rayne: but when the yéere comes about againe, they are founde the selfe same that they were left. And whatsoeuer is once consecrated there vnto the God, it is priuiledged for euer frō corruption of the aire. Letters written in the ashes continue tyll the Ceremonies of the next yéere. In the Country of Magnesia is the Towne of * Methone, in the siedge wherof *Phillip* the Father of great *Alexander* of Macedonie, lost hys eye by the stripe of an Arrow, which

Betweene Cæsar and Pompey.

Mount Olimpus

Modon.

a Townes-

a Townſman named *Aster* ſhot at him with his own name, and the name of the party that he ſhot it at, and the place that he wounded written thereuppon. That this people could ſkyll of Archery, we may beléeue by *Philoctetes*, foraſmuch as Melibæa is reckoned in the foote of thys Country. But to the intent we procéede no further then wee haue Poets for our defence, the fountaine Libethrus alſo appertaineth to Magneſia.

Philoctetes,

CAP. XIII.

Of Macedonie, *and the ſucceſſyon of the Kinges thereof: and of the ſtone* Peantis.

THe people which were ſometime the *Edonians*, and that which was the Lande of Migdony, or the Countrey of Pieria, or Aemathia, is nowe in one entyre terme the Realme of Macedonie. And the partitions which héeretofore were ſeuerally diſioyned, béeing nowe vnited in the name of *Macedones*, are become all one body. Macedonie therefore is bounded on the forepart with yͤ Marches of Thrace. The South Countrey of Theſſaly is inhabited by the *Epirots*. On the Weſtſide are the * *Dardanians* and *Illyrians*. Where the North beateth vpon it, it is fenced in with Pæony & Pelagony From the Triballs it ſhooteth foorth in Mountaines to the colde Northeaſte wynde. It is deuided from Thrace by the Riuer Strymon which runneth from yͤ Mountayne Hæmus.

The bounds of Macedonie

* The people of Seruia & Raſcia,

But to passe Rhodopee with silence which is a Mountaine of Mygdony, and Athos sayled through by the Persian fleete, and cutt of frõ the maine Land, by the mountenaunce of a myle & a halfe, together wyth the vaines of Gold and Siluer, wherof there are digged vppe verie good and great store in the fieldes of Macedonie, I wyll speake of the Countrey Orestide. There are a people which take the name of Orestides heerevpon. *Orestes* fleeing like an outlawe from Mycene after he had killed his mother, forasmuch as hee hadde determined to goe further of, commanded that a yong Sonne of hys, borne in Aemathia of Hermione whom he had taken to be his companion in all aduentures, should be brought vp priuilie heere. The Childe bearing his Fathers name, as he grew to mans estate so also grewe in courage and stomacke meete for hys royall race: and conquering all that extendeth to the Coast of Macedony, and the Adriatish Sea, hee called the Land (whereof he was ruler) Orestide.

The Orestides

Phlægra (in which place, before there was anye Towne there, the report goeth ý a battell was fought betweene the hoste of Heauen and the Gyants,) doth put vs in minde to declare throughlie with how great proofes of soueraigntie there, the tokens of that Heauenlie warfare haue and doo continue it vnto thys day. If at any time (as it commeth to passe indeede) the brookes ryse with foule weather, and the excesse of waters breaking theyr bankes doo shoote themselues ouer violently into the fields: they say that euen now through the gulling of the water, are discouered bones like to mens carkasses, but farre bigger, which for the vnmeasurable hugenesse of them, are reported to haue beene the bodies of that monstruous Army. And thys opinion is furthered with the euidence of excessyue great stones, wherewith heauen was thought to haue

The Gyants war agaynst Heauen.

beene

béene assaulted. I will procéede to the residue which extende into Thessaly and Aemony. For they be heigher then that in anie place, the height of the Mountain is able to reache therunto. Neither is there any thing in anie Land vnder Heauen, that may woorthely bee compared héereunto in height, as wherevnto only the rage of water neuer attained when ẏ flood ouerwhelmed all thinges els with woorse moistnesse. There remaine yet prints of no small credite, whereby it appeareth that these places were aboue the stormy flood. For in the darke Caues of the Hilles, which at that time were eaten hollow with the strugling of the water, the shelles of Fishes are left behinde, and many other things which are cast vppe by the working of the rowgh Sea: so that although (to sée to) the places bée mayne Land: yet they haue a resemblaunce of ẏ Sea shore.

Nowe will I speake of the Inhabiters. *Aemathius* who was the first that obtained soueraigntie in Amathia, (whither it be because the knowledge of his pedegrée is worne out by time, or because it is a matter farre fette) is counted to bee breede of the earth. After him the name of *Aemathia* which procéeded frō him, continued to the Realme of Macedony. But *Macedo* the Nephewe of *Deucalion* by the Mothers side, (who onelie with the familie of his housholde scaped from the general destruction) chaunged the name, and called it Macedony, after himselfe. After *Macedo* followed *Caranus* Captaine of a companie of Peloponesians: who according to the aunswere gyuen by *Apollo*, builded a Citty in the same place, where he had séene a hearde of Goates sitte, and named it * Ægæa, in which place the custome was to bury theyr Kings: neyther was it lawfull among the auncient Macedones, to burie their chiefe states in anie other place then

The descent of the kinges of Macedoni.

Which may be interpreted, Goteham.

than there. After *Caranus* succéeded *Perdicas* in ỹ two and twentith Olimpiad, who was the firste that bare the name of King: after whom came *Alexander* the Sonne of *Amintas*, who was counted rich, and not without cause. For he had so good successe in encreasing his substaunce, that he first of all men, sent Images of cleane golde for a gyft, one to *Apollo* at Delphos, and another to *Iupiter* at Elis. He was greatlie giuen to delight hys hearing: insomuch that for hys pleasures sake, he entertained with honourable pensions as long as he liued manie that were cunning vppon Instruments, among whom was *Pyndarus* the Harper. From this man *Archelaus* receiued the kingdome, who was a politick Prince in feates of warre, and the firste deuiser of battell vppon the Sea. Thys *Archelaus* was so great a louer of learning, ỹ he made *Euripides* the Tragicall Poet, one of his priuie Counsell. At whose burial, he was not content to follow the Herse onelie, but also he shore his hayre, and vttered in countenaunce the sorrowe that he conceiued in hys hart. The same *Archelaus* winning the wager in running with Chariots at the gaminges of Pythia and Olimpus, shewed himselfe rather to haue the hart of a glorious Greeke then of a royall King, in séeking that kind of prayse. After *Archelaus* the state of Macedony béeing troubled with dissention, at last was stayed in the raigne of *Amyntas*, who had thrée Sons, of whom *Alexander* succéeded his Father: who béeing dispatched out of the way, the fruition of that great preheminence was first giuen to *Perdicas*: by whose decease the Kingdome was left by inheritance vnto his Brother *Philip*, who (as we tolde you before) lost hys right eye at Methone, of which maime there had gone a fore token before.

King Alexander, a louer of Musick.

Kinge Archelaus a louer of Learning.

For at his marriage feaste it is reported that the Musicians

Muſitians which ſerued that daie, ſung (as it were in ſport) a ſong of the one eyed Gyants, called Cyclops. Thys *Phillip* begat great *Alexander*, howbeit that *Olympias Alexanders* Mother, coueting to purchaſe hym a nobler Father, auouched him to haue béene begotten by a Dragon. But howſoeuer the caſe ſtoode, *Alexander* ſo behaued himſelfe, that he was beléeued to be the Sonne of a God. He trauailed ouer the worlde, vſing the direction of *Ariſtotle* and *Calliſthenes*. Hee conquered Aſia the leſſe, Armeny, Iberia, Albany, Cappadocia, Syria, and Ægypt. He paſſed ouer ẏ Mountaines Taurus and Caucaſus: He ſubdued the *Bactrians*: hée raigned ouer the *Medes* and *Perſians*: Hée wan Inde, and went beyond all that *Liber* and *Hercules* reached vnto. He was of perſonage more ſtatelie than Man, with long and ſtraight necke, chéerefull & cléere eyes, chéekes ruddy with a pleaſantneſſe, and comely featured in all proportions of bodye, not without a certaine maieſtie. Béeing conqueror of all men, hee was hymſelfe a thrall to wyne and wrath. Through ſurfette of drunkenneſſe he died at Babylon, ſomewhat after a more baſe and vncomely ſorte then he had lyued. Wée finde that thoſe that came after him, were borne rather to increaſe the glory of the Romaines, then to inherite ſo great renowne. Macedony bringeth foorth a ſtone which they call Pæantis. The common reporte goeth, that this ſtone doth helpe Women, bothe in the time of theyr conception, and in the time of their labour. It is founde much about the Tombe of *Tyreſias*.

King Phillip

Great Alexander

The ſtone Pæantis.

Iulius Solinus Polyhiſtor.

CAP. XIIII.

Of the manners and cuſtomes of the Thracians. *Of the places and peoples of* Thrace. *Of Cranes and Swallowes. Of* Helleſpont. *Of the Ilande* Clarob, *and of the* Aegæum *Sea.*

* Romania

The manners and cuſtomes of the auncient Thracians.

NOw it is time to take our iourneye into * Thrace, and to ſette ſayle toward the puiſſanteſt Nations of Europe: which whoſoeuer will looke vpon aduiſedlie, ſhall eaſily finde that there is a contempt of life in the barbarous Thracians, through a certaine diſcipline of moother wytt. They agrée all to die willingly: ſome of them beléeuing that the ſoules of them that deceaſe returne againe, and otherſome thinking that they die not, but are in a more happie and bliſſful ſtate. Among moſt of them, the birth daies are ſorrowfull, and contrariwiſe the burialls are ioyfull. In ſomuch that the Fathers and Mothers fall a wéeping when theyr Children are newe borne, and reioyce when they are deade. The Menne doo glorie in the number of theyr Wiues, and count it an honour to haue manie bedfellowes. Such Women as are chare of their chaſtitie, doo leape into the fires where their dead Huſbandes are burned, and (which they thinke to be the greateſt token of chaſtity that may bee) runne headlong into the flame. When Women come to the time of marriage, they take not

Huſ-

Husbands at the appointment of their Parents: but such of them as excel others in beautie, set themselues foorth to sale, and making Proclamation who wyll giue moste, they marrie not to him that is of best conditions, but to him that is best Chapman. Those that are foule or deformed, bring dowries with them to bie Husbandes withall. When they feast, bothe sexes of them goe about the harthes, and cast the seede of certaine Hearbs growing among them into the fire. The fume of which Hearbes so striketh vp into their heads that it woundeth theyr sences, and maketh them like drunken folke, whereat they haue a good sporte. Thus much concerning their customes. Nowe shall ensue of their places and peoples. Along the Ryuer Strymo on the right hande thereof, inhabite the Denselats. There are also manie kinreds of the Besses, euen vnto the Ryuer Nestus, which runneth about the foote of the Mountaine Pangæus. The soyle of the Odryses sendeth foorth the Ryuer Hebrus which runneth amōg the *Briants*, *Dolonks*, *Thynes*, *Corpills*, and other barbarous nations, & toucheth also ye *Cycones*. Then is there Mount Hæmus, sixe myles high, the back part whereof is inhabited by the *Mæsians*, *Gets*, *Sarmats*, *Scythians*, and manie other Nations. The Ryuer Hebrus. Mount Hæmus.

On the sea coast of Pontus dwelleth the people of Sythony, the renowne whereof is augmented by *Orpheus* the Poet and Prophette that was borne there, who is reported to haue practised the secrets (whither it were of his Musicke or of his Ceremonies,) in the Promontorie Sperchius. Afterwarde is the Peole of Bilton, and not farre from thence the Country of Marony, wherein was the Towne of Tyrada sometime the stable of *Diomeds* horses. But nowe it hath giuen place to time, and there remaineth no more but the foundation of the Towre. Not farre from thence is

Abdera. the Citty Abdera which *Diomeds* sister builded, & called so after her owne name. Anon after, it became the house of *Democritus* ye natural Philosopher, & therfore to (say the truth) it is the more renowmed. This Abdera béeing by time decaied, was restored to a greater countenaunce by the *Clazomenians* comming out of Asia, the hundreth and one and thirty Olympiad, who abolishing the things that had passed before, restored it to the olde name againe. The comming of *Xerxes* made the place of Doriscon famous, because he mustered hys Armie there. Mount Hæmus hath ye tombe of *Polydore* to shewe, on that side which the *Scythians Aroteres* doo inhabit, and it hath the Cittie which in olde time was called Gerania, and is now called of the barbarous people Cattuza, from whence the reporte goeth that the Pygmæans were dryuen by Cranes.

Democritus.

Of the nature and order of Cranes.

Surely it is manifest that Cranes in the wynter time doo flye in great heards towards the North, and it shall not gréeue me to declare whither, and in what sort they direct their fight. They march in araye as it were an Armie vnder an Ensigne. And least the violence of the windes should driue them from the coaste to which they direct theyr course, they gorge thẽselues wyth Sande, and balace themselues by taking vppe stones of a measurable waight. Then they mount as high as they can, to the intent from thence (as from a hygh watchtowre) to aime the Landes which they would goe vnto. He that is surest of wyng goeth before the Hearde, and with his clarying rebuketh their slothfulnesse, and causeth the trayne behinde to make haste after. When he wexeth hoarce, another takes his roome. When they shall passe the Sea of Pontus, they séeke for the narrowest places, which they may easilie finde by eye sight, and they are betwéene Taurica and Paphlagonia, that is to say betwéene Carambis and the Rammes head. As soone as they knowe themselues to be past the mid channell, they disburden thẽselues of the stones in theyr feete. So the Shipmenne report, who by suddaine aduenture haue oftentymes béene rayned vppon wyth theyr stonie showers. As for theyr Sande, they put it not vp againe before they be well assured of theyr abyding. They are all alike carefull for such as are weary. Insomuch that if any of them tyre, the rest flocke altogether and beare them vppe that faint, until they may recouer their strength by resting. Neyther are they lesse circumspecte vppon the Land. For they kéepe watch a nights, in such wise that euery tenth of them waketh. Those that watche, holde little weyghts in their clawes, which reproue them of sléepe if they happen to let them fall. If aught be to be auoyded, they giue warning thereof by clarying. Theyr colour bewrayeth their age, for the elder they growe, the blacker they were.

Let vs come to the Promontorie * Chrysokeras, renowmed with the Cittie * Byzance héeretofore called Lygos, which is distaunt from * Dyrrachium seauen hundred and eleuen miles. For so much is ẏ space betwéene the Adriatish Sea, and * Propontis. In the Country of Cenik not far from Flauiople a Towne builded and peopled with Romaines, is the Towne of Byzia in tymes past the Palace of King *Tereus*, now hated and vnhaunted of Swallowes, and so foorth of other byrds: although it bee so that Swallowes doo shunne to come within Thebæ also, because the wals thereof haue béene so often taken. For among other thinges: that they haue a kinde of foreknowledge, it is knowne héereby, that they wyll not come neere a house that is like to fall, nor come vnder the roofe that by any means shal perish. Surely they are not chaced by rauening foules, neither are they a pray to any, but are as holy birds.

* It may be interpreted Goldenhorne.
* Constantinople.
* Durazo.
* The Sea of Constantinople

The nature of Swallowes.

There

There is an other * Isthmos in Thrace of lyke straightnesse, and hauing a narrow Sea of like wydenesse to that of Peloponnesus, vpon the shores wherof stande two Citties, on either side one. The shore toward the Sea of Constantinople is beautified wyth the Towne of Pactie, and Melane bay with the Cittie * Cardy: which hath that name because the platt of it is in fashion like a hart. All the great Sea of Hellespont is streightned into seauē furlonges, which space disseuereth the coast of Asia from Europe. Heere also stande two Citties, Abidos in Asia, and Sestos in Europe. And harde by are two Promontories one ouer against the other: Mastusia of Chersonesus, where endeth the thirde coast of Europe, and Sygeum of Asia, where is a little Hill called * Cynossema the Tombe of *Hecuba*, and the Tower of *Protesilaus*, put to ẏ vse of a Chappell.

That is to say a narrow balke of grounde betweene two seas.

It may be interpreted Hartsted,

* Dogs Tombe or dogs graue.

On the Northmarches of Thrace, beateth the Riuer * Ister, on the Easte Pontus and Propontis: and on the South, the Ægæan Sea. Betweene Tenedos and Chius, is the Iland Claros situate at such place as the Ægæan Sea wydneth. On the ryght hand, as men sayle to Antandros, there is a Rock (for so it deserues to be called rather then an Ile) which (to them that beholde it a farre of) seemeth to haue the shape of a Goate, which the Greekes call Æga, that is to saye a Goate. Of this Rocke the Ægæan Gulfe taketh hys name. From Phalarion a Promontorie of * Corcyra, hangeth out a Rock of the likenesse of a Ship, into the which *Vlysses* hys Shyppe was beleeued to haue beene transformed. Cythera which is fiue myles from Malea, was heeretofore named Porphyris.

* Danow or Tonware.

* Corfu.

CAP.

CAP. XV.

Of Creta, *and of many other thinges pertayning thereunto.*

MOre easie it is to to treate fully of * Creta, thẽ to say expresly in what Sea it lyeth. For ẏ Greeks haue so mingled the names of the Sea that enuironeth it, that while they thruste one in an others place, they haue almost drowned altogether. Neuerthelesse, I will bestowe my trauell with as much faithfulnesse as I canne, in buttelling it out, to the intent that nothing may hang in vncertaintie. It stretcheth out a great length betwéene ẏ East and the West, hauing Greece butting against it on the one side, and Cyrene on the other. On the North side it is beaten vpon with the * Ægæan Sea, and on the South with the Libicke and Ægiptian Seas. It was garnished with a hundred Citties (as they report which haue lauash tongues of theyr owne) but indéede with a hundred great and Lordly proud Townes: the chiefe whereof were Gortim, Cydon, Gnoson, Therapne, and Scylletion. Dosiades reporteth that it was named Crete, of the Lady *Crete*, the daughter of *Hesperus*. *Anaximander* saith, it was so called of *Cretes* K. of the *Curets*. *Crates* auoucheth that it hyght, first Aeria, and anon after Curetis. And manie also affyrme, that of the temperatenesse of the ayre, it was called

* Now Candie

The situation of Candy

* Or Gotesea

The auncient names of Candy

L. * Macaro-

The bleſſed Ile. * Macaroneſus. It was the firſt that could ſkil of ſea-matters and of ſhooting. It was the firſt that comprehended wordes in writing. It was the firſt that taught dauncing in Armor, called the Pyrrhicke daunce, of *Pyrrhus* the firſt deuiſer thereof. It was the firſt that trayned troupes of Horſmenne to winde and vnwinde themſelues in way of ſport and daliance, whereuppon was afterward founded the vſe of warlike diſcipline. The arte of Muſicke began firſt there, by meanes of the Dactyles of Ida, who finding out the diſtinction of tunes by the ſounding and tinckling of braſſe, brought it in order of ſonge, and ſunge ditties to it. It looketh whyte by reaſon of the ſnowie toppes of the Mountaines Dictimus and Cadiſcus, which are ſo exceeding white, that vnto ſuch as ſayle a farre off, they ſeeme rather clowdes then hilles. Beſides the others, there is Ida, which before the ryſing of the Sunne, ſeeth the Sunne.

Of things firſt founded in that Ile.

Mount Ida.

Varro in his worke intituled of the Seacoaſts, affirmeth that in his time, the Tombe of *Iupiter* was there to be ſeene. The people of Crete doo very deuoutlye worſhippe *Diana*, whom in their owne moother tongue they cal *Brithomartis*, which is as much to ſaie in our language, as Sweete maide. No man may lawfullie enter into the Goddeſſes Temple, but barefooted. The ſaide Temple ſheweth the workmanſhip of *Dædalus*. By Gortyn runneth the Riuer Læthey, at the which the Gortynes ſaie, that *Europa* was brought in vppon a Bulles back. The ſame Gortynes doo worſhippe *Cadmus*, *Europas* brother, of whō they report thus. He is ſeene, and meeteth folke, but in the ſhutting in of the Euenings toward night, he offereth himſelfe to ſight, with a countenaunce of much greater maieſtie. The Gnoſians account the Goddeſſe *Minerua* to be a Countriwoman of theirs, and affyrme that

The manners and cuſtomes of the auncient Candians.

Illuſion of the deuill by walking Ghoſtes.

that Corne was firste sowne among them, standing boldlie in contention with the Athenians for that matter. The fieldes of Crete are well stored wyth wylde Goates: but it wanteth Redde déere. It bréedeth not anie where Wolues, Foxes, and other fourefooted Beasts that be fearefull. There is no kind of serpents there. There is great store of Vynes. The soyle is wonderous batling. The increase of fruites of trées is aboundant. For in a part of this Ile onely, Cypresse Trées béeing felled doo spring againe. There is an Hearbe called * Alimos, whereof if a man champe a little, it kéepeth him from béeing a hungred for one whole daie, and therefore this also is peculiar to Crete. There is a kinde of Spider, called Phalangium. If yée demaund what force it hath: there is no strength at all in the bodie of it, but if you would learne what power it hath, the man whom it stingeth dyeth of the poyson. The stone also which is called * Idæus dactylus, is sayde to growe in this Ilande. It is of the colour of yron, and it is in shape like a mans thombe.

What thinges Candy breedeth.

* Hungarlesse

* The Finger-stone.

Crete hath no night Owles, and if any by brought thether, they dye out of hant.

CAP. XVI.

Of Caristos, *and the hote waters therein, and of the byrds called* Carists. *Of* Chalcis, *of the Circle Iles, and of the Ilands* Ios, *and* Delos,

C*Aristos* hath hote Bathes which they call Hellops, and byrdes called Carists, which flye into the fire without singing their feathers: and also a kynde of fine Lynnen which remaineth in the fire without perishing. This Ilande (as *Callidemus* auoucheth) was in olde time taken for * Chalces, because Brasse was there first founde. That the Titans raigned there time out of minde, the rytes of theyr Religions doo declare. For the Caristians doo diuine seruice to *Briareus*, like as the Chalcideans doo to Aegæon. For in a maner all * Euboia was in subiection to the Titans. It is supposed that those Ilands tooke the name of Cyclads, because that although they be situate some further then some from * Delos: yet they stand all in a Circle round about Delos, and the Greekes call a circle Cyclos. Ios is more famous then the rest by reason that *Homer* is buried there. It is héere to be remembred, that after the first flood, which is noted to haue béene in the time of *Ogyges*, when the day had continued as darke as night, by the space of nyne Monethes together: Delos before all other Lands

* Brasselande

* Negropont

Sdiles,

Landes was lightned with the Sunne beames, and thereof gate hys name, in that it was yͤ first that was restored to light. Nowe betweene *Ogiges* and *Deucalion* is accounted the space of sixe hundred yeeres.

CAP. XVII.

Of the Ilande Ortygia, *and of Quayles*.

D*Elos* is also called * Ortygia, the most renowned of all the Cyclads, beeing it selfe one of the number of them, and is named diuersly: sometime Asteria, of the honouring of *Apollo*, there: sometime Lagia, of hunting: and *Cynethus*, and *Perpole* because fire pannes, and fire it selfe also were founde there. In thys Iland were Quayles seene first which byrds the Greekes cal Ortyges. Men think that these foules are in the tuition of Latona. They are not to bee seene at all seasons, but haue theyr time of comming, which is when Sommer is gone. When they passe ouer the Seas, they flye leysurely at yͤ first, cherryshing theyr strength wyth flying softly for feare of a longer iourney. But as soone as they spy Lande, they cluster on a flock, and thronging close together, make all the speede they can: which hast of theyrs doth oftentimes turne to the destruction of them that are vpon the Sea. For it happeneth in the nights, that they rende the tackling, and bearing the saylecloathes

Quaylland.

Of Quayles and of theyr propertyes.

before them by violence, turne the bottomes of the keeles upwarde. They neuer sette forth whyle the Southerne winde bloweth, for feare of the force of a more swelling foggie blaste. They commonly cōmitt themselues to the Northerne wyndes, to the intent that the gale thereof bëeing more drie and more vehement, may the easlyer carrie their bodies which are somewhat fatte, and by reason therof somewhat slow also. Hëe that guydeth the flocke, is called * Ortygometra. As sone as he draweth towarde the Land, the Gossehawke (which watcheth for the nonce) seazeth uppon him, and therefore it is all theyr sëeking to get them a guyde of a straunge brode, by whom to escape the first daunger. Their chiefe delight is to fëede upō the sëede of venemous hearbs, and therefore wisemen haue forbidden them their Tables. And thys lyuinge creature onely (sauing manne) suffereth the falling sicknesse.

The quailguyde.

CAP. XVIII.

Of the Ile Eubæa, *nowe called* Nigropont.

The Ile of *Eubæa* is disseuered with so small a cut from the maine land of Bæotia, that it is to bee doubted whether it bee to be numbred amōg Ilands or no. For on that syde which they call Eurypus, it is ioyned to the Lande with a brydge, and is gone unto a fote by the frame of a very a very short Engine. It shooteth into the North with the Promontorie Cæneum, and with two other it extendeth into the South, whereof Gerastus faceth the Countrey of Athens, and Caphreus looketh into Hellespont, where after the destructiō of Troy (whether it were through the wrath of *Minerua*, or (as the certainer report goeth) through the influence of the Starre Arcturus) the Greekish Nauie suffered great losse by shipwrack.

The headlond of Caphreus

CAP. XIX.

Of the Ilande Paros, *and the stone* Sarda.

PAros is renowmed for the Marble that is in it. Next Delos it is the beste inhabited wt townes. But before it hadd ye name of Paros, it was called Minoia. For béeing conquered by *Minos*, as lōng as it cōtinued vnder the Cretish dominion, it was called Minoia. Besides the Marble, it yéeldeth the stone Sarda, which is better then Marble, but yet accounted as basest of all Jewels. Eyghtéene myle from Delos is the Ile of Naxos, wherin is the Towne of Srongyle. But before it was called Naxus, it bare the name of Dyonisia, eyther because it was the harborough of *Bacchus*, or els because it excelled the rest in fruitfulnes of Wines. Besides these, there be many moe of ye Circle Iles, but ye things that are chiefly worthy to be remembred are in the Iles aforesaid.

* The Stone Sarda.

Naxus now called Nixia.

Iulius Solinus Polyhistor.

CAP. XX.

Of the Ilande Icaros. *and of the Phylosopher* Pythagoras : *of the Ilands* Melos, Carpathos, Rhodes, *and* Lemnos, *and of the shaddowe of Mount* Athos.

Now it is called Nicaria.

I*Caros* also is one of the Ilands called Sporades, and gaue the name to the Icarish Sea. Thys Ile shooting forth in Rocks betwéene Samos and Myconus, is altogether harbourlesse : and because it hath no Bay nor Hauen to aryue at, it is ill spoken of for the daungerousnesse of the Coastes of it. *Varro* therefore is of opinion, that *Icarus* of Crete perished there by shipwrack, and that the place tooke hys name of the mis-fortune of the man. In Samos nothing is more notable then yͤ *Pythagoras* was that Countryman borne : who béeing offended at the Lordlinesse of the Tyrants, forsóoke hys natiue Country, and arryued in Italy in the tyme that *Brutus* which draue the Kings out of Rome was Consull * Melos (which *Callymachus* calleth Melanis) hard by Aeolia, is the roundest of all the Iles. For * Carpathus is the same whereof the Carpathian sea hath hys name. The ayre is neuer so clowdye but the Sunne shyneth vppon the Rhodes. The Lemnians worshippe *Vulcane*, and therefore the chiefe Cittie of

Samos. Pythagoras.

* Now called Mylo.

* Scarpanto.

* Lemnos

* Lemnos is called Hæphestia. There is also ẏ towne of Myrina, into ẏ Marketstéd wherof, the Mountaine Athos casteth his shaddowe out of Macedonie, which thing (not without cause) men haue noted for a wonder, forasmuch as Athos is fourescore and sixe miles of frõ Lemnos. Surely Athos is of such a height, ẏ it is supposed to bee higher then from whence the rayne falleth. Which opinion hath got credite héereupon, for that the ashes which are left vpon the Altars ẏ stande on the toppe of it, are neuer washt awaie, nor doo in anie wise diminish, but doo alwaies continue euen in the same heapes that they were raked vppe in. On the toppe of it was sometime ẏ Towne Acrothon, wherin the Inhabiters liued halfe so long againe as the inhabiters of other places: and therfore the Greekes cal the people thereof Macrobians, which is as much to say in our language, as longliued.

* Stalimene.

The exceeding height of Mount Athos.

CAP. XXI.

Of Hellespont, Propontis, *the Bosphor of* Thrace *and of the maruellous nature of the fishes called Dolphins.*

THe fourth coast of Europe beginneth at * Hellespont, and endeth at the mouth of Mæotis. All the saide widenesse which deuideth Europe and Asia a sunder, gathereth into a straight of seauẽ furlongs. This is Hellespont, héere

* Saint Georges arme.

did *Xerxes* make a brydge of shippes and passe ouer a foote. From thence stretcheth a narrowe arme of the Sea to a Cittie of Asia called Priapus, which *Alexander* the great sayled vnto, and gotte it into his handes, when he went about to conquer the worlde. From thence wydning into a mayne Sea, it groweth narrow againe toward * Propontis: and by and by gathereth into halfe a mile breadth, and is called the * Bosphor of Thrace, at which place *Darius* conuaied ouer his armie. These Seas haue manie Dolphins, which haue in them many straunge things to be wondred at. First and formost, the Seas breede not anie thing swifter or nimbler then them: insomuch as ofttimes in their leaping vpp, they shoote thēselues quite ouer the topps of the maine sailes of the ships. Wher-soeuer they become, they goe by couples. They bring forth pigs, and the tenth month is the ful time of their farrying, and they farroe euer in Sommertime, and giue their pigs sucke, and while they bee verie yonge they take them in at their mouth, and they wayt vpon them for a time till they were strong. They liue thirtie yeeres as hath beene tryed by experience in cutting of theyr tailes for a marke to knowe them by. They haue theyr mouthes not in ẏ same place where other Beastes haue, but almost in theyr bellies, and contrarie to the nature of Fishes they onely moue theyr tongues. They haue sharpe prickes on their backes, which stand vppe stiffe when they be moued to anger, and are hidden as it were in a sheath whē their minds be quiet. Men say they vent not in the water, nor take any breath but aboue in the aire. When ẏ Northwind bloweth they be light of hearing, & contrariwise thick of hearing whē ẏ wind is in the South. They delight in Musicke, reioysing to heare shalmes, & wher soeuer is harmonie, thither flock they together in heards. In the

* The Sea of Constantinople.
* The straighte of Constantiple, and it signifieth the Oxe-forde.
The wonderful nature of Dolphins and their loue towardes manne.

the raign of *Augustus*, a boy in Campane, first trayned a Dolphin wͭ shiuers of bread, & did so much by custom that he was contented to be fedde by hand. Afterward when yͤ boy wexed bold in playing with him, he carryed him frõ the land into yͤ lake of Laurine, & beare the boy as it were on horsback frõ the shore of yͤ bay, unto * Puteolis. This was done many yeeres together, so long til yͤ continual beholding therof made it to seeme no wonder. *Pozzolo. But when the lad was dead, the Dolphin mourning for yͤ want of him, died for sorow in yͤ sight of al men. I wold be lothe to vouch this thing, but yͭ it is registred in yͤ wrytings of *Mecænas*, & *Fabian*, & many others. Anon after, uppon the seacoast of Affrick at Hippon Dyarrhytun, a Dolphin beeing fed by yͤ men of Hippon, offred himself to be handled, and euer now an then caried such as were set upõ his back. And this thing was not doon by yͤ peoples hands only, for *Flauianus* yͤ Proconsul of Affrick handled him himselfe, and anointed him wͭ ointments, insomuch as the Dolphin being cast a sleepe with yͤ strangnes of the smell, was tumbled hither & thither for dead, and many monethes after desisted frõ his accustomed keeping of cõpany. At Iassus a cittie of Babilon, a Dolphin fel in loue with a lad, & in folowing him ouer eagerly after their accustomed sporting together, shot himself into yͤ sand and there stuck fast. *Alexander* yͤ great interpreting it to haue beene yͤ loue of the * God of the sea, made the lad chiefe priest to *Neptune* nere unto yͤ said citty, as *Egesidemus* maketh report. *Neptune. Another childe named *Hermias* likewise riding on a Dolphins back in the sea, & being drowned by violence of the waues, was caryed backe againe to lande by the Dolphin, who tooke such repentance, that he punished the fact with wilfull death, and neuer returned more into the Sea. There are store of other such examples, & yet I wyll not speake of *Arion*, whose aduenture is credibly auouched by Chronicles.

Furthermore, if theyr yong pygs at any time playe the wantons, theyr auncients sette one of the elder sorte to be guyde ouer the Hearde, by whose instruction they learne to slippe from the assault of greater fishes that rush in vppon them, howbeit that in those Seas there be very few great Fyshes except it be the Seale.

In Pontus there is great store of Tunnyes, and Tunnyes. they bréede not lightlie els where. For there is no place that they come sooner to their full growth in, then there: and ẏ is by reason of the plenty of swéete waters. Their comming into the Sea is in ẏ spring-time, and they enter in by the right side of the shore, and goe out by the left side: which thing they are thought to doo, because they sée better wyth the right eye then with the left.

CAP. XXII.

Of Ister: of the beaste called a Beuer, and of the precious stone of Pontus.

ISter riseth in the Hylles of Germanie, and *Danow or Tonware. issueth out of a Mountaine that lieth ouer against Turgew, a part of the ancient Gall. It receiueth into it thréescore Ryuers, almoste all able to beare Shippes, and it falleth into Pontus with seauen mouthes, wherof the first is called Peuce, the second Narcustoma, the thirde Calostoma, and the

fourth

fourth Pseudostoma: for Boreostoma the fift, and Stenostoma the sixt, are slower then the rest: and as for the seauenth, it is so dull and like vnto a Poole, that it hath not anie likelihoode of a streame. The firste foure are so great, that by the space of forty miles together they are not intermedled with the Saltwater, but kéepe theyr swéete taste with vncorrupted sauoure.

Through all Pontus there is great store of Beuers, which they call by the names of Fiber & Castor. Thys Beaste is like an Otter, and is a very sore byter, insomuch that if he fasten vpon a man, hee will not let goe his holde vntill he féele the bones crash betwéene hys téeth. Beuers.

His stones are greatly coueted for the medicinablenesse of them, and therefore when he findeth hymselfe put to the pinch, he byteth of his owne cods, and eateth them vp, to the intent men should haue no good of them when he is taken.

Pontus yeeldeth also precious stones of sundrye sortes, which of ths Countrey wee call Pontiks: for some haue starres of the colour of Golde, and some of the colour of bloode in them, and they are counted among the sacred: for they are gathered rather for a showe, then for anie vse that they serue to. They are not besprent in droppes, but are interlyned with long strokes of sundry colours. Agats and Porphyris.

CAP. XXIII.

Of the Ryuer Hypanis, *and the Fountaine* Exampeus.

THe Ryuer *Hypanis* springeth among the * Auchets. It is the prince of Riuers in Scythia, pure and verye wholesome to drinke, vntill such time as it entreth into the borders of the * Callipods, where the Fountaine Exampeus (which is iustly defamed for the bytternesse of hys spring) béeing mingled wyth the cléere streame, infecteth the Riuer with hys fault, so that hee falleth into the Sea vnlike to himselfe.

* They are nowe a part of Moscouia.

* May be interpreted Fayrfeete they are also a people of Moscouia.

Héereuppon groweth diuersitie of opinions among folke concerning Hypanis. For they that know hym at the beginning, do prayse him: and they that tast of hym at the ende haue good cause to curse hym.

CAP.

CAP. XXIIII.

Of the Ryuer Boristhenes, *and the people that dwell thereby: of the nature of dogges: of the manners of the* Scythians: *of the precious stones called the* Emerawd, Cyanie, *and* Crystall.

VIthin the Countrey of the * Neuers springeth the Ryuer * Borysthenes, wherein are Fyshes of excellent taste, without any bones, hauing nothing but very tender grystlys. But the Neuers (as wee haue heard) in the Sommertime are transformed into Wolues: and afterward when they haue passed a certaine time limitted for the continuaunce in that state, they returne to theyr former shape againe. The God of this people is *Mars*: in stedde of Images they worshippe Swordes: they offer menne in Sacrifice: and wyth theyr boanes make fire to burne the Sacrifices wythall. Next Neyghbours to these are the * Gelones: They make bothe rayment for themselues and furniture for their horses of theyr enemyes skinnes.

* Nepar.
The Neuers are now a part of Moscouia.
The manners and customes of the auncient Moscouites.

* These were afterward called Getes, and nowe are Tattarians.

Uppon the Gelones border the * Agathyrses, painting their faces with a blewe colour, and dying theyr hayre into a blewe colour. And this is not done without a difference. For the better man he is, ye déeper colour he dyeth himselfe: so that it is a token of lowe degrée to bee lightlie painted. After them are the * Anthropophags, who like cursed caytiues féede on Mans fleshe. The which custome of that wicked nation, the Countryes adioyning beare witnesse of, by lying continuallie waste, the inhabiters of them abandoning them, and running away for feare of that cruell outrage: and this is the cause that from thence to the sea, which they cal Tabis al along that coast which lyeth toward the Northeast, the land is vtterly without inhabiter and altogether wyldernesse, vntill yee come to the Seres.

* These also are now Tartarians

* Meneaters or Cannibals.

The Chalibyes and Dahyes which inhabit a part of that Scythia that is in Asia, doo differ nothing in cruelnesse from the most outragious of all. But the * Albanes inhabiters of the Seacoast by the Caspian Sea, who will haue themselues thought to be the posteritie of *Iason*) are borne with white hayre, and haue hore heads as soone as theyr hayre buddeth, the colour whereof hath giuen name to the nation. The apple of theyr eyes is of colour bright gray, and therefore they sée better by night then by day. The dogges that are bredde in this Countrey, excell all other beastes, for they pull downe Bulles, kill Lyons, and hold whatsoeuer they are put at. In consideration whereof, they deserued to be spoken of in Chronicles. We read that as *Alexander* was going toward Inde, the King of Albanie sent him two dogs for a present. Of which the one so disdained Swine and Beares brought before him, that béeing offended with the basenes of the pray he lay still a great while and would not once sturre at them:

Theyr Countrey is now called Zuira & Seroan.

Wonderful dogs & of the nature and property of dogs in general.

them: *Alexander* thinking him to bee but a cowardly curre (because he knewe not hys properties) commanded him to be killed. But the other at the information of them that brought the present, bæing put to a Lyon kylled him. And anon after, spying an Oliphant, hee made a great leaping and skypping for ioy, and beeing put to him, first tyred the Beaste with cunning fyght, and afterward (to the great feare of them that looked on) pulled him downe to the grounde. These kinde of Dogs groweth to a very large syse, and make a farre terribler noyse in theyr barking, then is the roaringe of a Lyon.

These things are peculiar to ẏ dogs of Albanie: the rest are common to all dogges. All dogs generally doo loue their Maisters, as is manifest by examples. In * Epyre a dogge descrying the murtherer of his Master in a great thronge, bewrayed him by barking. When *Iason* of Lycia was slayne, hys dogge forsaking meate dyed for hunger. When the fire was kindled wherein the corse of King *Lysimachus* should be burned, his dog threwe himselfe into the flame, & was consumed wyth him. Two hundred dogs brought home the King of the Garamants out of exile, and ouercame them in battell that withstoode them. The Colophonians & Castabalenses carryed dogges with them to the warres, and made theyr foreward alwayes of them. In the time that *Appius Iunius*, and *Publius Silius* were Consulles, a dogge folowed his Master that was condemned to pryson, and could not bee driuen away: and anone after, when he was executed, hee followed howling after him. And when the people of Rome for pittie gaue him meate, he carryed and layd it to his dead Masters mouth. Lastly when the carkasse was caste into Tiber, he swamme to it, and endeuoured to beare it aboue the streame. Onely dogges know their owne

Examples of the loue of dogges toward theyr Masters.

* It is nowe called Albanie

Dogs vsed in battell.

names, and remember the waies that they haue gone. The Indians when their Bitches goe proud, tie them in the Forrestes to haue them limed by Tygers: of whom they caste away the firste litter, and likewise the seconde, as the which will serue to no purpose because of their excéeding cruelnesse: the thyrde they kéepe vppe. The dogs of Ægypt neuer lap of the Nyle but running, for auoyding the Crocodiles which lye in wait for thẽ. Among the Anthropophags in ẏ part of Asia are numbred the Essedons, who likewise are embrewed with the same vngracious foode. It is the manner of the Essedons to follow the corses of theyr Parents singing: and calling together a knot of their next Neighbours, to teare the carkesses a sunder with their téeth, & dressing them with other flesh of beastes, to make a feast with them. The skulles of them they binde about with Golde, and vse them as mazers to drinke in. The Scythotaurians offer vppe straungers in sacrifice. The * Nomades giue themselues to grazing.

The Essedons deuourers of mans seshe.

* Grasyers.

The * Georges that are situate in Europe occupie Tillage. The Axiaks béeing likewise situate in Europe, neyther couet other mens goods, nor set anye store by their owne. The Satarches vtterly condemning the vse of Gold and Siluer, haue banished couetousnes out of their Cõmon weale for euer. The Scythians that dwell more into the firme lande, liue much more straightlie. They kéepe in Caues: they make themselues drinking Cuppes, not as the Essedons do, but of the skulls of their enemies: they loue fighting: they sucke the blood out of the woundes of them that are slayne: their reputation encreaseth by the number of slaughters, from which it is a reproche among them to haue cléere handes: they make leagues by drinking eche of others bloode: wherein they not onelie

* Tillmen.

The manners of the Vplandish Tartarians in olde time.

ly keepe the custome of theyr owne Countrey, but also borrowe the manner of the Medes. In that warre that was helde the fortie and nine Olympiade, which was the sixe hundred and fourth yeere after the wynning of Troy, betweene *Alyattes* King of Lydia, and *Astiages* King of Media, the league was confirmed after the same fashion. *Amphitus* and *Telchius*, the wagoners of *Castor* and *Pollux*, builded * *Dioscorias* the chiefe Cittie of Colchos, from whence the nation of the Henioches had their beginning. Beyond the Sauromats that are in Asia, where *Methridates* hid himselfe, and from whence the Medes had theyr originall.

* Sebastrople.

The Thalians march vpō those nations, which Eastward lie vpon the entring of the Caspian Sea, which entrance (after a maruellous manner) doth emptye by rayne, and encrease by drowght. Out of the Mountains of ỹ Henioches issueth Araxes, & out of ỹ mountaines of the Moscouits, issueth Phasis. But Araxes rayseth his head a little way from the spring of Euphrates, and from thence runneth into the Caspian Sea. The Arimaspes, which are situat about Gesglithron, are a people that haue but one eye. Beyonde them and the Mountaine Ryphey is a Countrey continually couered with Snowe, called * Pteropheron. For the incessant falling of the hore frosts and Snow maketh there a likelihood of fethers: a damned parte of the worlde is it, and drowned by nature it selfe in the clowde of endlesse darknes, and vtterly shut vppe in extreame colde as in a pryson, euen vnder the very North pole. Onelie of all Landes it knoweth no distinction of times, neyther receyueth it any thynge else of the ayre, then euerlastyng Winter. In the the Asiatik Scychia are rich Lands, but notwythstanding vninhabitable.

The wonderfull nature of the enterie into the Caspian Sea.

Araxes.

* The Arimaspes.

* It may be englished Fetherlande.

For wheras they abound in gold and precious stones: the Gryffons possesse all, a most fierce kinde of foule, and cruell beyond all cruelnesse: whose outragiousnesse is such a stoppe to all commers, that hardlie and seldome arryue any there: for as soone as they see thẽ they teare them in peeces, as creatures made of purpose to punish the rashnesse of couetous folke.

Gryffons.

The Arymaspes fight with them to get away theyr precious stones, the natures whereof I wyll not refuse to treate of. Thys Land is the natiue soyle of the Emerawdes, to which *Theophrast* gyueth the thyrd place of estimation among precious stones. For although there be of them in Ægypt, at Chalcedon, in Media, and about Lacedemon, yet those of Scythia are of chiefest reputation. The eye canne beholde nothing more pleasaunt, nor nothing more wholesome than them, first they glister greene aboue the moyste grasse, and aboue the hearbes that are in the Ryuers, and secondlie with the mildnes of theyr colour, they refresh the eyes that are wearyed with beholding other thinges. For they relieue and sharpen the sight that was dymmed or dulled wt the glosse of another stone. And there is none other cause why men think it not good to haue ought ingraued in them, but least the beautye of them should be perished wyth the cuttings of imagry: albeit that the right Emerawd wyll hardly bee cutte. They are tryed in this wise: if a man may see through them, if beeing rounde they caste theyr colour vpon the things that are next them by reflexion of the ayre, or if beeing holow they resemble the faces of them that beholde them, or if neyther in the shaddowe nor by candlelight, nor in the sunnelight is founde any alteration in them. Neuerthelesse they are of the best fashyon, which are plaine and leuell long. They are founde when the Eastern wyndes called Etesiæ do blowe, for then

Emerawdes

Etesiæ.

then the wynde discouereth the grounde, and they glyster through the fine sande easily: for those Easterne wyndes doo verie much remooue the sandes. Other of lesse valew appeare in the seames of stones in Rocks, or in brassemynes, which they call brazen Emerawds. The refuse sort of them haue certaine pranes within, like eyther to leade, or to hayre, or to salt. They are eased with Vineger, but they are much better amended with gréene Oyle, although they be spotted of nature. And the best sort of the stone called Cyanie commeth out of Scythia, it is of the colour of a bright Azure. They that be skilful Jewellers make two kinds of it, the Male and Female. *The Females are of chéere brightnesse: but the Males are fretted wyth little sparkes beautifull to beholde, hauing as it were dust of golde scattered betwixt them. There is also Crystall, which although the greater part of Europe, and some part of Asia also doo yéelde, yet Scythia yéeldeth the best.

Cyanies.

* This should seeme to be the stone called Lapis Lazulus.

Crystall.

It is much vsed to make drinking Glasses of, for it abydeth heate best, although it cannot well suffer any thyng but cold. It is found sixe cornered. They that choose it, couet the purest that no rednesse, no clowdynesse, nor frothinesse, hinder a man to sée through it: and moreouer that the ouermuch hardnes therof maketh it not subiect to brittlenes. Some think ẏ Ise congealeth and hardneth into Crystall, but ẏ is false. For if it were so, neither Aladand of Asia, nor the Ile of Cyprus shoulde engender thys kinde of stuffe, forasmuch as the heate in those Countreys is moste vehement. *Liuia* the wyfe of *Augustus* dedicated among the gifts of the Capitoll, a Crystall of a hundred and fiftie pounde weight.

CAP. XXV.

Of the people called Hiperboreans.

SVndrye thinges that haue béene reported of the Hyperboreans had béen but a fable and a flying tale if yͤ thinges that haue come from thence vnto vs hadde béene beléeued rashlie. But séeing the best Authors and such as are of sufficient credite do agrée in one constant report, no man néedes to feare any falshod. Of the Hyperboreans they speake in this wise. They inhabite almost the Pteropheron, which wee heare saie lyeth beyond the North pole, a most blessed Nation. They ascribe it rather vnto Asia then vnto Europe, and some do place it midwaie betwéene the Sunne rysing and the Sunne sette, that is tō wete, betwéene the West of the Antipodes, and our Easte, which thing reason reproueth, considering what a waste Sea runneth betwéene the two worlds. They are therefore in Europe, and among them are thought to be the poles of the worlde, and yͤ vttermost circuit of the starres, and halfe yéere light, lacking the Sunne but one day. Howbeit, there are that think the Sunne riseth not day by daie to them as it doth to vs, but that it riseth in the springtime, & goeth not downe againe before the fall of the leafe, so that they haue cō-tinuall daie by the space of sixe monthes together, and by the space of other sixe moneths continuall night. The aire is very milde, the blasts wholesome, and no hurtfull

The Hiperboreans.

hurtfull winde. Their houses are the wylde fieldes or the woods, and the trées yéelde them fóode from daie to daie. They knowe no debate, they are not troubled with diseases, all men haue one desire, which is to liue innocentlie. They hast death, and by wilfull fordoing thēselues, preuent the long taryance of their decease. For when they haue liued as long as they wold desire, then feasting and annointing themselues, they throwe themselues headlong from some knowne Rocke into the déepe Sea, and they beléeue this to be the best kind of buriall. The report goeth also, that they were accustomably wont to send the first fruits of their increase to *Apollo* of Delos, by the handes of their most chaste Maydens. But for because those Maides through the trecherie of them in whose houses they lodged, returned not vndefiled: they erected a Bishopricke wythin their owne Countrie for that deuotions sake, for the performance whereof they were faine before to sende abroade.

CAP. XXVI.

Of the Arimphæans, *of the* Caspian *Sea, of the Tygers, Panthers, and Pards.*

ANother Nation there is in Asia furthest Northeast, where the ridge of tho Mountaine Ryphey fayleth, like the Hyperboreans, which are called Arimpheans. These also delight in the leauie woodes, and féede vpon berryes.

he Arymphæ-Tans.

The Men and women are both alike weary of their hayre, and therefore bothe ſexes of them doo poll theyr heades. They loue quietnes and not to doo anie harme They are counted holie, and euen the wildeſt nations that be, doo thinke it an offence to touch them. Whoſoeuer feareth anie daunger among his owne Countrimen, if he flye to the Arimphæans, hee is as ſafe as in a Sanctuarie. Beyond theſe are the Cimmerians, and the nation of the Amazons, extending to the Caſpian Sea, which ſlyding along the backe part of Aſia, faleth into the Scythiſh Ocean. A great way of from thence is the mouth of the Ryuer Oxus: and there inhabite the Hircans, a Country full of rowgh woods, plentiful of cruell wilde Beaſtes, and ſtored aboundantly with Tygers, a kinde of Beaſtes notable for the goodlye ſpottes wherewith their coates are powdred, and for theyr ſwiftnes.

The Cimmerians and Amazons.

Hircanie.

Of Tygers.

Their colour is a bright yellowe: which béeing powdred with drops of black, make a very trim ſhow by reaſon of the varietie thereof. I am not able to ſay whither it be their nimbleneſſe or their eagernes that furthereth their ſwiftnes. For nothing is ſo long but they paſſe it ouer in ſhort time: nothing is gone ſo farre afore them but they ouertake it by and by. But moſt of all they ſhow what they are able to doo, when they haue littered, and when they purſue them that haue ſtolne away their whelps. For though poſte horſes be layd by the way, and that they worke neuer ſo ſubtillie to goe cléere away with theyr bootie, yet if the Sea be not at hand to reſcue them, all their endeuour is in vaine. And it is noted in them oftentimes, that if perchaunce they ſée the ſtealers that haue carryed away their welppes ſayling away againe: after they haue raged in vaine, they caſt themſelues headlong into the Sea, as it were to puniſh their owne ſlownes slownesse by wylful drowning themselues,and yet of all their whelps(which are manie in number)scarsely may one be côueied awaie. Of Panthers also is great store in Hyrcanie,which are spotted with little round specks,in such sort that the hayre of their skins,which is either white or of a skye colour,is beset with round eyes of yellow. It is reported that cattell are wonderfullie delighted with the sent & beholding of thẽ, and that as sone as they perceiue them, they hearde together in hast,and are not afraid but onely of the grimnesse of their looke. For which cause the Panthers hiding their heads,sette forth the rest of their bodyes to looke vpon,to the intent that when the Cattell are astonied in gazing,they may fall vpon them and deuour them without danger.

Panthers.

A Panther and a Lybard is all one kinde of Beaste

But the Hyrcans (as mans nature is euer full of deuises) kill them more commonly with poyson then with weapon. They stéepe flesh in ẏ iuyce of Lybardbane, and caste it in the waies where diuers pathes meete: the which as sone as the Panthers haue eaten,by & by their throats are troubled with ẏ squince, and therfore the wéede is called in Gréeke Pardalianches. But the Panthers against this venome deuoure mans dunge,and so by a remedie of their own finding withstande their destruction. They are very long in dying: in so much that they liue a greate while after that their bowels are taken out. In these woddy coũtries,are also Lybards a second kind of Panthers,sufficientlie knowne, and therfore not to be entreated of with further circumstaunce. Betwéene these and the Lyonesses matching against kinde,are engendred bastarde Lyons without force or courage.

This Hearbe is also called Woolfswort

Lybardes

CAP. XXVII.

From whence the Midland Seas haue theyr beginning.

FOraſmuch as we are in the matters of Pontus, it is not to bee omitted from whence the Mydland Seas do rayſe theyr heads. For ſome are of opiniõ that they take their beginning at the ſtreights of Marrok, and that they haue none other originall than the waues of the Ocean breaking in at that place, the liuely operation wherof ſheading it ſelfe abroade, cauſeth the flowings & ebbings of the tydes on diuers coaſts of the maynelande, as for examples ſake in a part of Italy. They that are of the contrarie opinion, ſay how all that flowing cõmeth from the mouth of Pontus: and thys they auouche wyth no tryfling argument, becauſe the tyde that commeth out of Pontus neuer ebbeth backe againe.

CAP. XXVIII.

Of certaine Iles in Scythia.

FOurſcore myles from the Boſphor of Thrace, is ỹ Iſle of the Apollonits, ſituate on thys ſide Iſter, frõ whence *Marcus Lucullus* brought vnto vs the *Apollo* of the Capitoll.

Againſt

Against the mouth of * Borysthenes is the Iland of *Achilles*, with a Church wherein commeth no byrde: and if any come by chaunce, shee flyeth away againe with all the speede she can make.

* Now called Nepar.

CAP. XXIX.

Of the North Ocean, of the Caspian *Sea, and of the Iland* Baltia,

THe North Ocean on that part where Paropamisus a Ryuer of Scythia washeth into it, is named of *Hecataeus Amalchium*: which in ẏ language of that nation, signifieth the Frozen sea. *Phylæmon* saith, that from the Cimbrians to the Promontorie Rubeas, it is called Morimarusa, which is as much to saie, as the dead Sea. Whatsoever is beyonde Rubeas is called Cronium. That the Caspian Sea on the otherside of Pontus beyonde the Massagets and the Scythians called Apellæans, in the coast of Asia, is sweete of taste, it was tried by *Alexander* the great, and afterwarde by *Pompey* the great, who in his warres against *Methridates* (as *Varro* one of his fellow Souldiours reporteth) would needes knowe whither it were true or no by drinking of it himselfe. It is reported that it commeth so to passe by reason of the number of Riuers, whereof there falleth such a sort into it, that they alter the nature of ẏ Sea.

The Frozen Sea.

The water of the Caspian Sea is sweete of taste.

I must not let passe, that at the same time the said *Alexander* was able to come in eyght daies out of Inde from Bactria unto the Riuer Icarus, which runneth into the Riuer Oxus, and from thence to ỹ Caspian sea, and so by the Caspian to passe into ỹ streame of the Ryuer Cyrus which runneth betwéene the marches of Iberia and Armenie. From Cyrus also conueying his Shippes after him by lande, hee came in fiue daies at the most to the Channell of Phasis: at whose issue it is manifestlie proued, that those which come out of Inde may be brought into Pontus. *Xenophon* of Lampsacum affirmeth that we may saile from the sea coast of Scythia, to the Ilande * Baltia in thrée dayes, the greatnesse whereof is unmeasurable, and almoste like unto a maine land, from whence it is not farre to the Ilands called Oones, the inhabiters whereof, liue by egges of Sea-foules, and the séede of wylde Oates: and that other Iles adioyning therevnto doo liue after the same sort: of which, the people that are called *Hyppopodes, béeing shaped in all points like men downe to the instep, haue féete like horses. He sayth also howe there are other Ilandes, and a nation called Phanesians, whose eares are of such an unmeasurable syse, that they couer the rest of theyr bodyes with thẽ, and néede none other apparrell to clothe theyr limbes with, then theyr owne flappes.

* It is nowe found to be many Ilands.

* They may be called Egge Ilands.

Hors-feete

Vnmeasurable eares.

CAP.

Iulius Solinus Polyhiſtor.

CAP. XXX.

Of Harts and Tragelaphes.

Before we ſteppe aſide frō Scythia, me thinks it a matter of conſcience, to paſſe ouer what beaſtes are petuliar to that Countrey. There is greate ſtore of Harts in this lande, & therefore we wil treate of Harts firſte. The male Deere of this kinde, when rutting time comes, are madd fonde ouer the Hyndes. Although the Hyndes bee bukt before, yet are they not wyth fawne vntill the ſtar Arcturus ryſe, neither do they bring vp their yong calues at aduenture. For they hyde them very charily while they be yong, and beate them with their feete to make them lye ſtill in the thicke buſhes or weedes where they haue laid them. When their ſtrength will ſerue them to followe about, they teache them to runne by exerciſe, and enure them to leape through places.

Of the nature of Harts,

When they heare the opening of a Hound, they flie with the winde, that the ſent may goe away with the. They like well the noyſe of pypes. When their eares ſtande vp, they heare verie lightly, and when they bee down, they heare nothing at all. They gaze at al thinges, and therfore it is an eaſie matter to haue a ſhoote at them. If they ſwymme ouer the Seas, they aime to lande, not by ſight but by ſmelling. They ſette the weakeſt behind, and beare vp the heades of them that are wearie vpon theyr haunches by turnes. Of theyr hornes the right hath moste efficacie in Medicine. If thou wilt driue away Serpents, burne which of them thou wilt, and besides that, the fume that ryseth of the burning thereof, will euidentlie bewray if the falling sicknesse be in anie bodie. According to their yeeres the tynes of their hornes increase, which multiplying cōtinueth sixe yeeres. For after that time, their hornes cannot increase in number of tynes, but they may bee thicker or broader palmed. If they bee gelded theyr hornes neuer increase, neyther doo they caste them.

Their teeth bewray their yeeres: for if they haue few or none then they be olde. They swallowe Serpents, and with the breath of theyr nostrells draw thē out of their lurking holes. The hearbe Dyttaine they brought to light, while by feeding theron they cast out arrowes & darts sticking in their bodyes. The hearbe also which men call an Artechoke they doo eate of against hurtfull weedes. The curds that are in ẏ maw of one of their Fawnes killed in his dammes belly, is a wonderfull preseruatiue against poyson. It is manifestlie knowne, that they are neuer troubled with any Feuer: and therefore oyntments made of their marroe, asswage the burning fits of those that haue the Agew. We reade that very many which were wont to breake their fast a mornings with redde Deere liued a long time, and neuer hadde Ague: but it taketh not effect, vnlesse the Hart be killed at one stripe. To dyscerne the continuaunce of theyr life, great *Alexander* put collers about many Stagges neckes, which were caught a hundred yeeres after, & yet had not any lykelihoode of age in them. In maner of the same shape are those which the Greekes call Tragelaphes, (but they are not to be seene els where thē about Phasis) sauing that they haue long haire on their shoulders, and long rough beards vnder their chynnes.

The Hearbe Dittayne.

The Artichoke

A speciall preseruatiue against poyson.

A remedy against the burning Ague.

Gotebucks

CAP.

Iulius Solinus Polyhiſtor.

CAP. XXXI.

Of Germanie, *and the wonderfull byrdes therein, and of the Bugles, Vres, and Alces. wylde Beaſtes.*

GErmanie takes his beginning at ẏ Mountaine Seuo which is greate of it ſelfe, and not leſſe then the Hilles of Ryphey. This hill is inhabited by the * Ingeuons, at whom firſt next after the Scithians beginneth the name of Germaines. It is a land rich of men, and inhabited with peoples innumerable and altogether ſauage. It ſtretcheth from the Forreſt of * Hercinia, to the Hils of Sarmatia. Where it beginneth it is watred with Danow, and where it endeth it is watred with the Rhyne. Out of the inward parts thereof, * Albis, Guttallus, and * Viſtula very deepe Ryuers runne into the Ocean. The Forreſt of Hertſwald breedeth byrds, whoſe fethers ſhyne and giue light in the darke, though the night be neuer ſo cloſe and clowdy. And therefore men of that Countrey, doo for the moſt parte ſo laye theyr outgoings by night, that they may vſe thē for a helpe to direct theyr iourney by: and caſting them before them in ẏ open pathes, doo finde howe to keepe theyr way by the glyſtring of thoſe feathers, which ſhewe them which way to goe. In this Region and in al the North coaſt, there is verye greate ſtore of Bugles: which are in manner lyke Oxen, bryſtled, wyth rough manes on their neckes, they are farre more ſwyfter then

The boūnds the auncient Germanie

* They were Indwellers.

* Hertſwalde

* Elb.

* Wixell.

Strange byrds

The be alſo called Buffles or wylde Oxen:

Bulles, and which béeing taken wil not by any means be made to come to hand. There are also Vres which the vnskilfull common sort cal Buffles, wheras Buffles are bredde in Affrick almoste altogether like a Hart. But these which we call Vres haue hornes like Bulles, of such length, that for the great receit therof, they are taken to make Cuppes for Kinges to drinke in. There is also a beast called Alce much resembling a Mule, with such a long vpper lippe, that he cannot féede but he must goe backward.

Vres.

Alce.

CAP. XXXII.

Of the Ilande Scandinauia, *of Amber, of the stone* Callais, *and of the precious stone called* Ceraunius.

Sconeland

* Munster taketh this beast to be the Alce

OVer against Germanie is the Ilande Scandinauia, which bréedeth a beast * much resembling an Alce, which like ỹ Oliphant boweth not the nether ioyntes of his legs, and therefore lyeth not downe when he sléepeth, but resteth himselfe when he is drowsie, against a Trée, the which is sawne almost a sunder, ready to fall, that when the beast leaneth to his accustomed staie, he may fall downe: and so is hee caught, for otherwise it is a hard matter to catch hym by hand. For although hys ioynts be so stiffe, yet is he of incomparable swiftnesse.

Of

Iulius Solinus Polyhistor.

Of the Germaine Iles, the greatest is Scandinauia, but there is nothing in it great sauing it selfe. The Ilande * Glessaria yéeldeth Crystall, and also Amber, which the Germaines in their Country spéeche call Glesse. The qualitie of this kinde of stuffe is touched briefly before. But at such time as *Germanicus Cæsar* searched all the corners of Germanie, there was found a Trée of the kind of Pynes, out of whose pyth euerie haruest issued a Gumme. Ye may vnderstande by the * name of it, that it is the iuyce of a Trée: and if yee burne it, the smell will bewray ŷ it comes of a Pyne Trée. It is worth the labour to procéede somewhat further, least men might surmise that the woods about Po, did weepe stones. The barbarous nation brought Amber into Illyrik, which through intercourse of Merchandise with the Paunonians, came to ŷ handes of the Italians beyond the Po, nowe because our Men sawe it there firste, they beléeued it had also growne there. Through the bounteousnesse of the Emperour *Nero*, no attire was gorgeous without Amber, which was no hard matter for him to doo, sithence that at the same time, the King of Germanie sent him thrée and thirtie thousande pounde thereof for a present. At the first it groweth rugged and with a barke, and afterward it is boyled in the greace of a sucking Pigg, and and so is pollished to that brightnesse that wee sée. According to ŷ colour, it hath diuers names. It is called Melleum and Phalernum, bothe which names it hath giuen vnto it for the likenesse it hath to that kinde of wine, or to honnie. It is manifest that it gathereth vp leaues and draweth chaffe vnto it: and the arte of phisicke hath taught, that it remedieth manie inconueniences of men. Inde also hath Amber, but Germanie hath the best, and best store. Because we were come to the Ile of Glessaria, we began with Amber: for in the

* Now called Sudawe.

Of Amber.

* That is to say by the latin name of it, which is Succinum.

P.i. inner

The stone Callais.

inner parts of Germanie is founde a stone called Callais, which men preferre before the precious stones of Arabie: for it passeth them in beautie. The Arabians saie it is not found anie where but in the nestes of the birds which they call * Melancoryphes: which no man beléeueth, forasmuch as they are to be found in the Regions of Germanie among stones, although very rarelie. In respect of the estimation and value of the Emerawd, it is of colour a faint gréene. Nothing dooth better beséeme golde. Furthermore, of the Ceraunies are diuers sorts, that of Germanie is white, with a bright blew: and if yée haue it abroade, it draweth the brightnes of the starres to it.

* They may bee interpreted black toppes.

The Ceraunie or thunderstone.

CAP. XXXIIII.

Of Gallia, *of the Countryes of* Rhetia *and* Noricum, *of* Pannonie *and* Mæsia, *and of the medicinable Oyle.*

The more part of it is now the Realme of Fraunce.

G*Allia* is situat betwéene the Ryuer Rhyne and the Mountaines Pyrenyes, and betwéene the Ocean and ẏ Mountaines * Gebenua and * Iura, fortunate for the fatnes of the soyle, and rich of increase of fruits, in many places also replenished with Uines and Orchyardes, and blessed with store of all things for the behoofe of manne. It is well watred with Ryuers and Fountaines, & of those Fountaines some in times past sacred and hote.

* The Mountaine of Geneua, or the Mountaines of Auuerne.

* The Mountaine of Saint Claude.

It

It is ill spoken of for the custome of the inhabiters, who (as is reported) for I auouch not my selfe to haue had triall of the truth, after a detestable manner, (not to the honor, but rather to the iniurie of Religion,) offer men in sacrifice. Out of this Countrey yée may goe into what part of the world yée wil: Into Spayne and Italy both by sea and lande: into Affrick by sea onely. If ye iourney into Thrace, yée must come to the fayre and fruitfull fieldes of * Rhetia, renowmed with the Lake * Brigantine: from thence into * Noricum, a colde Countrey and lesse fruitfull, but where it is far from the Alpes verie plentifull: Then * Pannonie, puissaunt in men, the soyle champion and rich, and inclosed with the two famous Riuers Drauus & Sauus, and lastlie the * Mæsians which our auncestors called worthelie the Gardner of Ceres. In one part wherof, (namelie of that which is toward Pontus) there groweth an hearbe wherwith they make an Oyle that they call the Chirurgions Oyle. This béeing sette a fire, if yée goe about to quench it with water, burneth the more, and cannot bee put out otherwyse then by casting on of duste.

Sweuia.
* The Lake of Constance.
* Bauyer.
* Austrich and Hungary
* Walachy

A wonderfull Oyle.

CAP. XXXIIII.

Of Britaine *and the other Iles about it, of the stone called Geate.*

THe Sea coast of *Gallia* had béene the ende of the worlde, but that the Ile of Brytaine for the largenesse therof euery way, deserueth the name almoste of an other Worlde,

Britayne which nowe is England & Scotland

for it is in length eyght hundred myles and more, so we measure it to the angle of * Calydon, in which nooke an Altar engrauen with Greeke Letters for a vowe, beareth witnes that *Vlisses* arriued at Calydon. It is enuironed with many Iles, and those not vnrenowmed: wherof Ireland draweth neerest to it in bygnesse, vnciuill for the sauage manners of the inhabiters, but otherwise so full of fat pasture, that if theyr Cattell in Sommer season be not now and then kept from feeding, they should run in daunger of bursting. There are no Snakes, and fewe byrdes: the people are harbourlesse, and warlike. When they haue ouercome theyr enemies, they first besmeere their faces in the blood of them that be slayne, and then drinke of it. Be it right or be it wrong, all is one to the. If a Woman be deliuered of a manchilde, shee layes his firste meate vppon her Husbands sworde, and putting it softlie to his pretie mouth, giueth him the first hansell of his foode vppon the very point of the weapon, praying (according to the manner of their Countrey) that he may not otherwise come to his death, then in battel and among weapons. They that loue to bee fine, doo trimme the hylts of theyr Swords with the teeth of monsters that swymme in the Sea: for they bee as white and as cleere as Iuorie. For the men doo chiefly glorie in the beautie of their Armour. There is not anie Bee among them: and if a man bring of the duste or the stones from thence, and strow them among Bee hyues, the swarmes forsake ẏ combes. The Sea that is betweene Ireland and Brytaine, beeing full of shallowes and rough all the yeere long, cannot be sayled but a fewe dayes in the Sommertime. They sayle in keeles of wicker doone ouer with Neats leather. How long soeuer their passage continueth, the passengers abstaine from meate. Such as haue discussed the certaintie

*Catenesse

Ireland and the manners of the Irish men in old time, not altogether altered to thys day.

This is founde nowe to be contrarie.

certaintie of the matter according to reason, haue esteemed the breadth of that narrow Sea, to be a hundred and twentie miles. The troublous Sea also deuideth the * Iland of the Silures, from the coast of Brytaine: the men of which Ile keepe their olde customes euen vnto this day. They vtterlie refuse buying and selling for money, and giue one thing for another, prouiding things necessary, rather by exchaunge then for ready mony. They worshyppe the Gods very deuoutly. As well the Women as the Men boast of the knowledge of prophesying.

It should seeme to be the Ile of Manne.

The Ile * Thanatos is beaten vpon with ỹ French Sea, and is deuided from Brytaine with a verye narrowe cutte, luckie for corne fieldes and fatte soyle, and not onely healthful to it selfe, but also to other places. For inasmuch as there is no snake creeping there, the earth thereof to what place soeuer it bee carried from thence, killeth snakes. There bee many other Iles about Brytaine, of which * Thule is ỹ furthest of, wherin, at such time as the Sun is at the hyghest in Sommer, and passeth through the signe of Cancer, there is almost no night at all. Againe in the deade of wynter, when the Sunne is at the lowest, the day is so shorte, that the rysing and going downe of the Sunne is both together. Beyond Thule wee learne is the deade and frozen Sea. From the Promontorie of Calydon, to the Iland Thule, is two dayes sayling. Next come the Iles called * Hebudes fiue in number, the inhabiters wherof, know not what corne meaneth, but liue onely by fishe and milke. They are all vnder the gauernment of one King. For as manie of them as bee, they are seuered but with a narrowe groope one from another. The King hath nothing of hys own, but taketh of euery mans. Hee is bounde to equitie by certaine lawes: and least he may start from right through co-

The Ile of Wyght.

* Iseland.

* Catenesse in Scotlande.

* The West Iles of Scotland, of them are now founde aboue fortie.

couetousnesse, he learneth Iustice by pouertie, as who may haue nothing proper or peculiar to himselfe, but is found at the charges of the Realme. Hee is not suffered to haue anie woman to himselfe, but whomsoeuer he hath minde vnto, he borroweth her for a tyme, and so others by turnes. Wherby it commeth to passe that he hath neither desire nor hope of issue. The seconde Harborough betwéene the maine lande and the Hebuds, is the * Orcades: which are frō the Hebuds, seauen dayes and as manie nyghts sayling. There bée but thrée of them: no man dwelleth in thē: they haue no woods: onelie they are ouergrowne with rushye wéedes: and the rest of them is nothing but sand and bare Rocks. From the Orcades vnto Thule is fyue dayes and fiue nights sayling. But Thule is plentiful in store of fruits that will last. Those that dwel there do in the beginning of the spring time liue on hearbs among Cattell, and afterward by milke, and againste Winter they lay vppe the fruites of their trées. They vse their women in common, and no manne hath any wife. The whole circuit of Britaine, is foure thousand eyght hundred, thréescore and fiftéene miles. In which space are great and manie Riuers, and hote Bathes, finelie kept to the vse of men; the soueraigne of which Bathes is the Goddesse *Minerua*, in whose Chappell the fire burneth continuallie, and the coles do neuer turne into ashes, but as soone as ẏ embers were dead, it is turned into balles of stone. Moreouer, to the intent to passe the large aboundance of sundry mettals, (wherof Britaine hath many rich veynes on all sides) Here is store of the stone called Geate, and ẏ best kind of it. If ye demaund ẏ beautie of it, it is a black Iewell: if the qualitie, it is of no weight: if the nature, it burneth in water, and goeth out in Oyle: if the power, rubbe it till it be warme, and it holdeth such things as

* Orkney of them be nowe xxx,

Bathe

Geate

as are laide to it, as Amber doth. The Realme is partlie inhabited of barbarous people, who euen frõ theyr childhoode haue shapes of diuers beastes cunninglye impressed and incorporate in theyr bodyes, so that béeing engraued as it were in theyr bowels, as the man groweth, so growe the marks painted vpon him, neyther do those Nations count any thing almost to be a greater token of patience, then ẏ their bodyes shoulde by manifest scarres drinke in the déepest colour.

CAP. XXXV.

Of Spayne, and the Iles about it: Of the Ocean, and the Midland Sea, and of theyr sundry names, and what the Phylosophers haue left in wryting, concerning the ebbing and flowing therof.

NOwe that I am come again to ẏ maine lãd the matters of Spayne call me. The coast of this Coũtrey is cõparable with the the beste, and inferiour to none, whether yee haue respecte to the fatnesse of the soyle, or to the reuenewes of the Vyneyardes, or to the fruitfulnes of the Trees. It aboundeth in all kind of things, whatsoeuer is costlie of price, or necessary to be occupyed. If yee séeke siluer or golde, it hath thẽ: the yron mynes neuer wast: it gyueth place to no Countrey for Wines; and for Oliues it passeth all others.

The plentifulnes of Spayne.

It is deuided into thrée prouinces, and in the second warres against Carthage it became ours. Nothing is in it idle, nothing barraine. Whatsoeuer grounde is not able to beare corne, beareth good pasture, euen the places that are drye and barraine, yéelde stuffe for ship men to make Cables of. They séeth not salt there, but dyg it out of the grounde. They scoure the fine sparks of dust and make Sinople of it, and therwith dye theyr wooll, that they may afterward make it the better into a scarlet engraynde.

In * Lusitania is a Promontorie which some cal Artabrum, and some call it the Promontory of Lysbone. It disseuereth both ayre, land, and Sea. By land it finisheth the one side of Spayne: and it deuideth the ayre and the Seas in such wyse, at the circuit thereof the French Ocean and the North coast begin, and the Athlantish Ocean and the West do end. There is the Cittie of Lysbone builded by *Vlisses*: and there is the Ryuer Tagus, preferred before other Ryuers for hys golden sandes. In the marches of Lysbone the Mares excéede in fruitfulnesse after a wondrous manner. For they conceiue by the blaste of the Southwest wynde, and theyr lust is as well spedde with the breath of the ayre, as if they were couered wyth Horses. The Ryuer Iberus gaue name to ye whole Realme of Spaine, and the Ryuer * Bætis to the prouince of * Bætica, bothe of them are famous streames. The Cittye Carthage in Spayne, was builded by the Carthagenenses of Affrick, and replenished also with people of that Countrey. The Scipios builded Tarracon, and therefore it is the head of the prouince called * Tarraconensis. The Seacoast of Lusitania hath greate plenty of the precious stones called * Ceraunie, which is preferred before the Ceraunie of Inde. The colour of this Ceraunie is like the Carbuncle: and the vertue ther-

* Portingale

This fable was made of the Genets because of theyr swiftnes

* Granat and Andolosia.

* Guadalqueuer

* Arragon.

The thunderstone.

of is tried by fire: the which if it be able to abide without perrishing or blemish, it is thought to bee good against the force of lightning. The Iles * Cassiterides but against ÿ side of * Celtiberia very fertile of leade: so do also the * fortunate Iles: of which there is nothing worth the noting saue the name onely. * Ebusus, one of the Iles called Baleares, which is distant frō Dianium seauen hundred furlongs, hath no Serpent, for the soile thereof driueth away Serpents. But the Ile * Colubraria which is towarde Sucro, swarmeth with Snakes. The * Baleares were sometime ÿ kingdome of Bocchariis, and there was such store of Connyes, that they vtterlie destroyed all kinde of fruites. At the Hearde of * Betica where as is the vttermoste point of the knowne world, there is an Ilande about seauen hundred paces from the mayne land, which the Tyrians (because they came from the red Sea) called * Erythræa, and the people of Affrick in theyr language called Gadir, that is to say the Hedge. There are many monuments to proue that *Gerion* dwelled héere, albeit some think that *Hercules* fetched his kyne out of another Iland, which lyeth ouer against * Lusitania. But the narrowe Sea betwéene Affricke and Spayne, tooke his name of the Ilands called * Gades. At that place, the Athlantish Ocean sendeth in our Sea which deuideth the world. For the Ocean (which the Greekes so call because of the swiftnesse thereof,) breaking in at the Sun going downe, raseth Europe on the left side and Affricke on the right: and hauing cut a sunder the Mountaines Calpe and Abila (which are called *Hercules* Pyllars) rusheth in betwéene the Mores and the Spanyards. And at this streight (which is in length fiftéene miles, and in breadth scarcely seauen,) as it were at a gate, he openeth the barres of the inner Sea, and wyndeth himselfe into the mydlande

* The Iles of Bayona.
* Byscay
* The Canaries
* Euisa.
* Adderland
* Mallorca and Menorca.
* Granado
Cales Males
* Portingale
* The streights of Gibraltar or Marocke:

coasts, which he beateth vppon from place to place, e-uen vnto the East. Where it beateth vppon Spaine, it beareth ẏ name of the Spanish & Balearish Sea, where it runneth by the prouince of Narbon, it is called the Sea of Gall: then * Lygusticum: & from thence to Si-cill, Tuscane, which ẏ Greekes call Ionian, or Tyrrhæ-niā, and the Italians the nether sea. From Sicill to the Ile of Candy it is called the sea of Sicill: from thence to Pamphylia and the Ægiptian Sea, it is called the Cretish sea. The same gulf of waters wrything hys side first into the North, and fetching great circuits by the Greeke lands, and by Illyrik through * Hellespont draweth into the straights of * Propontis: the which Propontis disseuering Europe and Asia, extendeth to * Mæontis. Of the originall of the names there is no one vniforme reason. It is called Asiaticke and Phæ-nician of the Countries: Carpathian, Ægæan, Icari-an, Balearick, and Cyprian of the Ilands: Ausonian, Dalmatian, Lygustian, and Thuscane of the nations: Adriatish, Argolicke, Corynthian, and Tyrian of the Townes: Myrtoan or Hellespontian of the mischan-ces of men: Ionian in remembraunce of a King of that name: Bosphor of the passing ouer of an Oxe, or of the streights which an Oxe might swim through: of the natures of the dwellers by * Euxinus, or as it was called before * Axenus: and of the order of the flowing Propontis. The Egyptian sea is allotted to Asia: the Gallik sea to Europe, and the Affrick sea to Lybia: and as the sea approcheth to any of the seueral parts of these Countries, so taketh it name therafter. These are in the bowels of the world. But the Ocean beclippeth the vttermost coastes, which according to the shoares it beateth vpon, is named Arabick, Persi-an, Indian, Easterne, Serick, Hercanish, Caspian, Scy-thick, German, French, or British, Athlantish, *Lybick*

Now the Sea of Fraunce.
* The Sea of Genoa.

Now the Candian Sea.

* Saint Georges arme.
The Sea of Cōstantinople.
* The Sea of Zabacca.

* Harboursome
* Harbourlesse.

and Æthiopick. The flowing of the tydes whereof, doth rise exceeding high about the Sea coasts of Inde, and make verie great breaches ther, which happeneth eyther because the waters swelling by force of heate, are helde vp beyond their stint, or els because that in that part of the world is farre greater aboundance of springs and Ryuers. The matter is yet in question, what should be the cause that the Ocean should swel or why it should fal again into it selfe, considering the superfluitie thereof: and it is euident yͤ many things haue béene vttered, rather to showe the wits of yͤ disputers, then to the setting forth of the trueth. But to omitte the doubtfull debatings of the Demurrers, we haue found these opinions to haue most likelihoode of trueth. The naturall Philosophers hold opinion, that the world is a liuing creature, and that being compact of the diuers bodies of the Elements, it is mooued by a soule, and gouerned by a minde: bothe which béeing shed through all the members, doo put in vre the force of theyr eternall moouing: and therefore that like as in our bodies there is an intercourse of the breath and the soule, so in the déepes of the Ocean, there are as it were, certaine nostrils appointed, at which yͤ breache béeing sent out, or drawne in againe, dooth one whyle puffe vppe the Seas, and another while call thē backe againe. But they that folow the knowledge of Astronomie, affyrme that these goings and comminges are mooued by the course of the Moone, and that the interchaungablenesse of the ebbings and flowinges, depende vppon the increasing and decreasing of her, insomuch as they keepe not alwaies one ordinary stint, but altar from tyme to tyme, according to her approching or going away.

Why the tydes be higher in the East parts of the worlde.

Reasons of the swelling of the Ocean.

Iulius Solinus Polyhiſtor.

CAP. XXXVI.

Of Lybia *: of the Orchyardes of the Siſters called* Heſperides *: and of Mount* Atlas.

Of Affrick and the ſundry names therof

OVt of Spayne my next ſtart is into Lybia. For when yee are loſened from Belon which is a Towne of Betica, the next arriuall on the furtherſide of that Sea which is thrée & thirty miles broade, is * Tingie nowe a Towne inhabited with people of Mauritanie, wherof *Antæus* was the founder. Moreouer, because in that circuit the Sea of Ægypt endeth, and the Sea of Lybie beginneth, it hath ſéemed good to me, to call Affrick by the name of Lybie. Some notwithſtanding haue auouched, that Lybie was ſo named of *Lybia*, the daughter of *Epaphus*, and Affrick of *Afer* the Sonne of *Hercules* the Lybian.

*Tanger.

Antæus.

Lix.

Lix alſo another newe inhabited Towne ſtandeth on the ſame coaſt, where was ſometime the Palace of *Antæus*: who béeing perfecter in wynding & vnwinding of knots vpon the ground then els where, as if he had béene the natiue Sonne of the earth, was there vanquiſhed and put to death by *Hercules*. As concerning the Orchyardes of the Heſperides, and ỹ waking Dragon, leaſt the liberty of Fame might be infringed this is the very truth. Out of the Sea commeth a crooked arme with ſo wreathed and wynding banks, that

The Orchards of the Heſperides.

to

to such as beholde the broken turnings of it a far of, it resembleth the glyding of a Snake: and it enuironeth the place that they called the Orchyard. Whereuppon interpreting it to bee the kéeper of the Apples, they opened a gappe to deuise lyes vpon. But thys Iland so wreathed about with the wynding Channell running forward and backward, which is situate in a certaine circle of the Sea, hath nothing in it to prolong the memoriall of antiquitie with, sauing a fewe Trées like wylde Olyues, and an Altar consecrated vnto *Hercules*. But this is a greater wonder then the golden fruite Trées or the leauie gold, that though the grounde be lower then the leuell of the Sea, yet the tyde neuer ouerfloweth it: but the water béeing kept off by the prouidence of nature as by a Iettie, stayeth at the very brimme, and the waues of theyr owne accorde stand still in a circle at the innermost brewes of the Sea bankes: and so through the wonderfull disposition of nature, the leuell grounde continueth styl dry, though the Seas come falling downeward vpon it. Upon the Ryuer Sala standeth the Towne of Sala. From hence by the nation of the Autolians the way lyeth to the * wyldernes of Atlas.

The deserts of Numidie

The description of Mount Atlas, called of those Countrimen Diris.

The Mountaine Atlas rising out of the mids of the waste and sandy Countries, and growing into a circle like the halfe moone, lifteth his head aboue ye clowdes. Where it reacheth to the Ocean that is named after him, no Fountaines spring out of him, but all lyeth horrible wast, all is stéepe cliffs and Rocks all is lothsome and barraine: the grounde bare, and no grasse growing thereon. But where he turneth backe to Affrick warde, he is rich of all kinde of fruites springing of theyr owne accorde, and he is shadowed with hygh Trées, the sent whereof is ranke, and ye leaues like Cypresse leaues, and they are couered with a kind

 of

of * downe, of no lesse value then silke. On that side also groweth plentiously the hearbe Euphrobia, ẏ iuyce whereof cleereth the eye sight, and many wayes preserueth health, and greatly expulseth the force of venims. The top of this hyll is euermore couered wyth snowe, the launes thereof are haunted with foure footed beastes, and Serpents, wyld beastes & Olyphants together. All day long there is no noyse but al is whist not without an horror. But in the night time he glystreth wyth fires, and rings with the noyse that the Ægyptians make in dauncing on a ryng. There are also hearde the sounde of shalmes, and playing vppon Cymballs all along the Seacoast, it is distaunt from Lyx two hundred and fiue miles, and Lyx is from the straights of Marock a hundred & twelue myles: sometime it was inhabited as the plat of the place witnesseth, and throughly occupyed, as where there remaine a fewe Vines and Date trees for a token. *Perseus* and *Hercules* made themselues passage ouer the toppe of it, but no man els came euer there, as the inscriptions of the Altars doo plainly manifest. Where it looketh Westward, betweene it and the Ryuer Anatis by the space of foure hundred, fourescore and sixteene myles together, is nothing but woods full of wylde beastes. There are Riuers about him, not to bee passed ouer wyth silence, which though they be seperated a greate waie one from another, yet they serue all after a sort to doo the Mount Atlas pleasure. Asaua is brackish of tast like the Sea water. Bambothum swarmeth with Waterhorses and Crocodiles: and beyond them another Ryuer, which beeing of colour blacke, runneth through the innermost and scorched deserts, that are broyled continually wyth vnmeasurable heate of the parching sunne burning, hoter then any fire, and is neuer wythdrawne from the heate.

Thus

* It shoulde seeme to be Cotton.

The herbe Euphorbia which some suppose to bee Eybright.

These seeme to be all one wyth the Fayries which appeared to men in the time of popyshe darknesse.

Waterhorses & Crocodyles

Thus much of Atlas: which the Mores call Dyris, according to the instructions of the Books of *Hanno* of Carthage, and of our owne Chronicles, and also of *Iuba* the Sonne of *Ptolome*, who helde the kingdome of both the Mauritanies. *Suetonius Paulinus* also hath finished the certaintie hereof, who first (and almost onely of all the Romaines) aduaunced hys banners beyonde Atlas.

CAP. XXXVII.

Of Mauritanie, *and of Oliphants, and Dragons and whereof Cinnabar is made.*

Called Sanguis Draconis.

Diuers are the prouinces of Mauritanie. The prouince of Tingie where it butteth vpon ẏ Northwest, and where it extendeth toward the midland Sea, ryseth with seuen Mountains which of their likenesse one to another, are called Brothers, and butt vpon the Sea. These Mountaines are full of Oliphants. Thys kinde of beast putteth me in remembraunce from the beginning to intreate of thē. Oliphants therefore, according to mans perceiueraunce, haue vnderstanding, and excell in memory, and obserue the discipline of the starres. When the Moone shineth bright, they goe in heards to the riuers and there hauing washed themselues with water they salute the sonrysing with such gestures as they can, and then return againe into the Forrests. There are two kindes of them: the nobler sorte are knowne by theyr greatnes, the lesser sort are called bastards.

Oliphants and of the natures and properties of them.

By the whyteneſſe of their téeth it is knowen that they be yong: whereof the one is euer occupyed, and the other is ſpared, leaſt béeing made blunt with continuall chauſing, it ſhoulde haue no force when they haue néede of it in fighting. When they bee chaced in hunting, they breake them both, to the intent ẏ when the Iuorie is gone, they may be purſued no further: for they vnderſtand that that is the cauſe of their danger. They goe together in heardes. The eldeſt of them leadeth the bande, and the eldeſt next him followeth the trayne. When they paſſe a Ryuer, they ſende the ſmalleſt before, leaſt the treading of the greater ſorte ſhould weare the channell, and make déepe gutts in the Foordes.

The Females goe not to make before they bee ten yéeres olde, nor the Males before they bee fiue. Two yéeres they giue themſelues to generation, whereabouts they ſpend fiue dayes in eche yéere & not aboue: and they returne not to the heard, before ſuch tyme as they haue waſhed thẽſelues in running water. They neuer ſtryue for the Females: for there is no adulterie knowne among them. They haue in them the vertue of pittie. For if they happen to finde a man going aſtray in the wilderneſſe, they guide him into ſome beaten and knowne way. Or if they méete wyth any Heards of Cattell as they are trauelling, themſelues, they make way gentlie and courteouſly with theyr hand, becauſe they woulde not kill any beaſt that meeteth them.

But if it ſo chaunce that they muſt fight, they haue no ſmall regard of them that be wounded: for they receiue the wearyed and wounded into the middes of them. When they are taken and come into mennes hands, they become tame with drinking meſhes made of Malt. When they ſhall paſſe the Seas, they wyll not

not take shypping before it bee sworne to them that they shall return. The Oliphants of Mauritanie feare the Oliphants of Inde, and as though their consciences grudged at theyr owne smalnesse, they are afraide to come in their sight. They growe in their dams bellies, not tenne yeeres (as the common reporte goeth) but two yeeres as *Aristotle* determineth. And they neuer ingender but one time, nor bring forth mo then one at that once. They liue three hundred yeres, but in anie wyse they can not awaie with cold. They eate the bodies of Trees, swallowe stones, and loue aboue all things to feede of Dates. Most of all things they shunne the sauour of a Mouse: and they wyl not eate of anie thing that Mise haue touched. If anie of them by chance deuoure a Camæleon (which worme is a poyson to Olyphants) he remedieth the mischiefe by eating a wilde Oliue. The hyde on theyr backs is very hard, and the skinne on their bellies is but soft, and they are altogether smooth without haire. Betweene them and the Dragons is continuall enmitie, and the ambush is laide for them in this wilie sorte. The Serpents lurke by yͤ waie sides, where the Olyphants vse to goe customablie: and letting yͤ formoste slippe by, they assaile the hindermost, to the intent the first should not be able to rescue the last, and first they wrythe their tailes in knottes about theyr feete, that hauing snarled their legges, they may staie them from going awaie. For the Oliphants if they be not preuēted and staied by this winding about their feete, doo leane themselues to trees or stones, and therewith enforcing themselues, treade the Dragons to death. The chiefe cause of their fighting is (as men saie) for that Olyphants haue great store of blood, which is colder then the blood of other beastes, and therefore the Dragons doo vnsatiatiably desire it in the excesse of heate. Finallie, they neuer sette vpon them, but when they haue drunk theyr bellies full, to the intent when their vaynes be well stuffed with moysture, they may suck the more out of them when they haue ouercom them. They séeke nothing so much as the eyes of thẽ, which alonelie they know may be perished: or els the inner parts of their eares, because that part cannot be defended with their snowte. But when the Dragons haue sucked out their bloode, they themselues are also ouerwhelmed with the fall of the beaste: and so the bloode that is shedde from them both soketh into the ground, and all the earth that is stéeped therewith, becommeth a vernish to paint withall, called Cinnabar. The firste time that euer Oliphants were séene in Italy, was the fourehundred, thréescore and twelfth yéere after the building of Rome, when *Pyrrhus* king of the Epirhots made warre against the Romaines: and because they were séene in Lucanie first, they called them Oxen of Lucanie.

In the Prouince Cæsariensis is the Towne of Cæsarea, peopled wyth Romaines, sent thither by the Emperour Claudius, héeretofore the Pallace of king *Bocchus*, which Towne afterwarde by the bountifulnesse of the Romaines, was gyuen to King *Iuba* for a rewarde. There is also the Towne * Siga, where *Syphax* dwelled. But wee must not passe mute from * Icosium. For as *Hercules* passed that way, twentie that forsooke his companie, chose a place, and laid foundation of the walles, and because no man should boast peculiarlie of gyuing the name by hymselfe alone, the name was gyuen it of the number of the builders.

* Seren.

* It signifieth the number of twenty

CAP.

CAP. XXXVIII.

Of Numidia *and of the Beares therein.*

HOwe much soeuer is from ẏ Ryuer Ampsaga, is attributed to Numidia. The Inhabiters heereof, as long as they straied abroade in grazing like wanderers, were called * Nomades. In it are many noble Cittyes, but Circa excelleth them all, and next Culloo, comparable to Tyre in dying Purple. All this Region bordereth wholie vpon the marches of Zeugitane. In such part of it as is wooddie, it nourisheth wilde Beasts, where it is high ground, it breedeth Horses, also it is cōmended for the excellent Marble that it hath. The Beares of Numidie excell all other Beares onely in fiercenes and deepe hayre, for the littering of them is like in all places, wheresoeuer they be bred. I will speake therof by and by. They couple not in like sort as other foure footed beastes doo: but inasmuch as they are formed apt to embracinges, they couple together as man and woman do. Winter stirreth vp their desire of generation. The Males seuering themselues for the tyme, doo reuerence the Females when they are bagged, and although they lie all in one den, yet they lie seuerallye by themselues in couches deuided one from an other with diches. The time of their whelping is very swift for they goe not past thirtie daies, whereby it cōmeth to passe, that their ouerhastie littering maketh them bring forth deformed whelps.

* That is to say, Grazyers.

Of the nature and property of Beares.

The things that they bring forth are little lumps of flesh, of colour white, without eyes. And (by reason of the hastie comming foorth before it be ripe) it is nothing but a shapelesse matter, sauing that it hath the proportion of nayles. These they fashion by little and little with licking, and sometimes they cherrish them by laying their warme breastes to them, to the intent that through the heate of their continuall rucking vppon them, they may gather the breath of lyfe. All that while they fast. Surelie for the first fouretéene daies, the dammes fall into so heauie a sléepe, that they cannot be waked with woundes. After they haue whelped, they kéepe home by the space of foure months together. Afterward when they goe abroade into the open daie, they can so ill awaie with the vnaccustomed light, that a man would think they were blinded.

Beares haue weake heades, and their greatest strength is in their fore pawes, and in their loynes, wherby it commeth to passe, that sometimes they will stande vpright vppon their hinder féete. They lye in waite for Béehiues, lusting greatlie for the Combes, and they snatch at nothing more gréedilie then at honnie. If they taste of the Apples of Mandrake they die. Neuerthelesse, they preuent the mischiefe before it growe too strong, and deuoure Ants to recouer theyr health. If at anie time they sette vppon Bulles, they knowe vppon what parts it is best for them to catche holde: and therefore they catch at no parte, but their hornes and theyr nostrils: their hornes to the intent to weigh them downe, theyr nostrilles to the intent to put them to greater payne in so tender a place. In the time that *Marcus Messala* was Consull, *Lucius Domitius Aenobardus* béeing Curulis Aedilis, shewed a hundred Beares of Numidie, and as manie Huntsmen of Aethiop, in ẏ great Theater at Rome: and

and that syght was regystred among hys honourable tytles.

CAP. XXXIX.

Of Affrick, *of Lyons, of the Hyene, of the sundry sorts of Serpents, of precious stones, of monstrous kindes of creatures, and of other notable thinges of that Countrey.*

ALl Affricke beginneth at the foote of Zeugitane, facing the Ilande Sardinia from the Promontorie of *Apollo*, and butting towarde Sicill from ẏ Promontorie of *Mercurie*.

Thus shooteth it forth wyth two heades, whereof the one is called the whyte Promontorie, and ẏ other which is in the region Cyrenaica, is called Phycus. The same béeing situate directlie against the Ile of Crete by the Cretish Sea, shooteth into the sandes toward Tænarus of Lacedemon. Catabathmos windeth into Aegypt. The next Country whereunto (which is Cyrenaica) lyeth betwéene the two Syrts, which the shallowe and uncertaine Sea maketh unaccessible. The Syrts or whasshes of Affrick.

The rysing and falling of which Salt water, it is no easie matter to finde: so uncertaine is the mouing thereof, one while breaking into shallow shelues, and another whyle ouerflowing like a spring tyde. *Varro* affyrmeth that the ground béeing there loose, is readye to be perced with euery wynd, by meanes whero the suddaine force of the swift blastes, doth eyther puffe out or sowpe in the Seas. All this coast is deuided frõ Aethiope & the borders of Asia, by the Ryuer * Nygris, which is the mother of Nilus, and from Spayne by the narrowe Sea. On that side that enclyneth to the South, it is voide of springs & altogether droughtie. On the other side that lyeth towarde the North, it is watred aboundantly, insomuch that in the Countrye Bizacene which is two hundred myles ouer or more, the soyle is so rich, that the séede there sowne yéeldeth increase of a hundred times as much fruite. That many straungers haue resorted thither to inhabite, we will showe you for a proofe the Cittyes and places there. The Promontorie Boreon which is beaten vppon wyth the Northwynde, was so named by Greeks that came thither. The Towne of * Hyppon, (which afterward was called Rhegium, and the other Hyppon called afterward Dyarrhyton of the narowe sea running by it, two noble Townes, were builded by Knights of Greece. The Sicilians builded the Citie * Clypea, and named it first Aspis, they builded Venerie also, whereunto they transferred the religion of *Venus* of Eryx. The Achæans in their language gaue the name of Trypolis, because of the number of ye thrée Citties Taphre, Abrotone, & the greater Lexcis.

* Senega

* Bona.

* Coros.

* Tripolie

The Philene brethren tooke that Greeke name, of the desire of praise. The people of Tyre were founders of Adrymet and Carthage. But now wyll I declare what true bookes haue reported of Carthage. This Cittie (as *Cato* in his Oration before the Senate, affirmeth) was builded at such time as *Hiarbas* raigned in Lybia. *Elyssa* a Lady of the Country Phænicia, who called it Carthad, which in the phænician tongue, is as much to say as a newe Cittie.

Carthage

Anon

Anon after as theyr speche turned into Punicke, both she was called *Elissa* & the Cittie Carthage: which was vtterly rased seauen hundred thirty and seauen yeeres after it was builded. Within a while after, being repayred againe by *Caius Gracchus*, and peopled wyth Italians, it was named by him Iunonia, and continued for a certain time without estimation, in a low and faint state. At length after a hundred and two yeeres respit, in the time that *Marcus Antonius* and *Publius Dolobella* were Consulls, it recouered the honour to be called the second Carthage, the second beautie of the whole world, next Rome. But to the intent to returne againe to * Affrick, it is an Angle seuerally enclosed by it selfe. The inner partes thereof are possessed with manie kyndes of wylde beasts, but speciallie with Lions, which alonely of yͤ kind of beastes yͭ men call toothed beastes, wͨ they (as *Aristotle* affyrmeth) doo see as soone as they bee whelped. Of them there is reckoned three sortes. For yͤ shorter sort with curled manes, are for the moste part weake and cowardlie. The longer sorte with smooth hayre, are more fierce and strong. But those that the Lybards begette, are of the rascallest sort, and haue no manes at all. All of them alike forbeare gorging of themselues: firste for that one day they feede, and another day they drink by turnes, and oftentimes, if they haue not good digestion, they forbeare meate a day longer: and secondly for that if they feele themselues greeued with rauening too much flesh, they put their pawes into theyr mouthes, and pull it out againe. And euen the like also doo they when they flee, if they bee to full. The falling away of their teeth, argueth age. And there bee many proofes of theyr pittifulnesse.

Of Lyons, and of the noble nature and properties of them.

For they spare them that humble themselues before them: and shewe theyr crueltie rather against men then women. As for sucking Children they kyll them not, vnlesse it be for extreame hungar. Neyther are they without mercie. For by daile examples from time to time it is manifest ẏ they haue shewed mercy inasmuch as manie prisoners méeting with some Lyons by the way, haue notwithstanding returned vntouched into theyr Countryes. And in the Bookes of King *Iuba* is recorded the name of a Woman of Getulia, who by entretaunce escaped vnhurt from ẏ Lyons that she mette. They engender backwarde: and not they onely, but also Lynxes, Camels, Oliphants, Rhynocerots, and Tygers. The Lyonesses at ẏ firste lytter bring forth fiue Whelps, and euery yéere after they diminish their number by one, and at the length when the dammes come to bringing forth but one at once, they become barraine for euer. The looke and the taile declare the courage of the Lyons, like as the stomacke of a horse is knowne by hys eares. For nature hath gyuen these two markes to euerie notable beaste to be knowne by. Their chiefest force is in their brest, and their chiefest stedinesse is in their heades. When they be chaced with dogs, they goe away disdainfully, and now and then staying, dissemble theyr force wyth pretence as though they cared not whither they went away or no: aud this they doo when they be followed in open and champion fields. But in woody places (as though they thought no body were able to beare wytnesse of their cowardlinesse) they runne away as fast as theyr legs can beare them. When they themselues pursue any thing, they further their pace with leaping. When they goe at leysure, they hyde the hookes of their talants betwéene the fleshe of their toes, as it were in sheathes. And this they obserue so warelye, that they runne not but wyth their talants turned inward. When they are enuironed and beset with hunters,

ters, they looke stedfastlie vpon the grounde, to the intent they will not be made afraid with the sight of the hunting staues. They neuer looke a squint, neyther can they abide that one shoulde looke a squint vppon them. They feare the crowing of a Cock, and the ratling of whéeles, but most of all they feare fire. Wee reade that there are little beasts called Lyonsbanes, which are caught and vncased, to the intent that flesh béeing powdred with the ashes of them, and caste in the pathes where wayes méete, may kill the Lyons, if they taste neuer so little thereof. And therefore Lyons pursue them with a naturall hatred, & when they get them at aduauntage, they forbeare byting of them but they teare them all to péeces with theyr pawes. *Scaeuola* the Sonne of *Publius* was the first that made a showe of them, in the time that he was Curulis Aedilis. Affrick bréedeth the Hyene, which beast cannot wrythe his necke a side, vnlesse hee moue his whole bodie, because his backbone is without ioyntes, and runneth so whole through his necke. Many wondrous things are reported of it. Firste that it haunteth shepheards cotages, and by continuall harkning, learneth some name, the which he expresseth by counterfeyting mans voyce, to the intent to worke his wrath vppon the man whom he tolleth out by his policie in ye night time. Also he counterfeiteth the vomiting of men, and thereby alluring out the dogs with his false sobbing, deuoureth them. Which dogs if perchance they touche his shaddowe in hunting of him, they lose their voice, and cannot barke. The same Hyene in séeking mens carkasses, scrapeth vpp theyr graues: and therefore it is the easier matter to take the Males. For the Females are of nature more subtill. There is great varietie in their eyes, and chaungablenes of colours, and in the bailes of them is founde a stone called Hyenie,

The beast called Lyons-bane.

The Hyene, and of hys wonderfull nature.

S. enduced

The stone called Hyenie.

endued with such power, ỹ vnder what mans tongue soeuer it be put, he shall prophesie of thinges to come. But what lyuing thing soeuer a Hyene compasseth in thrice about, cannot moue it selfe: and therfore it hath béene auouched for a certaintie, that there is a magicall power in him. In a parte of Aethyop it coupleth with a Lyonesse, and betwéene them is engendred a Monster named a Crocute. Which in likenesse also counterfetteth the spéech of man. He neuer stirreth the balles of his eyes, but stareth continually without twinckling.

A Crocute

He hath no gummes at all in hys mouth, but one whole and maine tooth, which is naturally closed vpp as it were in Caskets, because it should not bee blunted. Among those kinds of beasts that are called Grazers, the same Affrick hath wyld Asses, in which kind euery Male hath his heard of Females. They cannot abyde that any other shoulde haue to doo where they like. And therefore they wait very narrowly vppon their Mares when they be with foale, that (if it bee possible they may byte of the genetoryes from the Colts when they be new foaled: to the end they be not apt for generation. Whereof the Mares béeing ware, hyde their young ones out of the way. Affrick swarmeth in such wise with Serpents, that it may worthelie challenge the preheminence in that mischiefe from all the worlde. The Cærasts péere with foure little hornes, by shewing whereof (as it were wyth a bayte) they allure birds to them, and deuoure them. For they hide the rest of their bodyes for the nonce in the sand, discouering no part of thẽselues sauing that onely part wherwith they entice the birds deceitfully to féeding, when they lie in wait to kill them for theyr labor. The Amphisbene riseth with two heads wherof one is in his accustomed place, and the other where hys

Wyld Asses.

Serpents

The Cerast or Horneworme

The Amphisbene or doubleheade.

his taile shoulde bee. Whereupon it commeth to passe, that with both heads forward at once hee creepeth in a roundell. The Darters clymbe up uppon trees, from whence whirling themselues with as much violence as may be, they pearce through what beast soeuer happeneth to come within their dint. The Scytale hath such a glystering and speckled hide, that the beautie of the spots staie such as behold it, by means whereof, hee catcheth them as they stande gazing and wondring, whom he cannot ouertake by his slownes in creeping. Notwithstanding, as beautifull as his scales be, he is the first that casteth his wynter coate. There are many and sundry kinds of redde Adders, but they haue diuers effects in hurting. The Dipsas killeth wt thirst. The Hypuale killeth with sleepe, and *Cleopatra* may beare witnesse, that it is bought to kill folke. The poysons of others, forasmuch as they bee curable deserue lesse fame. The Hemorrhoyd byteth till it bleedes, and thereby breaking the intercourse of the vaynes, draweth out the life wyth bleeding. Whomsoeuer the Prester stingeth he is bloune, and beeing puffed up to unmeasurable hugenesse dyeth with swelling. Immediatlie uppon the stinging of the Seps ensueth rotting. There are also, ⋆ Ammodits, ⋆ Cheuchries, ⋆ Olyphantyes, ⋆ Chersydres, and ⋆ Chamedraconts. And finally as many sundry names as there bee, so manye sundry deathes there are.

The Darter. The Scytale. Red Adders A Thirstworme. A Sleepeworme, The bloodworm The Prester The rotworme. * A sandcreeper * A Leaperworme. * A watersnake * The Earthdragon,

For Scorpions, Scinks and Lucerts, are accounted among unhurtfull wormes, and not among serpents. These Monsters, if they drinke, doo sting the gentlier. They haue affections, for lightly they goe not but by couples. If the one be caught or kylled, the other that scapeth runneth madde. The heads of the Females are finer, theyr bellyes rownder, and theyr venime more hurtfull.

The Male is a like rounde in all places, and higher also, and more meeke. All Serpents are dull sighted They seldome looke right before them: and not wythout a cause, forasmuch as their eyes stand not in theyr foreheads, but in their temples, so as they are lighter of hearing, then of seeing any thing. As concerning the precious stone called Helitrope, there hath beene contention betweene Aethyop, Affrick, & Cyprus, which of them should yeelde the excellentest of that kynd: and it is founde by manie tryals, that the stone of Æthiop or of Libie hath ẏ prerogatiue. It is of a greene colour not altogether verye fresh, but somewhat more clowdie and deepe, powdred aboue with spots of scarlett. The stone taketh hys name of hys operatiō and power. Beeing cast into a brasse panne, it altereth ẏ colour of the Sunne beames, making them to haue a bloody reflexion: and it casteth the glymering brightnesse of the ayre out of the water, and turneth it aside. Moreouer it is reported to haue this vertue, ẏ beeing mingled wyth the herbe of the same name, and consecrated before with the accustomable enchantmēts, it maketh the bearer thereof to goe inuisible. They that trauell the Syrts, though theyr iourney lie by lande, yet must they direct theyr course by the starres, otherwise they shall neuer come to the place appointed. For ẏ ground is so rotten, that the aire altereth the vpper part thereof, and if there whiske neuer so small a wynd, ẏ blaste thereof maketh such an alteration, that it leaueth no token whereby to knowe a mans way. For it euermore turneth vpside downe, the plats of the places in such wyse, that those which were euen nowe full of hygh hils, sinck into vallies: and those that euen now were vallies, are heaped vp with sande like hyls. And the maine land beareth the nature of the sea that beateth vppon it. Neyther makes it any matter where

The stone Helytrope or Turnstone.

The alteration of the land like to the tydes of the Sea.

stormes

stormes rather bée, séeing that the elements conspyre the destruction of trauellers, so as the wynd rageth vpon the land, and the land as the sea. The two Syrts are seperated two hundred and fiftie myles a sonder: the lesse of them is somewhat calmer. Wee reade that in the time that *Cneus Seruilius*, and *Caius Sempronius* were Consuls, the Romaine fléete passed harmles betwéene these shallowes. In this Coast is the Ile Meninx, where *Caius Marius* hid himself after he came out of the Fennes of Minturne. Beyonde the Garamants were the Psylls, fortified with a wonderfull strength of body against hurtfull poyson. They onelie dyed not of the byting of Snakes: and although they were stunge with their deadly tongues, yet they continued in vnappayred health. Yea they layde theyr newe borne babes to Serpents, and if they were misbegotten, the adulterie of the Mothers was punished wyth the destruction of ỳ Children. But if they were right begotten, the priuiledge of theyr fathers bloode saued the innocent babes from death. Thus they put the assurance of theyr issue to the triall of poyson. But the Nasamons conquered this country, and destroyed it, insomuch that nowe the Psylls haue left nothing whereby to be remembred, sauing onely theyr bare name. The Nasamones yeelde a stone which is called a Nasamonite, altogether bloode shaddowed with blacke vaynes. In the innermost part of the bigger Syrt, about the Philenes Altars, (as we learne) inhabited the Loteaters, and it is so indéede. Not farre from the Philenes Alters, is a Lake whereinto ỳ Ryuer Tryton runneth, where men haue beléeued that * the Goddesse of arts was first séene. The greater Syrt vaunteth of a Cittie called Cyrene, which *Battus* the Lacedemonian builded, the fiue and fortith Olimpyade, when *Ancus Marcius* raigned ouer ỳ Romains,

The Syrts or Whasshes.

Meninx

The Psylls

The Nasamones

The Loteaters.

Mineruа.

Cyrene.

the fiue hundred, fourscore and sixe yeere after the destruction of Troy: the which Cyrene was the natyue Country and dwelling place of *Callimachus* the Poet. Betweene this Towne and the Temple of *Ammon*, are fourehundred myles, harde by the Temple is a Fountaine consecrated to the Sunne, which with the moysture of his water byndeth the ground, and hardneth ashes also into a clod, wherin (not without wonder) the place glistreth rounde about none otherwyse then if it were the greene fields. There is also gathered the stone called Ammons horne. For it is so warpped and crooked, that it is shaped like a Rams horne. It is as bright as gold. Beeing layde vnder a mannes head when he sleepeth, it is said to represent vnto him heauenly dreames. Also there is a Tree called Metops out of which floweth a clammy gumme, which of the place it commeth fro, we call Ammoniack. Furthermore among the Cyrenenses groweth Syrpe ÿ rootes whereof haue a pleasant flauor, and it is more like a shrubbie hearbe then a fruite Tree. Out of the stalke thereof, yssueth in the summer time a fatte dew, which cleaueth to the beards of Goates that feede thereon, and when it is there throughly dryed, it is gathered in dropps like Isicles to serue vppon Tables, or rather to serue for medicine.

Ammions horne.

Ammoniacke.

Syrpe.

It was first called the mylke of Syrpe, because it ozeth in the manner of Mylke. Afterward (custome drawing it thereunto,) it was named Laser. Thys Herbe was afterwarde almoste vtterlie dygged vppe by the Inhabiters of the Countrey, by reason of the intolerable burthen of trybute that was layde vppon them, when their Countrey was wasted at the firste inuasion of strange nations.

On the left hande of Cyrene is * Affrick, on the right side Egypt, on the foreside the rough and harborowlesse

* This is Affrick the lesse, where Carthage stoode.

borowlesse sea, on the backpart diuers barbarous nations, and a wildernesse not to be come vnto, vninhabited and forlorne which breedeth the Cockatrice, such a singuler mischiefe as is not in all the whole worlde beside. It is a serpent almost halfe a foote long, white, wyth, as it were a little myter, proportioned in lynes on his heade. Hee is giuen to the vtter destruction not onely of man and beast, or whatsoeuer hath life, but also euen of the earth it selfe, which he stayneth & burneth vppe, and seareth away, wheresoeuer he hath his deadlie denne. To be short, he destroyeth hearbs, kylleth Trees, and infecteth the very aire: insomuch that no byrd is able to flye ouer the place which he hath infected wyth hys pestilent breath. When hee mooueth himselfe, he creepeth wyth hys one halfe, and wyth the other halfe auaunceth himselfe aloft. All other Serpents are horriblie afraide to heare his hyssing: and as soone as they heare him, they flee euerye one wyth as much haste as they can, euery one hys way. Whatsoeuer is kylled of his byting, no wylde beaste will feede of it, no foule wyll touche it And yet for all this, he is ouercome of Weasels, which menne bring thether, and sende them into the dennes, where he lurketh. Notwithstanding, he wanteth not power euen when he is dead. The Cittizens of Pergamus gaue a full * Sestertium for the carkasse of a Cockatrice, and hanged it vpp in a nette of gold in the Temple of *Apollo*, which was notable for the great workmanshypp thereof: to the intent that neyther Spyders shoulde spynne there, nor byrds flye in there. About the vttermost nooke of the Syrtes, there runneth by the Cittye Berenice the Riuer Lethon, which (as is supposed) issueth from the springes of hell, and is renowmed among the auncient Poets for his forgetfull waters.

The Cockatrice and of his horrible nature.

God hath prouided a remedye for euery mischiefe.

Fiue pounde sterling.

The Ryuer Lethon.

Berenice.

The foresaide Cittie was builded and fortified in

 the

the great Syrte by *Berenice* that was marryed to the third *Ptolomie*. All the large contry that lyeth betwéen Egypt Aethyope, and Lybia, as farre as there is anye woods to cast shaddowe, is replenished wyth sundry kyndes of Apes: and I would not that any man shold be gréeued at the mistaking of the name. For surely it is not expedient to omit any thing, wherein the prouidence of nature is to be séene. Among these is the common sorte of Apes which we sée euery where, not without great aptnesse to counterfet, by means wher of they are the easier taken. For while they desirouslie practise the gestures of Hunters, who for the nonce leaue byrdlime to noynt them withall, they dawbe vp theyr eyes as they had séene them pretende to doo before, and so when theyr sight is stopped vppe, they are easie to be caught.

Apes.

They make merry at the newe of the Moone, and they become sadde when shee is in the wane. They loue their yong ones out of all measure, in so much as they easiler loose the whelps that they are most chare ouer and carry in theyr armes, because those that are not set by, doo euer folow their dam hard at her bréech. The Moonkyes haue tayles: and this is the onely difference betwéene them and the Apes. The Dogheads are also of the number of Apes, most plenteous in the parts of Æthyop, sprightish in leaping, cruel in byting, neuer so tamed, but that they be more rather wyld.

Monkyes
Dogheads

Among Apes are also accounted the Sphinxes, shacke hayred, side and déepe dugged, apt to be taught to forget theyr wyldnesse. There are also that menne call Satyres, very swéete faced, and full of mopping and toying continually. The Callytriches are almost altogether vnlike the other. On their face is a bearde, and on their rumpe a broade tayle. To catch these is no hard

Sphinxes
Satyres.
The fairhayres.

hard matter, but to bring them out of the Country is a rare thing. For they liue not but in the soyle of Aethiop, that is to say in their owne soyle.

CAP. XL.

Of the nation of the Hammanients, *and of the houses therein builded of salt.*

BEtween the Nasamonits and the Troglodits, is the nation of the Hammanients, which build theyr houses of Salt, which they heawe out of ye Mountaines in manner of stone, and laye it with morter. Such is the aboundance of this vaine, that they make them houses of Saltstones. These are the Hammanients which haue intercourse of Merchandise wyth the Troglodits. The precious stones called Carbuncles are on this side the Hammanients, more neerer the Nasamones. The Asbysts lyue by Laser. This is their nourishment, and this is their foode.

* Cauecreepers

Carbuncles

The Asbysts

CAP. XLI,

Of the Garamants, *and of a wonderfull fountayne among them.*

AMong the Garamants is the Towne Debris, with a wonderfull Fountaine in it, which by turnes is

A wonderfull Fountaine,

cold a day times and hote a night times,one while ſée-
thing like water on the fire,and another while becom
ming as cold as Iſe,both contrarieties procéeding out
of yͤ ſelfe ſame veynes.It is a meruailous thing to be
ſpoken of,yͭ in ſo ſhort a time,nature ſhould ſo ſtrang-
ly diſagrée with her ſelfe,that whoſoeuer tried her doings in the dark,would think there were a continuall
fire in the ſpring: and he that felt it in the day,would
beléeue it were none other thing then a winters Water continually frozen.By meanes whereof (not with
out good cauſe) Debris is famous among thoſe nations,for that the waters change their propertie according to the mouing of the heauen,though after a maner cleane contrarie to the diſpoſition of the Planets.
For whereas the euentide aſſwageth the heate of the
world: this ſpring beginneth to heate in ſuch wiſe at
the Sunne going downe,that if yee touch it,yee ſhall
find it ſcalding. Againe, when the Sunne is ryſen a-
boue the ground,and all things are chauffed with hys
rayes,the water thereof is ſo excéeding colde, that no
man is able to drinke it,be he neuer ſo thirſtie. Who
then would not wonder at a Fountaine yͭ becommeth
The Garamants. cold through heate,and hote through cold? The heade
of the Garamant Regyon is Garaman , whereunto
for a long whyle the way was very comberſome,and
not able to be paſſed. For the théeues couered the pyts
with ſande,to the intent that withdrawing yͤ waters
deceitfully for a time,no man might be able to trauell
to them for famine and thirſt. But in the raigne of
Veſpaſian,in the warre that was againſt the Oyans,
this diſtreſſe was taken away,by finding a nerer paſ-
ſage. *Cornelius Balbus* was the firſt that ſubdued the
Garamants,and for his victory firſte tryumphed ouer
them. Surely he was the firſt of ſtraungers (for hee
was borne in one of the Ilands Gades) that attayned
the

the honor of a tryumphant conqueror. The great cattell of this Countrey feede with their necks awry, for if they should graze with their heads right forwarde, their hornes bowing downe, with the tynes into the ground, would hinder their feeding. On the same part that Cercina lyeth, the reporte goeth that there is an Ile called Gaulos, wherein breedeth no serpent, neyther lyueth any ẏ is brought in thither. And therefore the dust thereof being strewed in any place of the worlde, keepeth away Snakes: and being cast vpon Scorpions, it killeth them out of hande.

Strange Cattell.

The Ilande Gaulos.

CAP. XLII.

Of Aethyop*: of the filthy fashions of the people of that Countrey, and of theyr monstrous shapes: of the Dragons, and other wylde beastes of wonderfull nature there: of the spyce Cinnomom, and of the* Iacint *stone.*

THe *Aethiopians*, and the Nations that inhabite the Countryes bounding vpon the Mountaine Atlas, are parted a sunder with the Ryuer * Nigris, which is thought to bee parte of Nyle.

* Senega.

It is so greene with Rushes wherof paper is made it is so clad wyth Reede, it bringeth forth ẏ same kind

of

of liuing thinges, it floweth ouer at ÿ same times, and returneth againe with his banks euen then when Nilus is content with his own channel. The Garamants of Aethyop know no seuerall marriage, but vse their women in common, who that list. Thereon it commeth that the Children acknowledge onely their mothers. For the name of Father hath no reuerence at all among them. For who is able to knowe hys Father, where such incestous lecherie runneth at large. Therfore are the Garamants of Aethyop counted a bastard people among all nations: and not without cause, considering how they haue infringed the discipline of chastitie, and by a wicked custome destroyed the knowledge of their succession. The name of Aethiopians extendeth large.

The beastly manners of the Garamants of Æthyope.

The Æthiopians

On Affrick side, where Lybie faceth the Ilande Meroe, there be many and sundry nations of them. Of the number of them the Nomades liue by the mylk of the Dogheades. The Syrbots are lazie things of a 12. foote long. The Asaches take Oliphants in hunting, and deuoure them. Among the Sambres no fourfooted beast hath eares, no not so much as the Olyphants. Theyr next neighbours, make a Dog theyr King: by whose gesture they diuine what he cōmaundeth them to do. The Aethiopyans on the Sea coast are reported to haue foure eyes a péece, but the trueth is otherwyse, namelie that they are verye sharpe sighted, and ayme the throwing of theyr darts most certainly. Toward the West dwell the Agriophags which feede onely on the flesh of Lybards and Lyons, and haue a King that hath but one eye, which standes in hys forhead. There are also Pamphags who féede of al things that may be chewed, and all things that grow vnsett. There be also Anthropophages, whose name expresseth their conditions. They say that the Cynamolgies haue

The Nomads The Syrbots, The Asaches The Sambres.

The Agriophages or wyld-eaters,

The Pamphags or eateals Meneaters or Cannibals Bytch mylkers

haue chaps like Dogs, and long snowts. The Arthabathits, goe groueling like foure footed beastes, and wander abroade without dwelling place, as beastes doo. The borderers vpon Mauritanie gather Locusts, in time of yeere, and powdring them, doo lay them vp as their onely foode to liue by: But none of them lyueth aboue fortie yeeres. From this Ocean vnto * Meroe (which is an Ilande that Nyle maketh where he first parteth and meeteth againe) are sixe hundred and twenty miles. Beyond Meroe toward the Sunne rysing, are the * Macrobian Aethyopians. For theyr life is longer then ours by the one halfe. These Macrobians, execute Iustice, loue vpright dealing, excell in strength, are very comely and beautifull of personage, are decked wyth brasse, and make giues of golde for offenders. There is among them a place called * Heliutrapæza cōtinually furnished with daintie fare, whereof all men eate without difference, for they vpholde that they are encreased by the power of God. There is also in the same place a Lake, wherwith the bodyes that are washed, shyne as if they were anointed wyth Oyle. This Lake is moste wholesome to drinke. Surely it is so sheere, that it wyl not beare the leaues falne from the Trees, but letteth them sinke downe to the bottome, by reason of the thinnes of the liquor. Beyond these lye desert and vninhabited wildernesses, euen vnto the coast of Arabie. And then in the furthest part of all the East, are nations of Monstrous shape, some hauing yll fauoured visages, altogether plain without noses: & othersome hauing theyr mouthes growne together sauing onely a little hole to put in an Oaten Reede, whereat they draw in their sustenaunce. Some haue no tongues: but vse beckenings and gestures in steede of speeche. Certaine of these nations neuer knewe the vse of fire, before the

Arthabathits.

Guaguera.

The Macrobians or long lyued and their manners.

* The Sunnes Table.

A strange Lake

Monstrous Nations,

time of *Ptolomeus Lathyrus* King of Egypt. Aethyop contayneth all ẏ is from the South east, to the South west. As much of it as is vnder ẏ South coast, is garnished wyth thicke woods, which are gréenest in winter. On the South part there hangeth into the Sea a high Hyll, continually hote with gentle fire, and burning on the toppe wyth restlesse flames, among which continuall hote fires, there is great store of Dragons. Furthermore, the true Dragons haue smal mouthes, and not gaping wyde to byte with, but of a narrowe conduit, by which they drawe breath, and spirt out their tongues. For their force lyeth not in theyr téeth, but in their tayles, and they hurt with beating, rather then with byting. There is cut out of the Dragons braynes a stone called Draconce, but it is not a stone vnlesse it be taken from them while they are alyue. For if the Serpent die before, the hardnesse resolueth and vanisheth away wyth hys life. The Kinges of the East doo chiefely vaunt themselues of the wearing thereof, although it be so hard, that no man can deuise to imprint or engraue any thing in it: and whatsoeuer is beautifull in it, is not made by mans hand, because there should none other colour stayne the pure naturall whitenesse thereof. An Author named *Sothacus*, sayth that he hath séene this Iewel, & declareth by what meanes it is come by. Men of excellent courage and audacitie serche out by holes where the Serpents lie, and also their haunts. Then watching tyll they come forth to féede, and passing by them wyth as much spéede as they can, they cast them hearbes stéeped in thinges that haue as much force as may bee to prouoke sléepe. So when they be fast a sléepe, they cutt the stones out of their heades, and getting the booty of their heady enterprise, enioy the reward of their rashnesse. The places which the Aethyopians possesse, is full of wyld Beastes, whereof one is the Nabis which

Dragons.

The stone called Draconce

wée

we call a Camelopardalis. It is necked like a horse, foted like an Oxe, headed like a Camell, & of a bryght bay colour powdred with white spottes. This beast was shewed first in Rome at the gamings that *Cæsar* the Dictator made in the Lysts. Almost about ẏ same time also were brought from thence monsters called Celphies, whose hinder féete from the ancle upp to the toppe of the calfe, where like a mans legge, and lykewyse hys forefeete resembled a mans hande: notwithstanding, these were neuer séene of the Romaines but once. Before the showes of *Cneus Pompeius*: the Romaines had neuer séene the Rhynoceros openly. Thys beast is of a pale russet colour: in hys nose is a horne that boweth upward: the which hee maketh sharpe pointed like a bodkyn, by whetting it upon stones, and fighteth wyth it against the Olyphants, béeing almost ful as long as they, but somewhat shorter legged, and with this his naturall weapon hee pusheth at theyr bellyes, as the onely part which he knoweth may bee perced with striking. By the Riuer Nigris bréedeth the Catoblepe, a little sluggish beast, with a great heauie ioll, and a venemous sight For they that happen to come in hys sight die. There bee Ants as big as a Mastiffe, that haue talents like Lyons, wherewyth they scrape up sand of golde, which they kéepe that no man may fetch it away, & if any man aduenture, they pursue them to death. The same Aethiop bréedeth ẏ Lycaon, which is a woolfe with a mane on his necke, & so pied, ẏ men say there is no colour, but he hath parte of it. It bréedeth also ẏ Tarand, of the bignes of an Oxe, clouen foted, with tined hornes, headed like a stag, coloured like a Beare, & shacke hayred. It is saide ẏ thys Tarand changeth his complexion for feare, and ẏ whẽ he hideth himselfe, he becõmeth like unto the thing ẏ he is next unto, whither it be a quarrie of white stone, or a groue of gréene trées, or what thing soeuer it be, of any other likenes. The

The Nabis.
Celphies.
The Hornynose.
The Catoblepe
Wonderfull Ants.
The Lycaon
The Tarrande

The Fish Polipus.
* Landlyons

The same thing also dooth the Fyshe Polypus in the Sea, and the * Chameleons on the lande. But the Polypus and the Chameleon haue a sheere skinne, and therefore it is the easier for them to resemble things next vnto them, because of theyr thin smug skynnes, which are like glasse. But it is a straunge and singuler case, that harsh hayre should alter colour, heereby it comes to passe, that they are hardly taken.

The Woolues of Aethiop.

It is a peculiar propertie to the Wolues of Aethyop, to be as nimble in leaping, as a byrde, so as they ridde not more ground by running, then by going, but yet they neuer assault a man. In Winter time they are hayrie, and in Sommertime naked. Menne call them Thoes.

The Porkpyne

The Porkpine also is very ryfe in those Countries a beast like a Hedghog, wyth a hyde full of rough brystles, which he oftentimes looseneth of his owne accorde, and darteth them foorth so thicke as it were a showre of pricks, and therewyth woundeth the Dogs that pursue him.

The bird Pegasus.

Of that coast is the byrde Pegasus: but this bird hath nothing of a horse but his eares. So is also the Tragop, a byrde bigger then an Egle, vaunting himselfe with an armed head, besett with hornes like a Rammes hornes.

The Tragop or Goteface.
Of Cynnamom

The Aethiopyans gather Cynnamom. Thys shrub groweth on a short stalke, wyth low and flatte boughes, neuer aboue two cubits high. That which groweth slenderest is counted the excellentest: and that that swelleth into thicknes, is nothing sette by. But it is gathered by the priestes, who make sacrifice before. Which doone, they take good heede that they beginne not theyr haruest before the Sunne rise, nor continue it after the Sunne sette. He that is Primate among them, deuideth the heapes of sticks wyth a speare, which is consecrated to ye same vse. And so a portion of the faggots is dedicated to the Sunne,

Sunne, which if it bee rightlie deuided, taketh fire alone. Among these things that we haue treated of, is found the Iacint, in colour a bright azure, a precious stone, if it may be found faultlesse: for it is not a little subiect to faultines. *The Iacint.* For diuers times it is eyther vernished with a violet colour, or darkned with a mistynesse, or wanzing into a watry sheerenesse, the best fashion of it is, if it be not dimmed with two deepe a die nor ouer lighte with too pure a sheerenesse, but haue a sweete orient colour of lightsomenesse and purple equallie mixed together. This is he that feeleth ÿ ayre, and altereth with it: insomuch as it is not a like bright when the wether is clowdy, as whē it is fayre. Moreouer, beeing put into ones mouth, it becommeth colder. And for ingrauing it is nothing meete, because it wyll abide no chafing, yet is it not altogether inuincible: for with a Diamonde a man may write in it, and drawe what he list in it. Where as is the Iacint, there is also the Chrysolamp, which stone the light hydeth, *Crysolamp.* and the dark discouereth. For this diuersitie is in him that in the night he is fierie and in the day he is pale. *The Hæmatite or bloodstone* Out of that soyle also we take the Hæmatite, a stone as redde as blood, and therfore called the Hæmatite.

CAP. XLIII.

VVonderfull things of the nations of Lybia, *and of the stone called* Hexacontalythos.

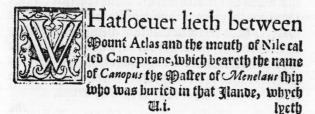

WHatsoeuer lieth between Mount Atlas and the mouth of Nile called Canopitane, which beareth the name of *Canopus* the Master of *Menelaus* ship who was buried in that Ilande, whych lyeth against the said mouth of Nyle, where Libie endeth, and Egypt beginneth, is inhabited by nations of sundry languages, which are withdrawne into wayllesse wildernesses. Of these the Athlantians are altogether void of manners méete for men. None hath anie proper calling, none hath any speciall name. They curse the Sun at his rising, and curse him likwise at his going downe: and because they are scorched wyth the heate of his burning beames, they hate the God of light. It is affirmed that they dreame not, and that they vtterlie abstaine from all thinges bearing lyfe. The Troglodits dig them caues vnder the grounde, and house themselues in them. There is no couetousnesse of getting, for they haue bound themselues from riches, by wilful pouertie. Onely they glory in one stone which is called Hexacontalythos so powdred with diuers sparks, ẏ the colours of thréescore sundrie stones are perceiued in his little compasse. All these liue by the flesh of Serpents, and béeing ignoraunt of spéech, do rather iabber and gnarre then speake. The Augyles worship none but the deuils. The first nyght that they are married, they compell theyr wyues to haue to do with as many as will come: and from that time forward, they bind them by most straight lawes to continuall chastitie. The Gamphasants abstayne from warres, eschew intercourse of merchandise, and will not abide to intermedle with any straunger. It is thought that ẏ Blemmyes (but not those Blemmyes that dwell by the Red sea) are borne headlesse, & that they haue theyr mouth and eyes in their breste. The Satyres haue no resemblance of menne sauing onely shape. The Egypanes are the very same that wée see them painted. The Hymamtopodes hauing ẏ ioynts of their legges bowed, do rather créepe then goe, and in walking vse rather to slyde then to steppe.

The Athlantians

The Troglodites or Cauecreepers.

The stone called the threescore stone, or the Sixtistone.

The Augyles

The Gamphasants.

The Blemmyes

The Satyrs or Woodwards

The Goatefeete

The crookelegs

the

The Pharusians hauing brought *Hercules* on the waie as he was going toward the Hesperids, were so wearie of the iourney, that they taryed there. And thus much of Lybie. The Pharusians

CAP. XLIIII.

Of Egypt, *of the head, encrease, & mouthes of* Nile, *of the Oxe Apis: of the Crocodiles: of the bird Trochyle: of the Skinks, waterhorses, and the bird Ibis, of the wonderfull trees of* Egypt, *of* Alexandria, *and of Pyramyds or Broches.*

EGypt runneth to the South inward, vntill it méete with the Aethiopyans. Behind it floweth Nile about the lower part thereof. The which Riuer béeing deuided at the place that is named Delta, embraceth a péece of groũd within it like an Ile, and it is almost vnknowne where the head is from whence it commeth, as we shall declare. It hath hys beginning from a Mountaine of the lower Mauritanie, that is nèere the Ocean. Thus affirme the Punick bookes, and so reported King *Iuba* as I vnderstand. By and by therefore it maketh a Lake which they call Nilides. Of Nyle.

And it is coniectured that Nile commeth frõ thence.

because thys Poole bringeth forth the same kinds of hearbs, fishes, and beasts that we see in Nyle, and that if Mauritanie from whence it hath his originall, happen to bee watred eyther with ouer deepe snowe, or rage of raine, the flood in Egypt is thereby increased: But the Nyle when he runneth out of his Lake is sucked into the sandes, and hydden in the loose moulde of the earth, and afterward, bursting foorth in the Caue of Cæsarea, larger then hee was before, bringeth the same tokens with him which we noted in him at hys first spring.

Afterward hee sinketh downe againe, and venteth not aboue the ground, till after a long weary iourney, he come to the Aethyopians. Where it ryseth vppe againe, it maketh the Ryuer Nygris which we told you before bounded the borders of Affrick. The Inhabiters there call it Astapus, which is as much to say, as a water flowing out of darknesse. It inuironeth many and great Iles, whereof some are of so large and huge bignesse, that a man can scarce lakey through them in fiue dayes, runne he as fast as he can. The noblest of them is * Meroe, about which, the Ryuer béeing deuided, is named on the right Channell Astusapes, and on the left Astabores. Then also trauelling through great Countryes a long iourney, as soone as ẏ Rocks méeting him by the way make him rough, hee caryeth his waters with such violence through the cragged cliffs, that he may séeme to fal rather then to flow; and at length when he hath passed the last leape (for so the Egyptians call certaine straights of hys) there is no daunger in him. Then leauing the name of Syris behinde him, he runneth from thenceforth playne without any stoppe. Lastly he is deuided into seauen channels: and so turning towarde the North, is receiued into the Sea of Egypt.

* Nowe called Guaguera.

Such

Coniectures of the increase of Nyle.

Such as are ignorant of Astronomie and Cosmographie, haue aledged manie causes of his increase. Some affyrme that the East wyndes called Etesiæ, do driue great store of clowdes to the place where the Ryuer springeth, and that the spring rysing by the moysture comming from aboue, afoordeth so much water to the flowing of the Riuer as the clowdes haue let fal moysture to the féeding of the spring. Othersome reporte, that béeing driuen backe by the violence of wyndes, when hee cannot vtter his waues, which kéepe their accustomed swiftnesse, the water béeing pent in the straight ouerfloweth his banckes, and the more the blasts of the contrarie wynds resist, so much the higher dooth the swift Riuer (being beaten backe) mount aloft, because that neyther the accustomed course can emptie the channel, and yet the weyght of the streame commeth on still from the head of the spring vpon the Ryuer which is dammed vp: And that thus by the agréeable violence of the Element on the oneside stryuing forward, and on the otherside beating backward, the waues swell, and gather into a heape, whereby is made the floodde.

Diuers hold opinion, that this spring which is called Phiala, is raysed by the influence of the stars, and that béeing haled out by the Sunne beames, it is heaued vpp by the celestiall fire, but not wythout a sure and orderly custome, that is to say, at the newe of the Moone, howbeit that the Sunne is the verye grounde of hys excesse. For the first rysing and swelling thereof beginneth when the Sunne mooueth through ẏ signe of Cancer: and afterwarde, when the thirty partes thereof are runne out, so as the Sunne is entred into Leo, and the starre called Sirius ryseth in then the Riuer flushing forth wyth so great a violence, breaketh ouer his bancks: which time the Priests iudged to be the byrth day of the worlde, that is to weete betweene the * thirteenth of the Calends of August, and the eleuenth day of August, and that afterward all the excesse is called back againe, when the Sunne passeth into Virgo, and is driuen cleane againe within hys banks, when the Sunne is entred into Libra. They adde this moreouer, that he hurteth both wayes, whether he swell too high or too lowe, forasmuch as hys scantnes bringeth small store of increase, and his ouer great aboundance hindreth the tyllage by to long continuance of moistnes. They say that his greatest excesse riseth to eighteene cubits, and his measurablest to sixteene: and ŷ at fifteene wanteth no store of fruite. But if it be vnder, it causeth derth. They attribute also this maiestie vnto him, that hee shoulde foreshewe thinges to come: grounding their argument heerevpon, that at ŷ battell of Pharsalie, it exceeded not fyue fathome. This is most certaine, that hee onely of all Riuers breatheth forth no ayres. It beginneth to appertaine to the Realme of Egypt from Syene, wherein is ŷ vttermost bounde of Aethyop, & so from thence vntill it fal into the Sea, it keepeth the name of Nyle. Among all the thinges that Egypt hath woorthye to be spoken of, they make a wonder specially of the Oxe which they call Apis.

* The nineteenth day of Iuly.

Apis the God of Egypt.

Him they worshyppe as a God, and hee is notable for the whyte specke which groweth naturally on hys right side, representing the likenesse of the horned Moone. The time is appointed howe long hee shall liue, which beeing expyred, hee is drowned in the bottome of a holy Well, because hee shoulde not liue any longer then is lawfull for him. By and by not wythout solemne mourning of all the whole Realme another is sought.

Assoone as he is founde, a hundred Priestes wayte

vpon him to Memphis, to the intent that taking orders there, he may begin to become holye. The Temples into which he entereth or where he resteth, they misticallie name bryde Chambers. Hee giueth manifest foretokens of things to come: and that inespecially if he take meate of their handes that come to aske counsel. By refusing *Germanicus Cæsars* hande, hee bewrayed that which hung ouer his head, for it was not long after, but *Cæsar* was dispatched of his life. The boyes followe flocking after Apis, and suddainly, as though they were mooued with some spirit, they tell of things to come. Once in a yéere a Cowe is shewed him, and shée also is not without certaine marks, the which is kylled the same day that she is found, assoone as she hath béene shewed to him. The people of Memphis solemnize the byrth day of Apis, by casting a cup of golde into Nyle. This solemnitie is helde seauen dayes together, during which time the Crocodyles kéepe as it were a truce with the Priestes, and touch them not in their washings. But the eyght day, when the Ceremonies are nowe finished, (as though open warre were proclaimed again) they take to thē theyr former crueltie. The Crocodile a fourefooted myschiefe, hath force both vpon land and water alike. Hée hath no tongue, and he mooueth ẏ vpper Jaw. Where he byteth he taketh horrible fast holde, his téeth shutting Checquerwise one wythin another. For the most part he groweth to the bignes of twenty fathoms, and they lay Egs like Géece Egs. Hee chooseth a place to builde his neste in, where the water of Nyle cannot come when it is at the fullest. In cheryshing vp theyr young, the Male and Female kéepe theyr turnes. Beside hys wyde chappes, hée is also armed with outragious long talants. A nights hee kéepeth in ẏ waters, and a dayes he resteth vppon the lande.

See howe the deuil can delude Idolaters by false Miracles.

Of Crocodyles.

He is clad in a meruailous strong hyde, in so much as a péece of artillarie shotte at him out of any engine reboundeth backe againe from hys skynne. There is a little prettie byrde called Trochylos, which in seeking to féede vpon the flesh that sticketh in the Crocodyles téeth, doth by little and little scrape his mouth, and so delyghting him easily with hys soft tyckling, maketh him gape, that hee may stande betwéene his chappes. Which thing the Enhydre (which is a kynd of water Ratte) perceiuing, whyppeth into the beasts belly, and eateth vp hys inwardes, and then grating through his paunche commeth out againe. There is also a kind of Dolphins in Nyle, that haue finnes like sawes vpon theyr backs. These Dolphins egge foorth the Crocodiles for the nonce to swymme, and then diuing subtillie, they poppe vppe vnder them, and cutting theyr bellies kyll them. Moreouer in a certaine Iland of Nyle, there dwell men of a very low stature, but of such a boldnesse, that they offer to méete ẏ Crocodyles, for these Monsters pursue them that flée from them, and flée from them that follow them. Therfore are they caught, and béeing made tame become slaues in their owne waters, and when they be throughlye brought in awe, they are so obedient for feare, that forgetting their wildnesse, they carry theyr Maisters ryding on their backs. As soone therefore as they escrye this Iland or this nation by the smell, they flée far of. In the water they are dull of sight, and on the lande most sharpe sighted. All the Winter long they eate no meate: but from the beginning of the short dayes, they continue fasting by the space of foure Monethes together. Ther is also about Nile great store of Skinks which are like Crocodiles, but of a lesser making, and shorter, howbeit they are very necessarye for the preseruation of helth. For Physicions make drinkes of them

The bird called Trochylos.

The beast called the Enhydre.

The Dolphins of Nyle.

Skinks

them to ease the numnes of sinewes, and kil the force of poyson. In the same Ryuer, and in the same soyle, bréedeth the Water horse, lyke a Horse in back, mane, and neying: wyth a snoute turning vpwarde, clouen cleés, tusshes like a Boare, and a writhed tayle. Hee eateth vppe the Corne in the night, whereunto of a subtiltie hee goeth backwarde, that by the deceitfull print of his foote, hée may not bee laide for in hys way homeward. The Waterhorse

The same beast, when he is ouerfull with féeding gettes him to the Réedes that are newe cutte downe, and trots so long vppe and downe vppon them, vntill the sharpe stumppes haue so wounded his féete, that with bléeding he may abate the burthen of his bellye. Afterwarde hée stoppeth the wounde with clay, vntill it growe to a dry scarre. *Marcus Scaurus* was ẙ first that brought Water horses and Crocodiles to Rome. About the same bankes is a Byrde called Ibis, which maketh haucke of Serpents Egges, and carryes them as a most delectable meate to her young ones in her nest: by meanes whereof the increase of hurtfull thinges is diminished. Neyther doo these birdes good wythin ẙ coast of Egypt onelie. For wheras swarms of winged Snakes come out of the Fennes of Arabie whose poyson is so swift of operation, that menne dye of their stinging before they féele anie paine, the birds béeing mooued with a certaine foresight (wherewith they are endued for the same purpose) goe altogether in aray, and before the saide forraine mischiefe caune waste the bounds of theyr owne Country, they méete the pestilent flocks in the ayre, and there deuoure all the whole hoste of them. For which deserte they are counted holie, and no man may hurt them. They lay their Egges at theyr mouth. Onelie Pelusium bree-deth them blacke, the reste of Egypt bréedeth them white. The bird Ibis white. Of the trees which only Egypt beareth, ẏ chiefe is the Figge tree of Egypt, which hath leaues lyke a Mulberrie Tree, and beareth fruite not onely on the boughes, but also on the body of the Tree. It is so bou̅teous in fruitfulnesse, that in one yeere it beareth seauen times. Wheresoeuer yee pull of one Fyg, by and by buddeth vppe another. The woode thereof beeing put into the water sinketh downe to the bottome: and afterward, when it hath lyen long soking in the water, as though it were made lighter, it ryseth vppe and fleeteth vpon the brym: and cleane contrary to the nature of all other woods, moistnes maketh it dry.

The Fygtree of Egypt.

The Date tree of Egypt, is also a thing worthy to bee spoken of, properly it is called Adipsos, and so it ought to bee called: for beeing tasted it putteth away thirste. The sauor therof is like a Quince: but it stauncheth not thirst, vnlesse it be gathered somwhat before it bee ripe. For if it be taken full ripe, it perisheth the memorie, takes away ones going, makes ones tongue trippe, and weakening the powers both of the minde and of the body, cou̅terfetteth the vice of drunkennes.

The Date Tree of Egypt. Thirstlesse,

The Marches of Egypt where it ryseth in height toward the vppermost point of Kakecaumen, are inhabited by a people, which find out the moment wherin the yeere beginneth first his ordinarie course by thys deuice. There is chosen a holy groue, whereinto they driue beastes of all kinds. These beastes, at such time as the motion of heauen is come about to his determinate point, expresse their vnderstandings by such outward signes and tokens as they are able. Some howle, some lowe, some roare, some bray, and diuers runne together into the myre, and theyr wallowe.

A straunge finding of the beginning of the yeere.

Thys experiment is a rule to them, wherby to finde out the beginning of the time. The same

people

people reporte also, that it hath beene left vnto them for a certaintie by the first founders of their Nation, that the Sunne rysing was there, wheras is now the going downe. Among the Citties of Egypt, Thebe is notable for the number of Gates, vnto which Cittie the Arabians bring merchandise from all parts of the worlde. Hereof the Countrey Thebaica taketh hys name. Abydos also sometime renowmed wyth the Palace of Memnon, and nowe beautified with the Temple of *Osyris*. Both the hugenesse of the work it selfe, and the King of Macedonie the founder thereof, do ennoble Alexandria, and *Dimocrates* the maister of the workes, deserued the seconde place of fame next vnto the builder, for setting out the platt thereof. Alexandria was builded in the hundred and twelfth Olympiade, when *L. Papyrius* the Sonne of *Spurius* and C. P*etilius* the Sonne of *Caius* were Consulles of Rome, not farre from the mouth of the Ryuer Nyle, which some call Heracleotick, and othersome Canopick. There is also Pharos, peopled with inhabiters sette there by *Cæsar* the Dictator, where lights are sette vppe a nights for men, to sayle safely in and out of the Hauen by. For the comming to Alexandria is subtill, full of deceitfull shelues, an vncertaine Sea, and arriuable onely at three Channels, Tegamus, Posidonius, and Taurus. Heereupon therefore such beakons or engines as are framed in Hauens to giue light, are called Phari. The * Pyramides are Broches in Egypt, raysed with sharpe spyres aboue the height of any thing that can be made by mans hand: and forasmuch as they passe the measure of shaddowes, they haue no shadowes at all. Now let vs turne our talke from Egypt.

Thebæ of Egypt

Abydos in Egypt.

Alexandria.

Pharos

Pyramides

CAP. XLV.

Of Arabic *and of the Frankencence and Myrrhe in it, of the byrds called Phænix and Cynamolgies. Of the manners of the* Arabians, *and of the kynds of theyr precious stones.*

BEyonde the mouth of Nylus called Pelusiacum is Arabie stretching to ẏ Red sea, which *Varro* affirmeth to be called Erythræum, of King *Erythrus* the sonne of *Perseus* & *Andromeda*, and not onely red of the colour, thereof. The sayde Author auoucheth also, that on ẏ shore of this Sea, is a Fountaine, whereof if Shéepe drinke, they chaunge the colour of theyr fléeces: and wheras they were white before, they lose that which they had vntill they drunke, and afterward become a déepe yellow colour. Vppon the Redde Sea, standeth the Cittie Arsinoe. And thys Arabie extendeth to that spicebearing and rich Land, which the Cutabanes and * Scænits possesse. The Arabians are renowmed with the Mountain Casius. The cause why these Scænits are so named, is for that they dwell in Tents, and haue none other houses. Theyr Tents are couered with haires made of Goates haire wouen.

This is Arabie the Desert.

A strange spring

Arsinoe.

* Dwellers in Tents.

Moreouer, they vtterly abstaine from Swynes flesh. Surelie if this kind of beast bee brought thither, it it dieth by and by. This Arabie the Greckes call * Eudæmon, and we call it by interpretation blessed. It is inhabited wyth a Hyll made by hand, betweene ẏ Ryuer Tygris, and the Riuer Eulæus: which springing among the Medes, is so renowmed for the cleereneſſe of hys water, that all the Kings of that Realme, drink none other thing then the liquor thereof. That it was not unworthelie surnamed Eudæmon or blessed, yee may gather heereby: that besides the spyces whereof it hath great store, that Countrey onely and none other, yeeldeth Frankencence, and yet not al the whole Countrey neither. For in the mids of it are the Atranits a shiere of the Sabæans, from whence about eight remouings of, is the Countrey that beareth ẏ Frankencence. It is called Arabie, that is to say holy, for so the name signifieth by interpretatiō. These low trees are not cōmon: but (which is a strange thing among barbarous nations) they goe by right of inheritaunce in the succession of certaine Families. And therefore those that haue the possession of thys groue, are called in the Arabian tongue holy. The same persons also at such time as they doo eyther crop or fell these groues, come not nigh any coarse, nor defile themselues wyth the companie of women. Before the trueth of the matter was certainlie knowne, some likened thys tree to the Mastick Tree, and some to the Turpentine Tree, untill such time as by the Bookes of King *Iuba*, wrytten to *Cæsar* the Sonne of *Augustus*, it was plainlie declared, that it was a Tree wyth a crooked stock, and boughes like a Maple, yeelding a iuyce like ẏ Almond Tree, and that it is wont to be cutte in the beginning of the Dogdaies, when the Sunne burneth hotest. In the same lands groweth also Myrrhe: the rootes wher of doo thriue with dyging, and delight to bee proyned: and when they be layd bare, they yeelde ẏ fatter gum.

* Blessed or happy.

The estimation had in old time to the water of the Riuer Eulæus.

Of Frankencence.

What the worde Arabie signifieth.

Myrrhe.

The iuyce that issueth of his owne accord is ẏ more precious: and that which is drayned forth by slitting the barke, is counted the worser. The barke wyndeth rounde like a whirlepoole, and is full of rough pricks: the leafe is like an Olife, sauing that it is somewhat more rough. The vttermost height that it groweth vnto, is fiue Cubits. The Arabians make fire wyth the shreddes of it: the fume whereof is so noysome, that if they preuented not the mischiefe with the sent of burnt Storax, diuers times they shoulde catch vncurable diseases. Among the same people bréedeth the byrd called the Phænix, of the bignesse of an Eagle,

The Phænix

his head garnished with a plume of feathers sticking vppe like a crest, with tufted chéekes, and with a ring about his necke, shyning like gold. All his hinder part is purple, sauing his trayne, the feathers whereof are of a rose colour, medled with a bright Azure. It is prooued that he lyueth fiue hundred and fortye yéeres. Hée maketh hys herse of Cynnamom, which he trimmeth néere vnto Panchaia, bringing his pyle of sticks into the Cittie of the Sunne, and there laying it vppon the Altar.

Heliopolis.
What a great yeere is.

It is a matter of doubtfull credite among Authors, whither a great yéere be accomplished with the life of this yéere or no. The most part of thē affyrme, that a great yéere consisteth not of fiue hundred and fortie, but of twelue thousand, nine hundred fiftie and foure of our yéeres. Finally, when *Quintus Plautius*, and *Sextus Papinius* were Consuls, the Phænix flewe into Egypt, and béeing taken the eight hundreth yeere after the building of the Cyttie, was by the commaundement of *Claudius* the Emperour, shewed openlie at the election of the Officers. The which deede, besydes the decrée that remaynes concerning the same, is also enrolled among the Acts of the Cittie.

The

The Cynnamolgus likewyse a byrd of Arabia, maketh hys neste of the twygges of Cynnamom in the trées that be highest, whereunto because there is no clymbing by reason of the height of the trées, and brittlenesse of the boughes, the inhabiters throwe lynes with plummets of lead on the endes of them into the nestes, and so pulling them downe, sel them farre déerer, because the Merchants like that Cynnamom better then any other. The Arabians haue a large and a wyde Countrey euery way, and liue after diuers maners, with diuers kinds of Religion. Many goe wyth powled heads, and hoodes like myters, and in apparel fashyon like to the same: and some shaue their beards to the hard skyns. They giue themselues to Merchandise: not bying other folks wares, but vttering theyr owne. For they bee rich bothe in woods and waters. The shadowes which lye to vs on the ryght hande, lie to them on the left. Some of them that liue hardlye eate Snakes flesh. They haue neither regard of body nor soule, and therfore they are named Ophiophags. From the Seacoast of thys Countrey was brought vnto King *Polycrates*, a precious stone called a Sardonix, which first stirred vppe the firebrand of excesse in our part of the worlde. But the Sardonix is so well knowne of all men, that I thinke not méete to make long processe about it. The vpperpart thereof is allowable if it be a shéere red: but it is reproued if it be thicke like dregges. The mids of it is girded wyth a whytish circle, the grace whereof is if it neither shed his colour into the next, nor be himselfe borow of the other. The rest of him is finished with a black, which (if it giue a light through it,) is counted a fault: but if it let from séeing through, it giueth it the greater grace. The Arabian also findeth the Molochite of a deeper greene then is the Emerawde, hauing a

The Cinnamom Byrde.

The manners of the Arabians.

Not at all tymes of the yeere, but openly while the Sun is in Cancer, and that is but in the South part of Arabie onely.

Snakeaters.

Sardonix.

The Molochyte.

natiue vertue against the perrills of infants. Hee findeth likewise the Iris in the Red sea, sixe cornered as the Crystall: which béeing touched with the Sunnebeames, casteth out of him a bryght reflexion of the ayre like the Raynebowe. The same Arabians gather the Androdamant bright as Siluer, with sides equallie square, which yée would thinke to haue borrowed somewhat of the Diamond. It is thought ẏ hys name is gyuen him of that hee asswageth ẏ passions of hote mindes, and restrayneth the rage of anger. Wee haue from thence also the Arabish * Pederote: which (to sée to) is like Iuorie, and will not be filed. It helpeth them that beare it, against paines of the sinewes. In the pederote is conueyed whatsoeuer is excellent, with a certaine prerogatiue of comlines. It is cleere, like Crystal: it is ruddy like purple: glystring in the vttermost verges as it were out of water, with a border yellowe like Saffron. With this swéetnesse it rauisheth the eyes, allureth the sight, deteyneth the beholders: and for this beautie, it pleaseth also the Indians. This is inough concerning Arabie, nowe let vs retyre againe to Pelusium.

The Iris or Rainbowstone

The Androdamant or Male Diamond

The Pederote called also Opalius,

CAP.

Iulius Solinus Polyhistor.

CAP. XLVI.

Of Mount Casius *: of the great* Pompeis *tombe: and of the Towne* Ioppa.

FRom *Pelusium* is Mount Casius, and ẏ Chappell of *Iupiter Casius*, and also the place of Ostracina, ennobled with the Tombe of the great *Pompey*. From thence beginneth * Idumæa, fruitful of Date trées. Afterward comes * Ioppa, the aunncientest Towne in all the worlde, as which was builded before the generall flood. In that Towne is to be séene a Rocke, which kéepeth yet the print of the chaynes of *Andromeda*, who (as is reported, and that by no vaine rumor) was sette foorth there to bee deuoured of a Monster.

*Edom

*Now called Port Iaffe

Of Andromada and the Monster

For *Marcus Scaurus* in his Aedileshyppe showed the bones of that Monster openly at Rome. The thing is regystred in Chronicles. The measure of thē also is contayned in true Bookes: that is to say, that the length of his ribbes was more then fortie foote, and that hee was farre higher then the Olyphants of Inde. Moreouer, euery ioynt of hys ridgbone were aboue halfe a foote broade.

Iulius Solinus Polyhistor.

CAP. XLVII.

Of Iewry *: of the Ryuers and Lakes therein : of Balme : of* Sodom *and* Gomorrhe *: and of the Essane Nations.*

The Ryuer Iordan.

IEwrie is famous for waters, but all the waters are not of one nature. The Ryuer Iordan béeing of excellent swéetnes, and flowing out of yͤ fountaine Peneas, runneth by moste pleasant Countries, vntill that falling into the Lake

The dead Sea.

* Asphaltites, which ingendreth Bitumen, it is there corrupted with the standing water. This Lake hath no lyuing thing in it, nothing can drowne in it. Buls and Cammels swym without daunger in it. There is

The Lake of Genezareth

The Lake of Tyberias

also a Lake called Genezar, sixtéene myles long, besett with many goodly Citties, and himselfe fellowe with the best. But the Lake of Tyberias is preferred before all these, wholsome for his milde tast, and effectuall of operation for health. The heade of Iewry hath

Ierusalem.

Iericho.

béene Ierusalem, but it is vtterly destroyed. In stedde thereof, succéeded Iericho, and this also hath ceased to be the head, since it was conquered in the warres of *Artaxerxes.*

* Fairestreame.

Néere vnto Ierusalem is the Fountaine * Callyrhoe, greatly commended for the medicinable heate thereof, which taketh hys name of the renowne of his

Of Balme

water. Onely in thys Lande groweth Balme, which

kinde

kynde of Trée was not to be founde out of ye compasse of twenty acres of grounde, vnto the time that wee conquered the Countrey. But after that we had gotten Iewry, those groues were so spredde abroade, that nowe very large Hylles doe yeelde vs Balme.

The stocks of them are like vines: they are sette of slyppes: they were lustie with dygging about the rootes: they delight in water: they loue proyning, and are shadowed continually with their own leaues which stick fast.

The wood of the stemme béeing touched wyth yron, dyeth without delay: and therefore they be cunningly slytted eyther with glasse or with knyues of boane, and that onely in the Barke, out of which issueth a Gumme of excellent swiftnesse. Next after the Gum, the second place of price is gyuen to ye Apples, the thyrd to the rynde, and the last to the woode. A great way from Ierusalem lyeth a sorrowful coaste, which was striken from heauen, as appeareth by the soyle thereof, which is black, and resolued into Ashes.

There were two Townes, the one named Sodom, the other Gomorrhe: and there groweth an Apple which though it séeme to bee rype, yet canne it not bee eaten. For wythin the skynne that goeth about it, there is contayned a cindrye soote, whych at euerye lyght touch puffeth out lyke a smoke, and crumbleth into loose dust.

Sodom and Gomorrhe.

The inner partes of Iewrye towarde the West, are possessed by ye Essænes: who vsing a notable trade of dyscypline by themselues, haue departed from the custome of all other Nations, ordeyned heereunto (as I thynke) by the prouidence of the diuine maiestie.

The secte of the Esseyes.

There are no Women among them: they haue

vtterly renounced fleſhlie luſt : they occupy no mony, they liue by Dates : no manne is there borne, and yet there wanteth no ſtore of men. The place it ſelfe is deputed to chaſtitie : whereunto though many reſorte from all places about, yet is none admitted vnleſſe his approoued chaſtitie and innocent life make him woorthie. For hee that is guiltie of neuer ſo light a fault, cannot get in there, make he neuer ſo much ſute : but is remooued by the power of God.

Thus time without minde (a wonderfull thing to bée ſpoken) the nation continueth, and yet no chyldbeddes among them. Beneath the Eſſænes was the Towne of Engaddie, which nowe is vtterly raſed. Neuertheleſſe, the notable woods kéepe theyr reputation ſtill, and the high groues of Date trées are nothing at all defaced, neither by time nor by warres. The vttermoſt bounde of Iewry is the Caſtle of Maſſada.

CAP. XLVIII.

Of the Towne Scythopolis, *and the Mountaine* Caſius.

I Paſſe ouer Damaſco, Philadelphia, and Raphana, and will tel who were the firſte inhabyters, and who was the founder of Scythopolis. At ſuche time as *Bacchus* had buried his Nourſe, he builded this Towne, to the intent by rearing

Scythopolis.

rearing the walles thereof, to aduaunce the renowme of her Sepulture. And forasmuch as inhabiters wanted, he chose out of his company the Scythians: and the more to encourage them to defende the Cittie, hee gaue it their name.

In the Countrey Selucia is another Mount Casius, harde by Antioche, from the toppe whereof a manne may in the fourth watch sée the Globe of the Sunne, Mount Casius. and with turning his body about a little aside, behold day on his one side, by meanes of the Sun dispersing the darknesse wyth his bright beames, & on hys other side still night. Such a prospect is there out of Mount Casius, that yée may sée the light before the day appeare.

CAP. XLIX.

Of the Ryuers Euphrates *and* Tygris, *and of sundry sorts of precious stones.*

Euphrates cōmeth out of the greater Armenia, rysing aboue Zimara vnder the foote of a Mountayne that is next Scythia, which the dwellers by call Capotes. This Riuer receiuing certaine others vnto him, wereth bigge, and béeing encreased with forraine waters, wrestleth wyth the straights of the Mountaine Taurus, whom he cutteth through at Eligea, albeit he withstand hym twelue Euphrates myles broade: and so running still foorth a long way, leaueth Comagene on his right side, and Arabic on his left. Afterwarde, sweeping by many Nations, hee deuideth Babylon sometime the heade Citty of Chaldey. Hee enricheth Mesopotamia with the excesse of his yeerely ouerflowing, and maketh the soile fruitful by shedding himselfe vpon the land, in the like sort as the Riuer of Egypt doth. He passeth ouer his bankes in a manner the same time that Nylus doth, namelye when the Sunne is in the twentye degree of Cancer. And it falleth againe at such time as the Sunne hauing trauailed ouer Leo, is setting foote into the vttermost Marches of Virgo.

The Cosmographers holde opinion, that it happeneth so vnto like paralleles, which by the plat bothe of the heauen and of the earth, meete iust and euen together, according to the order of the imaginitiue line. Whereby it appeareth that these two Ryuers, beeing situate plomme vnder one parallele, albeit they flowe out of sundry quarters, haue neuerthelesse one selfe same cause of both theyr increasings. It is conuenient also to speake of Tygris in this place. In the Realme of the greater Armenie, it lyfteth vppe hys head wyth a meruailous fayre and cleere spring, in a hygh ground, which is named Elongosine: and yet is hee not bygge from the beginning.

Tygris.

Fyrst he goeth slowly, not wyth hys owne name: but as soone as he entreth the borders of Medea, hee is forthwyth called Tygris: for so do the Medes call an arrowe. Hee runneth into the Lake Arethusa, which sustaineth all weyghts: the Fysh whereof neuer come within the Channell of Tygris, lyke as the Fysh of Tygris neuer passe into the Poole of Arethusa, through which hee shooteth vnlyke of colour, and a very swift pace.

A strange Lake

Anon

Anon after béeing letted by the Mountaine Taurus, hée sinketh into a déepe Caue, and so running vnder him, venteth againe on the otherside of hym at Zoroanda, bearing before him wéedes & other drosse, and a little way of sinketh againe, and afterwarde aduauncing himselfe, hee runneth by the Adiabines and Arabians, embraceth Mesopotamia, receiueth the noble Ryuer Choaspes into him, and carryeth Euphrates into the Sea of Persia. As many Countryes as drinke of Euphrates, doo glyster wyth sundry precious stones. The Smilax is gathered in Euphrates owne Channell, a Jewell like to the Marble of Procomiesus, but that in the belly of thys stone, there shynes a yellow, like the ball of ones eye. The Sagda commeth to vs from the Chaldyes, not easie to bee founde, but that (as they affyrme) it offereth it selfe to be taken. For by the naturall operation of the spyrite thereof, it ryseth out of the bottome to the shyps that sayle ouer it, and cleaueth so fast to theyr Kéeles, that it can hardly bee seperated from them wythout scraping away part of the timber. This Sagda for the effects that they knowe it hath, is hyghly estéemed of the Chaldyes: and it hath such an orient gréene, that the beauty thereof maketh it to bee liked aboue all others. The Myrrhite is common among the Parthyans. If yée should iudge thys stone by the eye, it is of the colour of Myrrhe, and hath nothing that may delight the sight. But if ye try him throughly, and chase hym tyll hée bee hote, hee hath as sweete a flauor as Nardus. In Persia is such aboundance of stones, and such varietie, that it woulde bee a long matter to reporte theyr names. The Mythridax béeing strycken wyth the Sunne, glystereth wyth sundry sorts of colours.

The Smilax

The Sagda

The Myrrhite

The Mythridax

The Tecolythe

The Tecolythe beeing lyke the kernell of an

Olyue,

an Oliue, is despised in sight: but in goodnes for medicine it excelleth the beautie of other stones. For béeing beaten into powder and drunke, it breaketh the stone, and easeth the diseases of the rayne and ÿ bladder. The Ammochryse béeing medled wyth sparkes of golde and fine grauell together, hath héere and there little square spots of goldfoyle and dust. The Ætite is both yellow, and round of proportion, contayning another stone within it, which maketh a noyse when it is styrred, albeit that the cunningest Jewellers say, it is not the little stone within it that maketh that tingling, but a spirite. This Ætite *Zoroaster* preferreth before all other stones, and attributeth very great vertue vnto it. It is founde eyther in Egles nestes, or els on the shoares of the Ocean: but most of all in Persia. Béeing worne about a woman wyth chylde, it preserueth her from deliuerance before her time. The Pyrrhite is of the colour of golde, and wyll not suffer himselfe to bee helde ouer close in ones hande, for if it chaunce to be strayned ouer hard, it burneth ÿ fingers. The Chalazias pretendeth both the whytnes and the fashyon of a Haylestone, of hardnesse most sounde and inuinsible.

The Ammochrise or goldsand.

The Aetite or Aeglestone.

The Pyrrhite or Fyrestone.

The Chalazias or Haylstone.

The Echite is spotted like a Viper. The Dyonisias is browne, besprinckled with red specks: the same béeing broken in powder and mingled with water, hath the flauor of wyne, and (which in that sent is a wonder) it resisteth drunkennes. The Glossopetre falleth from the skye in the wane of the Moone, lyke to a mans tongue, and it is of no small power as the Magicians affirme: who thinke that the motions of the Moone are stirred out of it. The Jewell of ÿ Sun is very white, after the manner of a streaming starre and spreadeth out ruddy beames. The hayre of *Venus* is of glossy black, resembling inwardly the likenes of redde

The Echite or Adderstone.

The Dyonisias or Winestone

The Glossopetre or Tonguestone.

The Iewell of the Sunne

Venus hayre.

red hayres. The Selenite is of a shéere white colour, medled with the colour of honny, contayning in it the Image of the Moone, which is reported to growe or diminish from day to day, according to the course of the Planet.

Selenite or the Moonestone.

The Meconite resembleth Poppie. The Myrmecite is marked with the likenesse of an Ant créeping. The Chalcophthong ringeth like Brasse beaten vppon. Béeing carryed chastly, it preserueth the voice cléere. The Syderite (to sée to) differeth nothing from yron: but like a makebate, wheresoeuer it is brought in, it styrreth discorde. The Phlogite representeth as it were flames of fire burning within it. The Anthracias glistereth as it were with sparkling stars. The Enydros sweateth in such wyse, as yée woulde thinke there were some spring of water shut vp within it.

The Meconite or Poppy stone
The Myrmecite or Antstone
The Chalcophthong or brasse-sounde.
The Syderite or Ironstone
The Phlogite or flame stone
The Authracias or the colestone.
The Enydros or Waterstone

CAP. L.

Of Cilicia, *and the Denne* Coricium, *and of the Mountaine* Taurus.

COncerning *Cilicia* which now is in hande, if wee treate of it as it is nowe, we shall séeme to discredite antiquitie. Againe, if we followe the bounds it had in olde time, it is cleane contrarye from the state of thinges present. And therefoꝛe to auoyde both inconueniences, the beſt that wee can doo is to repoꝛt the ſtates of both times. In olde time Cilicia extended euen vnto Pelusium of Egypt, and the Lydians, Medes, Armenians, Pamphilians, and Cappadocians, were vnder the dominion of the Cilicians. Anon after, beeing ſubdued by the Aſſyrians, it was ſtreightened into a narower roome. It lyeth foꝛ the moſt part in Champion ground, receiuing the Sea of Iſſos in a large Bay: and on the back it is encloſed wyth the ridges of the Mountaines Taurus, and Amanus. It tooke the name of *Cilix*, whom auncient time hath hidden quite beyond the reache of remembꝛaunce. They ſay he was the Sonne of P*hœnix*, who is counted auncienter then *Iupiter*, and one of the firſt that euer was bꝛedde vppon the earth. It hath the mother of Citties Tarſus, which *Perſeus* the noble ympe of *Danae* founded. The Ryuer Cydnus cutteth thꝛough thys Cittie. Some haue left in wꝛyting, that this Cydnus falleth from the Mountaine Taurus: and otherſome ſay it is deriued out of the Channell of Choaſpis: the which Choaſpis is of ſo ſweete taſt, that as long as it runneth wythin ẏ boꝛ-boꝛders of Perſia, the Kinges of Perſia reſerued it only foꝛ their owne dꝛinking: and when they ſhould go a pꝛogreſſe any whither, they carryed of the water of it with them. Of ſuch parent therefoꝛe doth Cydnus take hys wonderfull ſweetnes. Whatſoeuer is white the Syrians in their natiue language call it Cydnus: wherof the name was giuen this Ryuer. Hee ſwelleth in the ſpꝛing time when the ſnowes are melted, the reſt of the yeere he is ſlender and quiet. About Corycus in Cilicia groweth much Saffron, and very good, foꝛ though Sicill, though Syrena, though Lycia yeelde Saffron to, yet is the Saffron of Cilicia ẏ moſt pꝛincipall. It hath a moꝛe fragrant ſmell, it is of a

The bounds of Cilicia in olde time.

Tarſus.

The Ryuer Cydnus.

Choaſpes.

Corycus.

moꝛe

more golden colour, and the iuyce thereof is more effectuous in medicine.

There is also the Towne Coricus, and a Caue which maketh hollow the Mountaine that butteth vpon the Sea, from the very toppe to the hard bottom, wyth a most large and open roome wythin. For hauing both sides pitched fast in the déepe of the ground, it commeth ouer the midspace that is emptie in manner of a vault, wyth greene trées hanging inwarde wyth their toppes downe. The descent into it is two myles and a halfe long, hauing the open day al ẏ way, and springes of fountaines flowing out on both sides. When ye come to the bottome of the first vault, there openeth againe another Caue: the entry whereof is at the first wyde and lightsome, but afterwarde in going further in, it wareth darke by reason of the narrownes.

A description of the Caue of Corycus

In it is a holye Chappell of *Iupiter*: in the innermost retreit whereof, the dwellers by do beleeue that the cowche of the Gyant *Typhon* standeth. There was in Cilicia an auncient Towne called Soloe: the natiue place of Chrysippus Prince of the Stoick Philosophers: which béeing wonne by *Tygranes* King of Armenia, was long after named Pompeyople by *Cneus Pompeyus* the great, who conquered Cilicia to the Romaine Empire. The Mountaine Taurus riseth first at the Indian Sea, and so bearing hys ryght side towarde the North, and his left side toward ẏ South, and hys frunt full into ẏ West, shooteth himselfe betweene the Sea of Egypt and the Sea of Pamphilia at the Rocks of Chelidonie.

Soloe

The description of Mount Taurus.

It is manyfest hee woulde haue contynued the mayne Lande styll foorthe, but for the deepe Seas, which wyll not suffer hym to extend his rootes any farther.

Surelie they that treate of the natures of places, doo proue that with his promontories, he hath assaide all meanes possible, to finde passage. For wheresoeuer he is washed with the Sea, hee runneth out in Promontoryes. But he is stopped, sometime by the Phænician Sea, sometime by the Sea of Pontus, somtime by the Caspian or Hyrcan Sea: through whose resistaunce béeing often broken of hys wyll, hee wrytheth towarde the Lake of Mæotis: and béeing as it were tired with so manie distreses, ioyneth hymselfe wyth the Mountaines Riphæi. According to the diuersitie of nations, and varietie of tongues that hee passeth by, he is diuerslie named. Among the Indians he is called Imaus, and afterwarde Paropanisus: among the Parthians, Choatras: from thence Niphates: then Taurus: and where hee ryseth of greatest height Caucasus. By the way also he taketh names of peoples. On the right side he is called Caspius or Hircanus, and on the left side Amazonicus, Moschicus, and Scythicus. Besides these, he hath also many other names, where he gapeth with riuen cliffs, hee maketh Gates, whereof the first is called the Armenian, the seconde the Caspian: and the thyrd the Cilician. Hée beareth hys heade towarde Greece also, where hée is called Ceraunius. From the Coast of Cilicia, hee looketh downe into the Marches of Affricke As much of him as lyeth to the South, is scorched wyth the Sun, and whatsoeuer butteth vpon the North, is punished with winde and frost. Where it is woodye, is is replenished wyth wylde Beastes, and most cruell Lyons.

The names of Mount Taurus.

CAP.

CAP. LI.

Of Lycia, *and the Fable of the Monster* Chymæra.

THat which *Vesuuius* is in Campane, & Ætna in Sicill, the same is Chimera in Lycia. This Hyll breatheth vp smokie flames in the night times. Whereupon rose the Fable of the thréeformed monster amōg the common people, beléeuing that Chimæra was a liuely beaste. And because the place is of a firie nature, the Lycians dedicated the next Citty vnto *Vulcane*, and called it Ephæstia, after the originall of his name. Among other thinges, there was also the noble Towne of Olympus: but it is decayed, and nowe it is but a Castle. Mount Chimæra

Beneathe the which are the Kinges waters, a wonder to such as beholde them, for the beautifulnesse of them.

Iulius Solinus Polyhistor.

CAP. LII.

Of the lesser Asia *: of the Temple of* Diana *at Ephesus : of the birth of great* Alexander, *of the famous wryters of* Asia: *of* Phrygia, *of the fourefooted beast called* Bonasus, *of the tymes of* Homer *and* Hesiodus, *of* Memnons *byrds, of the Chameleon, of Storks: and of the originall of the* Galathians.

Asia the lesse now called Natolia.

NOwe followeth Asia: but I meane not that Asia which béeing the thyrd part of the worlde, is from the Egyptian Sea bounded wyth the Ryuer Nyle, and from the Lake Mæotis with the Ryuer Tanais : but I meane that Asia which beginneth at Telmessus of Lycia, from whence the Gulfe of Carpathus also taketh hys beginning. This Asia therefore is enclosed on the East wyth Lycia and Phrygia, on the West wyth the Aegæan Sea, on the South with the Egyptian Sea, and on the North with Paphlagonia. In it is the most famous Cittie Ephesus. The beauty of Ephesus is the Temple of *Diana*, buylded by the Amozons, such a royall péece of worke, that when *Xerxes* sette fyre on all the Temples of Asia, thys one onlie hee spared.

Ephesus.

But thys gentlenesse of *Xerxes* exempted not thys holy

holy Church vtterly from that mys-fortune. For one *Herostratus* to the intent (to purchase himselfe an euerlasting famė by hys mischieuous déede) did sette this noble péece of work on fire wyth his own hands, and when he had donne it, confessed it to wyn hymselfe a continuall name. The desire of vaine glory

It is therefore noted that the Temple of Ephesus was burned the selfe same day that Alexander the great was borne in Pella, which (as *Nepos* reporteth) was in the Consulshyppe of *Marcus Fabius Ambustus* and *Titus Quintius Capitolinus*, the thrée hundred fourescore and fift yéere after the building of Rome. At such time as the Ephesians afterward repayred it, more beautifull and stately then it was before. *Dinocrates* was chiefe maister of the workes, euen ẏ same *Dinocrates* who by the commaundement of *Alexander* builded Alexandria in Egypt, as we tolde you before. The great ruines of Asia beare wytnesse that there neuer happened so continual earthquakes, and so manie ouerthrowes of Citties in any place of the whole worlde, as in Asia. In somuch that in the raygne of *Tiberius*, twelue Citties were ouerthrowne at one tyme wyth earthquake. The byrth of Alexander the great. Dinocrates Horrible earthquakes.

The wyts of Asia haue béene renowmed ouer all the world. Fyrst for Poetrie *Anacreon*: then *Mimnermus* and *Antimachus*: after them *Hipponax*: then *Alcæus*: and among them also one *Sappho* a woman. Famous Poets

For wryting of Hystoryes, *Xanthus*, *Hecateus*, *Herodotus*, and wyth them *Ephorus* and *Theopompus*. Also of the seauen Sages, there were *Bias*, *Thales* and *Pittacus*, and of Philosophers, *Cleanthes* one of the excellentest Stoicks, *Anaxagoras* a sercher of nature, and *Heraclitus* also that bestowed all hys tyme in the secrets of a subtiler doctrine. The famous wryters of Hystories Sages Philosophers

Phrygie.

Next Asia, steppeth in Phrygia: wherein was Celenæ, which hauing abolished hys former name, fleeted into Apamæa, a Towne builded afterward by *Seleucus.*

Heere was *Marsias* borne, and heere was hee buried: of whom the Ryuer thereby tooke his name. For in remembrance of his vngracious chalenge, and ouer malapart contention wyth the God of Musicke, in playing vpon a shalme, there is a Valley wyth a Well in it not far from thence, which beareth marks of the thing that was doone, and is a tenne myles of from Apamæa, bearing the name of * Aulocrene vnto thys day. Out of a Mount of this Towne, the Ryuer Mæander lifteth his heade: which running forwarde and backward in crooked banks, falleth headlong betweene Caria, and Ionia, into the Gulfe that deuideth Miletum and Priene.

* Pypewell
The crooked Riuer Mæander

Phrigya.

Phrygia it selfe lyeth aboue Troas, and bordereth Northwarde vpon Galatia, and Southwarde vppon Lycaoma, Pisidia, and Mygdonia. The same is on the Easte, next Neighbor vnto Lydia, and on ÿ North to Mysia and Caria. On that side that is towarde the midday, is the Mountain Tmolus florished ouer with Saffron, and the Riuer Pactolus, whom they call by another name * Chrysoroa, because he caryeth golde in his streame. In these Countries breedeth a beaste called Bonasus, who hath the heade and all the bodie foorth on, like a Bull. Onely hee hath a mane lyke a Horse, and hys hornes are so manie times twysted rounde one within an other, that if a man light vppon them he cannot be wounded. But that defence that the front denyeth thys Monster, hys paunche recompenceth. For when he is put to the chase, hee gyrdeth out the dung of his loose belly, the length of three acres of ground: the heate whereof is such, that it scaldeth what-

Pactolus.
* Goldstreame
The beaste Bonasus.

whatsoeuer it toucheth, and so with his mischieuous squirt, hée kéepeth of such as pursue him. The head of Ionia is Miletus, sometime the house of *Cadmus*, the same that first founde the order to wryte in prose. Not farre from Ephesus is the Cittie Colophon, renowmed with the Oracle of *Apollo Clarius*. And wythin a little way of that, ryseth Mount Mimas, which giueth knowledge of the alteration of the wether by the clowdes that flye ouer the toppe of it. The heade of Mæonia is Sypilus, called héertofore Tantalis, and for the longer continuaunce of that name, commeth *Niobe*, borne to the losse of her husbande and children. About Smyrna runneth the Ryuer Melas, without all controuersie, the prince of all the Ryuers in Asia.

Ionia

Colophon

Mæonic

The prince of all Ryuers in the lesser Asia.

Through the fieldes of *Smyrna*, cutteth also the Riuer Hermus: which rysing at Dorilaum in Phrigya, cutteth Phrigya of from Caria. Antiquitie was in a beléefe, that this Hermus also flowed with golden streames.

Hermus.

Smyrna (which is the greatest beautie of all to it) was the Countrey of the Poet *Homer*, who departed out of this world, the two hundred, thréescore, & tenth yeere after the taking of Troy, *Agrippa Siluius*, the Sonne of *Tyberinus* then raigning in Alba, which was the hundred and threescore yeere before the building of Rome. Betwéene whom and the Poet *Hesiodus* (who dyed in the beginning of the firste Olympiad,) there were a hundred and eyght & thirty yeeres. In the Rhetæan shore, the Athenians and Mytileneans at the Tombe of the * Thessalian Captaine builded the Towne Achylleon, which is almost decayed. And about a forty furlonges from thence, in another nooke of the same shore, the Rhodians builded another Towne in the honor of *Aiax* the Sonne of *Telamon*, which they named Aeantion.

Homers byrth and death.

Hesiodus

* Achilles.

 But

But hard by Troy standeth the Tombe of *Memnon*, whereunto come certaine Byrds flying continuallie out of Aethyop in flocks, which the Troyans cal *Memnons* Byrdes. *Cremutius* is mine Author that these Birds euerie fifth yéere, assemble in flocks from all quarters wheresoeuer they be in all the worlde, to the Palace of *Memnon*. In the vplande Countrey, aboue a part of Troas, lyeth the region of Teutranie, which was the first dwelling of the Mysians. Teutranie is watred wyth the Ryuer Caicus. Through all Asia is great store of * Chameleons, a fourefooted beast, in making like a Lucert, but that hee hath straight and somewhat longer legges growing to hys belly, wyth a long tayle wrythed rounde in, with hooked talants finely bowing inwarde, slowe of gate, and in a manner trayling like a Snayle: rough bodyed, wyth such a hyde as we sée Crocodiles haue, and hollowe eyes suncke farre into his head, which he neuer shadoweth wyth twinckling. Moreouer, he beholdeth thinges not wyth rolling the bals of his eies, but with staring continually forward. His mouth is euer gaping, and serueth to doo no kind of thing wyth all: for he neyther eateth meate, nor is nourished with drink but liueth onely by drawing in the ayre, which is hys onely sustenaunce. Hys colour is variable, and euerie moment chaungable: so that to what thing so euer he leaneth himselfe, hee becommeth of the same colour. Two colours there are which hee is not able to counterfett, redde and white: all other he counterfetteth with ease. Hys body is almost without flesh, and hys intrailes without spléene: neither is there any blood to be founde in him, saue in his hart, and thereof is verie little. He hydes himselfe in wynter, and comes abroade in the spring time. The Rauen hath greate spight at him, but if he taste of him, hee béeing deade, killeth

Memnons birds

Teuthranie.

* The Chameleon or earthlyon.

kylleth his enemie that hath kylled hym. For if the Rauen eate neuer so little of him, he dyeth by and by. But the Rauen hath his defensiue, by meanes of nature it selfe, which putteth foorth her hande to heale him. For as soone as he feeleth himselfe diseased, hee eateth a Bay leafe, and so recouereth hys health.

There is in Asia a grounde called Pythous * Come, a plott in the Champion fieldes, to which at the very firste time of theyr arriuall, the Storks assemble, and there all of them fall vppon him that commeth laste, & teare him in peeces. They say these foules haue no tongues, but that the crocking which they make, is rather a sounde of the mouth then a voyce. There is in them a singuler naturalnesse. For looke how much time they bestowe in bringing vppe theyr yong birds, so much time doo their birdes bestowe in cherrishyng them againe. For they are so fonde in keeping theyr nestes, that by continuaunce of sitting, they cast theyr feathers. They thinke it a haynous matter in all places to hurt them, but specially in Thessaly, where is vnmeasurable store of Serpents, which they persecuting to feede vppon, doo greatly ease the Countries of Thessaly of that mischiefe.

* Village.

Of Storks

Galatia was in auncient time conquered by the olde Inhabyters of Gallia, namely by the Tolistobogians, Voturians, and * Ambians, which names remaine vnto this day, albeit that Galatia by the verye sounde of the name, declareth from whence it is deriued.

Galatia.

* People of Amiens.

Iulius Solinus Polyhistor.

CAP. LIII.

Of Bythinia, *and the rauishing of* Hylas: *and of the death and buriall of* Hanniball.

BIthinia at the enterance of the Sea Pontus, toward the Sunne rysing, oueragainst Thrace, welthie, and garnished richlye with Citties, taketh hys beginning at the heade of the Riuer Sangarius. It was in olde time named Bebrycia, afterwarde Mygdonia, and lastly (of King *Bithynus*) Bithynia.

The names of Bithinia.

In this Countrey by the Cittie Prusias, runneth the Ryuer Hylas, and likewyse there is the Lake Hylas, wherein it is thought that the Chylde *Hylas Hercules* delight whom the Nimphes hadde rauished was drowned. In remembraunce of whom, the people vnto this day runne solemnlie a scatterloping about the Lake, and cry *Hylas* as loude as they can. In Bithynia also is a place called Lybissa, néere to Nicomedia, registred in the Booke of fame for the Tombe of *Hanniball*, who after the iudgment gyuen vppon him at Carthage, resorting first to King *Antiochus*, and after the vnfortunate battell of *Antiochus* at Thermopyles and hys vtter discouragement through the vnconstancie of Fortune, béeing retayned a guestwise by King *Prusias*, because hee woulde not bee deliuered to

The place where Hanniball was buried.

to *Titus Quintius* who was sent into Bithynia for the same purpose, and bée caryed prisoner to Rome: poysoned hymselfe, and by wilfull death defended his bodie from the yrons that should haue béene laide vppon hym by the Romaines.

CAP. LIIII.

Of the Coast of Pontus.

IN the Coast of Pontus beyond yͤ straights of Bosphorus, and the Ryuer Rhæsus, and the Hauen of Calpas: the Ryuer Sangaris (called of manye Sangarius) which ryseth in Phrigya, maketh the beginninge of the Mariandine Gulfe, wherein is the Towne of Heraclea, standing vppon the Ryuer Lycus, and the Hauen Acone, so notable for the increase of wycked wéedes, that of the name of that Towne, wee call all hurtfull hearbes Aconite. Next vnto that is the Caue of Acheruse, where (as men say) is a darke déepe hole, that goeth downe to hell.

The Ryuer Sangaris

The Hauen of Acone.

The Caue of Acheruse.

CAP. LV.

Of Paphlagonia, *and of the originall of the* Venetians

THe Marches of Galatia inclose Paphlagonia on the backe part. Thys Paphlagonia from the promontorie of Carambis, loo- ** Precop* keth vnto * Taurica Chersonesus. It ryseth in height with the Mountaine Cytorus, the space of thréescore and thrée miles, *The originall of the Venetians* famous for the place called Henett, from whence (as *Cornelius Nepos* affyrmeth) the Paphlagonians passing ouer into Italy, were anon after named Venetians. The Milesians builded many Citties in that Realme. And *Mithridates* builded Eupatoria, which béeing subdued by *Pompey*, was named Pompeyople.

CAP. LVI.

Of Capadocia, *and the nature of horses in the same.*

OF all the Realmes that border vpõ Pontus, Cappadocia drawe- *The bounds of Cappadocia.* eth furthest into the firme land. On the left side it lyeth all along both the Armenies and Comagene: on the right side

side it hath the Marches of many people of Asia. It ryseth at the rydges of Mount Taurus, and the sunne rysing. It passeth all along by Lycaonia, Pisidia, and Cilicia. It goeth beyond the Coast of Syrya that is about Antioche, stretching euen unto Scythia at another part of the Realme, and is deuided from ẏ greater Armenie wyth the Ryuer Euphrates, which Armenie taketh hys beginning at the Mountaines Pariedric. There be manie famous Cities in Cappadocia: But to passe ouer the rest, the Ryuer Halys runneth by Archelais, which *Claudius Cæsar* peopled. The Ryuer Lycus wassheth by Neocæsaria. *Semyramis* builded Melita. Mazacha which is situate under Mount Argæus, the Cappadocians call the mother of Citties. The which Argæus beeing very high, hath his tops so couered wyth snowe, that euen in the whotest of all Sommer he is frozen, and the Inhabiters of the countrey beléeue there is a God dwelling in it. This countrey is a speciall bréeder of horses, and most commodious for increase of them, the natures of whome I thinke meete to be treated of in this place. For it is manifest by the sundry proofes, that there is discretion in horses, forasmuch as there haue béene some founde, that woulde not bee acquainted wyth any but wyth theyr first owners: utterly forgetting theyr accustomed tamenes, if at any time they happened to change their olde maisters. They knowe who bee enemies to theyr syde, in so much that in incountering in battell, they runne uppon them with open mouth to byte them. But this is a greater matter, that when they haue lost theyr former Keepers whom they dyd caste a loue unto, they starue themselues for hungar. These conditions are founde in the excellentest kinde of horses: for those that are of the baser sorte, haue shewed no examples of themselues.

The Ryuer Lycus.

The nature of horses.

But becauſe we will not ſéeme to take liberty to ſpeake more then we are able to auouche, wee will propounde diuers examples.

Bucephalus the horſe of great Alexander.

Great *Alexanders* horſe which (eyther of the ſtowreneſſe of his looke, or of hys marke becauſe hee hadde a Bulles heade bronded on hys ſhoulder, or els becauſe certaine bunches like little hornes ſwelled in hys forehead when he was angry,) was called Beucephalus, whereas at all other times he would gentlie ſuffer hys kéeper to ryde him, as ſoone as the kings ſaddle was ſette vpon his backe, hée diſdained to beare any man at all sauing his Lord and Maſter. He ſhewed manie proofes of himſelfe in battels, by bringing *Alexander* ſafe, out of moſt ſharpe incounters: for which his deſert it came to paſſe, that when hee dyed in Inde, the king kept his funeralls, and made a coſtly Tombe ouer him, and moreouer builded a Cittye which in remembraunce of hys horſes name he called Bucephala.

The horſe of Caius Cæſar

The horſe of *Caius Cæſar* would ſuffer no man to take hys backe but *Cæſar*. And it is ſaid, that his foreféete were like the féete of a man, as ſhoulde ſéeme by the Image of the horſe, which was placed by hym in that ſhape, before the Image of his mother *Venus*.

A Kings horſe of Scythia.

When one that killed a King of Scythia in combatt hande to hande, woulde haue ſpoyled hym, the Kinges horſe felled him with hys héeles, and tare him in péeces wyth hys téeth. The Country of Agrigent alſo hath many Tombes of horſes in it, which buriall they think was no more then the horſes had deſerued. The ſights in the great Theatre beare witnes ẏ they haue a delight in pleaſant thinges. For ſome of them at the playing vppon ſhalmes, ſome at ſinging, ſome at the varietie of colours, and diuers alſo at the ſight of burning Creſſets, are prouoked to running.

There

That there is affection in horses their teares doo declare. After that King *Nicomedes* was slaine, hys horse dyed for hunger. When *Antiochus* had vanquished the Galathians in battel, as he was about to haue gotten vppon the horse of their Captaine *Centaretrius*, (who was slaine in the fielde) to haue vaunted him selfe in a lustie brauerie: the horse did sette so little by hys rayning of him, that falling downe for the nonce, he threwe hymselfe and hys ryder both to the ground. The sights that *Claudius Cæsar* shewed in the greate Theatre, declared the wytt of horses, for when ye wagoner was ouerthrowne, they ouerranne theyr aduersaries that contended with them, not more by swyftnesse then by pollicie, and after running theyr full course orderlie, staied of themselues at the races ende, as it were to claime the reward of victorie. Moreouer hauing so cast of theyr Ruler (who was named *Ratumena*) they forsooke the gaming place, and ranne full flyght to the Capitoll, neuer stinting (although they had manie lets by the way) before such time as they had gone thrise about *Iupiter Tarpeius* righthandwise. In this kynde of beast the Males are longest lyued. We reade that a horse hath liued full thréescore and tenne yéeres. And this is out of all question, that they ingender till they be thrée and thirtie yéeres olde, and that after the twentith yéere they are purposely kept to couer Mares. Also we finde it noted, that a Horse named *Opus*, did hold out in seruing the race, vntil he was fortie yéeres olde.

The horse of king Nicomedes

The horse of Centaretrius.

A horse named Opus.

The lust of Mares is extinguished by shearyng their manes: and in the foles there bréedeth a poyson that prouoketh loue, which is in the Colts foreheade when he is newe foled, and is of colour yellowe lyke a dry Figge, and it is named * Hyppomanes: and if the same be taken from the Colt, the Damme wyll neuer

* It is called the knappe.

giue it suck. The fiercer that anie horse is, and of greater courage, the déeper dooth he thrust his nose into the water when he drinketh. The Scythians neuer bring horses to battell, but Mares: because the Mares can stale and run neuerthelesse. Mares doo conceiue and bring forth Colts by the wind, but those neuer lyue aboue thrée yéeres.

CAP. LVII.

Of Assyria, *and of the first comming vppe of oyntments.*

The place of encounter between Alexander and Darius

THe beginning of Assyria is Adiabene in a part whereof is the Countrey Arbelite, which place the victorie of great *Alexander* will not suffer to bee forslipped. For there he vanquished the power of *Darius*, and ouercame him, and in ryffling his Campe, among other of his princelye furniture, found a Casket full of Oyntments, which thing afterward opened first the gappe of excesse vnto the Romains, to delight in forraine perfumes. Neuerthelesse we were defended for a while from the allurement of vices, by the vertues of our auncestors, and that euen vnto the Censureshippe of *Publius Crassus*, and *Iulius Cæsar*, who in the fiue hundred thréescore and fift yéere of the building of the Cittie, forbidde by open proclamation, that no man should bring forraine Oyntments into the Cittie. Afterward our vices gott the vpperhand, and the Senate grew to such a delight

Perfumes open the Gate to excesse.

in

in the pleasantnesse of the sents, that they used them euen in theyr priuie Chambers: as it appeared by *Lucius Plotius* the brother of *Lacius* that hadde binne twise Consull: whom béeing proclaimed Traytor by the Thréemen, the sent of his oyntments bewrayed where he lay hidden in a hole at Salerne.

CAP. LVIII.

Of the tree called Medica.

AFter this rowe of Countryes followeth Media, the Trée whereof hath béene celebrated euē by the verses of *Virgill.* It is a great trée, and hath leaues almost like the leaues of a Crabbe Trée, sauing onely in this one poynt, that they bee rough with sharpe pricks. It beareth an Apple which is enemie to venim, of harsh taste, and of wonderfull bytternesse. The sent of this odour is very fragrant and excéedingly pleasant, and sensible a farre of. But the Trée is so plentifull of bearing, that it is allwaies ouercharged with the burthen of his fruite. For as soone as euer his fruite is ripe and falne of, newe spring forth, and it tarrieth no longer without increase, then while the first growne fruite may fall of. Other nations haue endeuoured to plant these Trées in their grounds, and slips and ympes haue béen fetched from thence and graffed. But nature is so coye in that behalfe, that no other soyle coulde borrowe that benefite from the Land of Media. The Apple of Media.

CAP. LIX.

Of the Gates of Mount Caspius.

ALl the Caspian Gates are a way cut out by mans hande, eight myles of length : and it is scarce so broade as a Carte may goe through. In these streights among other things, this also is verie difficult : that yͤ stones on eache side which are ragged, by meanes of the vaynes of salt that melt in them, yeelde foorth moysture aboundantly, which soone after beeing hardened by force of heate, congealeth into Ise. By meanes whereof it becommeth so slypperie, that no man can passe them. Moreouer, by the space of eyght and twenty myles, all the Coaste. which way soeuer ye goe from thence, hath no welles nor springs, but dry ground without any reskewe against thirst. Also the Serpents that breede in all coūtries there about, flocke thither as soone as euer the spring time beginneth. Thus through the conspiracie of the difficultnesse and of the daungerousnesse, there is no comming to the Caspians but in the wynter.

Iulius Solinus Polyhistor.

CAP. LX.

Of Direum, *and of the Countrey* Margiana.

FRom the Caspians Eastwarde, is a place that they cal Direum, to the plentifulnesse wherof, there is no place any where to be cōpared: about which dwel the Tapyres, the Anariaks, and the Hyrcanes. There bordereth also vppon it, the Countrey Margiana, notable for the wholsomnesse of the ayre, and commodities of the soyle, in so much as in all that large Coast, yͤ Countrey onely hath vynes It is enclosed round about like a Theatre with hyls, the compasse of a thousand and fiue hundred furlongs, almost vnpossible to be come vnto, for the sandy desert, which enuironeth it euery way round about, by the space of a hundred and twenty myles. *Alexander* the great liked so well of the pleasantnesse of this Region, that he builded the first Alexandria there, which was anon after rased by the barbarous people, and repayed againe by *Antiochus* the Sonne of *Seleucus*, who according to the name of hys progenie called it Seleucia: the circuit of which Cittie containeth threescore and fifteene furlongs. Into this Citie did *Orodes* conuey the Romaines that were taken at the slaughter of *Crassus*. *Alexander* reared another Towne also among the Caspians, which was called Heraclea as

Margiana

long as it ſtoode. But this alſo béeing beaten downe by the ſame nations, was afterward repayred by *Antiochus*, and (as it liked him beſt) was named Achais.

CAP. LXI.

Of the Ryuer Oxus, *and the nations about it: of the voyages of* Liber Pater, Hercules *and* Semyramis, *of the bounds of King* Cyrus, *and of the nature of Cammels.*

THe Ryuer *Oxus* ſpringeth out of the Lake Oxus, the brimmes wherof are inhabited about by the Henioches, Batenes, & Oxiſtages: but the chiefeſt part is inhabited by the Bactrians. The Bactrians alſo haue a peculiar Riuer of theyr owne called Bactrus, and a Towne thereupon which they inhabit named Bactrum. The nations that are behynde this, are enuironed with the hyls of Paropamiſus, which endeth againſt the heade of the Ryuer Indus: the reſt is encloſed by the Ryuer Oxus. Beyond theſe, is Panda a Towne of the Sogdians, in the borders of whom great *Alexander* builded the thyrde Alexandria, to teſtifie the bounds of hys iourney. For this is the place where Altars were erected firſt by *Liber Pater*, ſecondly by *Hercules*, thirdly by *Semyramis*, and laſtly by *Cyrus*: and therefore it was counted one of the greateſt commendations of *Alexander*, that he ſet out the bounds of his voyage ſo farre as yͤ place.

The Bactrians.

The bounds of Liber, Hercules, Semyramis and Cyrus.

The

The Ryuer Iaxartes disseuereth the borders of all the Countryes that lie in that tract onely: which Ryuer neuerthelesse the Bactrians onely call Iaxartes, for the Scythians call it Silys. The Souldiours of great *Alexanders* hoste, tooke this Iaxartes to be the same Ryuer that is Tanais. But *Demodamas* a Captaine of *Seleuchus*, and *Antiochus*, a sufficient Author in thys behalfe, passing ouer this Ryuer, went beyond the tytles of all that were before him, and found it to be an other Ryuer then Tanais: in remembrance of which hys renowmed enterprise, for the more aduauncment of his owne fame, he reared Altars to *Apollo Didymaus* in the same place. This is the battable grounde where the Marches of Persia and Scythia, meete. The which Scythians, the Persians in their language call Saks, and the Scythians on the otherside name ẏ Persians Chorsars: and the Mountaine Caucasus they cal Graucasus, that is to say white with snowe. Numbers of people innumerable thereabouts keepe the same Lawes and customs that the Parthians doo, if an vniuersall consent from the beginning, without breaking or alteration of order. Of which the famousest are the Massagets, the Essedons, the Saks, the Dahes, and the Assæans. Beyond whom by reason of most cruell and barbarous nations that lye betwixt, we finde great vncertaintie in the report of the customes of other nations.

The Ryuer Iaxartes.

Demodamas

Out of Bactria come strongest Cammels, albeit that Arabie breede of them too. But this is the difference betwixt them: that the Camels of Arabie haue two bunches on theyr backs, and they of Bactria haue but one.

Of Cammels

These doo neuer were theyr feete: for the feete of the other haue as it were little palmes of fleshe turning backe againe. By meanes whereof they haue a contrary fault in theyr going, in that there is no help for them to sette theyr féete stedfast vpon the ground. They serue to double vse. For some bee good for the burthen, and some are light & swyft in running. But neither wyll those receiue more then a reasonable burthen, nor these goe aboue their ordinarie pace. For desire of generation they become madd, in so much as they are outragious cruell when they woulde goe to make. They hate horses, and they will forbeare drink by the space of foure dayes together. But when the time serues that they may drink, they hale in as much as wyll bothe staunche the drought that is past, and moyst them for the thirst that is long to come. They couet soyled waters, and refuse the cléere. And if it bee not muddie of it selfe, they will rayse vppe the mudde with continual stamping, & make it troubled. They endure an hundred yeeres, vnlesse it be so that they be conueied into strange Countryes, and so the chaunge of ayre make them diseased. The Females are prepared for the warres, and meanes is found howe to kill the desire of generation in them by gelding them. For it is thought they become the stronger, if they be kept from the Males.

Iulius Solinus Polyhistor.

CAP. LXII.

Of the Seres *and of theyr silks.*

AS yee turne from the Sythick Ocean, and the Caspian Sea towarde the East Ocean : from the beginning of this Coast, firste dæpe snowes, then long desertes, beyond that the Cannibals a most cruell kind of people, and lastly places ful of moste outragious wilde Beastes, make almost the one halfe of the way vnpassible. The which distresses haue their ende at a Mount that butteth vppon the Sea, which the barbarous people call Tabis, beyonde which, the wyldernesses doo neuerthelesse continue a great way on styll. So in that Coast which faceth the Northeast, beyond those waste & vninhabitable Countreys, the first men that we haue heard of, are the Seres : who sprinckling water vppon the leaues of theyr Træs, doo by the helpe of that liquor kembe of certain flæces, and wyth moysture so carde that fine Cotten, that they make what they wyll thereof. This is that silke admitted to be worne commonly, to the hinderaunce of grauitie, and wherewith the luste of excesse hath perswaded first women, and nowe also menne to apparell themselues, rather to sette out the bodyes to sale then to cloth it. The Seres are meeke and very quiet among themselues : but otherwise they eschew the company of all men besides : insomuch that they

Of Sylke.

refuse to haue any traffick or intercourse of Merchandise with other nations. For those that occupy yͤ trade of merchandise with them, doo passe ouer the first Ryuer of their Countrey: vpon the banks whereof (without anie communication of talke betwéene the Chapmen, the Seres considering by eie-sight, the price that they bid for the things laid downe, vtter theyr owne wares, but by not ours.

CAP. LXIII.

Of the Attacene *Nations.*

NOwe followeth the Coast of Attacene, and the nation of the Attacenes who haue a singuler prerogatiue for the temperatnes and gentlesse of theyr ayre. The hilles kéepe of the hurtfull blasts: which hils béeing cast rounde about them euery way, doo with theyr wholsome opennesse to the Sunne, fence them from all pestilent ayres. And therfore (as *Amomatus* affyrmeth) their life and the life of the Hyperboreans is a like. Betwéene these and Inde, the skylfullest Cosmographers haue placed the Cycones.

Iulius Solinus Polyhistor.

CAP. LXIIII.

Of Inde, *and the maners of the* Indians *of the temperate ayre of that Country, of the Ryuers of* Inde, *of the wonderfull beasts, trees, kynds of odours, and precious stones in the same.*

INde beginneth at the hyls called Emodii, and extendeth from yͤ south sea to the East Ocean, and from the North to yͤ Mountaine Caucasus, most healthfull wyth the blastes of the South west winde. It hath Sommer twyse a yere, and twyse a yere haruest: and in stedd of Wynter, it hath the Eastern wyndes called Etesiæ. *Posidonius* placeth this Countrey directly against Fraunce, and surely there is no doubt at all in the matter. For firste béeing found by the warres of great *Alexander*, and since hys time trauelled through and through by the diligence of Kings, it is nowe come full and wholy to our knowledge.

The bouuds of East India.

Megasthenes hauing continued a good whyle among the Kinges of Inde, wrate the acts of yͤ Countrey, to the intent to leaue to his posterity the certaintie of those things that himselfe hadde seene wyth hys eyes. *Dennys* also (who in likewise was by king *Philadelphus* sent to sée whither those things were true or no,) wrytt the like.

They report therfore that there were in Inde thrée thouſand Townes of very large receit, and nyne thouſand ſundry ſorts of people. Moreouer it was beléeued a long time to be the third part of the world. It is no wonder that there ſhould bee ſuch ſtore of men & Citties in Inde, conſidering that alonely the Indians neuer flœted out of their natiue ſoyle.

The firſt forreyners that entred into Inde.

The firſt that entred into Inde was *Liber Pater*, who ſubduing the Indians tryumphed firſt ouer them. From him vnto great *Alexander* are numbred ſixe thouſand, foure hundred, fiftie and one yéeres, & thrée monethes ouer, making account by the raignes of the Kings, of whom there are found to haue paſſed in the meane time a hundred fiftie and thrée. The greateſt Ryuers in that Countrey are Ganges and Indus: of which, Ganges (by ſome mens report) riſeth no man can tell where, and ouerfloweth after the manner of Nyle. Otherſome will haue it riſe out of the Mountaines of Scythia. There is alſo a very noble Ryuer called Hypaſis, the vttermoſt part of great *Alexanders* iourney, as the Altars ſtanding on the bankes thereof teſtifie. The leaſt bredth of Ganges is eight miles, and the greateſt is twenty. The depth of him where he is ſhalloweſt, draweth a hundred fœte plom. The Gangarides are the vttermoſt people of Inde: the King of which Countrey furniſheth to the warres a thouſand horſmen, ſeauen hundred Olyphants, and thréeſcore and tenne thouſand footemen. Of the Indians, ſome occupy tyllage and huſbandry, moſt goe a warfare, and otherſome vſe traffick and merchandiſe. The beſt and welthieſt take charge of the Common weale, miniſtring iuſtice and aſſiſting the Kinges. There is a quiet kind of moſt excellent wyſdome among them: that is to ſay: to make great fires when they are glutted with life, and to haſten theyr owne deathes by caſting

Ganges.

The Gangarids.

The manners of the Indians.

sting themselues thereinto. But they that giue themselues to a more sauage life, and kéepe in the woodes doo hunt after Oliphants, & when they haue throughlie tamed them, they either breake them to the plough or to the saddle. In the Ryuer Ganges, there is an Ile containing a most populous and large nation, whose King kéepeth in wages fifty thousand footemen, and foure thousand horsemen. Surely as manie as haue the preheminence of kings, goe not to warfare wythout a verie great number of Olyphants, Horsemenne and footemen.

The Prasians a very puissaunt nation, inhabite the City Palibotra, wherupon some haue named the nation Palibotres: whose king kéepeth dailye in wages, sixe hundred thousand footemen, thirty thousand horsemen, and eyght thousand Oliphants. Beyond Palibotra is the Mountaine Maleus, the shadow whereof lyeth one halfe of the yéere into the North, and the other halfe of the yeere into the South. The Prasians

Charles wayne appeareth but once in the yéere in that Coast, and not aboue fiftéene daies as *Bethon* wryteth, who reporteth that this commeth to passe in dyuers places of Inde. The borderers vpon the Southside of the Ryuer Indus, are aboue others scorched wyth heate: and the colour of the people bewrayeth the force of the Planet. The Pygmæans possesse the hyll Countreys. But they that dwell vpon the Ocean, liue wythout Kings. The Nation of the Pandeans is gouerned of Women: of whom ẏ first Quéene is déemed to be *Hercules* daughter, and the Cittie Nysa is alotted to this Realme, and also a Mountaine hallowed vnto *Iupiter* named * Meros, in a Caue whereof the auncient Indians affyrme that *Bacchus* was fostered: vpon authoritie of the which terme, it is thought that fame taking occasion to ouer reache, reported that

Pygmæans

Pandeans.

* It signifieth a thygh.

Bacchus was borne of *Iupiters* thigh. Without the mouth of the Ryuer Indus, are two Ilands, * Chryse and * Argyre, so plentiful of mettals, that diuers haue reported them to haue soyles of gold and siluer. All the Indians weare long hayre, stayned with a blewish or yellowish colour. Their chiefe attyre is in precious stones.

*Goldland
*Siluer land
The Manners and behauiour of the Indians

No coste is bestowed in buriall of the deade. Furthermore (as is expressed in the bookes of King *Iuba* and King *Archelaus*) as much as the people disagree in manners and conditions, so great difference is there in theyr attyre. Some weare lynnen garments some wollen, some goe all naked, some couer but theyr priuie members, and many goe clad in barks of trees. Some people are so tall, that they wyll as easily vault ouer Oliphants, as if they were horses. Many thinke it good neyther to kill anie lyuing thing, nor to eate anie flesh. Some eate only fish, & liue by ẏ Sea. There are that make as it were a sacrifice of theyr Parents and kinsfolke, before they become bare with sicknes or age, and then make a feast wyth their flesh, which thing in that Countrey is not counted a wyckednesse, but a godlinesse.

There are also that in extremitie of sicknesse, or when diseases lynger vppon them, get themselues into some secrete corner farre from resorte, and there quietlie abyde for death.

The Aspagons

The Nation of the Aspagones haue goodly woods of greene Bay and Box, and as for vynes and all other trees, wherein is pleasure and beautie to delight, it hath most plentious store of them. The Indians haue Philosophers whom they call Gynmosophists, who from the rysing of the Sunne to the going down therof, behold the Globe of that burning Planet with fixed eyes, serching in that fierye circle for certayne

Gymnosophists

secrete

secrete thinges, and standing all day long vppon the scalding sande, nowe on the one foote and nowe on the other. At the Hyll that is called Milo, dwell people that haue their féete turned backward, wyth eyght toes on eche foote.

Strange kynd of people.

Megasthenes sayth, that in diuers Mountaines in Inde, are Nations that haue hands like Dogs, armed wyth talants, clad in hydes, hauing no likelihoode of mans speeche, but vttring a noise of barking, wyth rough chappes. We reade in Ctesias, that certayne Women beare Childe but once, and that the Babes as soone as they be borne, become by and by grayheaded: and that there is againe another nation which in theyr youth are hoare headed, and were black in their age, which endureth farre beyonde the race of our yeres. We reade also of a people called Monoscelans, borne there wyth one legge a péece, of singuler swyftnesse: who when they will defende themselues from the heate, lay themselues downe vppon their backes, and shadow them with the largenesse of theyr feete. They that dwell at the fountaine of Ganges, néede no maner of victuals to féede vpon. They liue by the sent of Stobfruite and Crabbes, and when they haue anie long iourney to goe, they carry the same with thẽ for theyr baite, to refresh themselues with the smel of thẽ And if it happen them to take any corrupt ayre, certain it is, that they die of it by & by. There is reported also to be a nation of women which beare Children at fiue yéeres of age, but their life endureth not aboue 8. yeeres. There are ẏ want heades, and haue their eyes in their shoulders. There are also wild menne, rough skinned, toothed like dogs, & that make a terrible gnarring. But among them that haue some more care to liue according to reason, many women are marryed to one man, and when the husband is deceased, each of

The Monoscelans or one legged people.

them pleadeth before most graue Judges, concerning her deserts, & she that by the sentence of ye Judges is deemed to haue béene more dutifull & seruicable then the rest, receiueth thys reward of her victory, that at her pleasure shee may leape into the fire where her Husbande is a burning, and offer herselfe as a sacrifice vpon hys herse. The rest lyue wyth infamie.

The hugenesse of Serpents

The hugenesse of theyr Serpents is so excessyue, that they swallow vp Harts, and other beasts of lyke bygnesse whole, yea and as great as the Indian Ocean is, they swym through it, and passe ouer into Ilands a great way distant from the firme lande to séeke feeding. And the selfe same thing is a good argument to proue theyr hugenesse, that they haue force to passe ouer such a bredth of salt water, and to attaine to the places that they ayme at. There are many and wonderfull beasts, out of the which multitude I wyll pick some to treate of.

The Leucocrote.

The Leucocrote passeth all wylde Beastes in swiftnesse. It is of the bygnesse of an Asse, haunched like a Stagge, breasted and legged like a Lyon, headed like a Cammell, clouen cléed, mouthed vp to bothe the eares, and wyth one whole round bone instéede of téeth. Thus much as to his shape. In voyce hee counterfetteth the spéech of man.

The Eale.

There is an Eale, otherwyse like a horse, tayled like an Olyphant, of colour blacke, chapped like a Bore, armed with hornes aboue a cubit long, plyable to what vse soeuer he lyst to put them. For they are not stife, but are bowed as neede shall require in fighting: of which he putteth out the one when he fighteth, and rolleth vp the other, that if by any stripe the point of the one be blunted, the other may succéede sharpe in hys roome. He is compared to the Waterhorses, and to say ye truth, he delighteth in waters to.

The

The Bulls of Inde

The Bulls of Inde are of colour bright yellowe, exceeding wight of foote, with their hayre growing the contrarie way, and as much mouth as head. These also beare hornes plyable to what purpose they liste, so hard hyded, that nothing is able to enter, so vnmercifullie cruell, that beeing caught, they kill themselues for moodinesse.

The Manticora,

Among these breedeth also ẏ Manticora, wyth three sette of teeth in his head checkquerwise one against another, faced like a man, gray eyed, sanguine coloured bodied like a Lyon, tayled like a Scorpion wyth a stinging pricke in the ende, with so shrill a voyce that it counterfetteth the tunes of pypes, and the harmony of Trumpets. Hee seeketh most greedilie after mans flesh. He is so swift of foote, and so nimble in leaping, that there is no space so long that may forslowe hym, nor anie thing so broade that can let him of hys way.

Strange Oxen

There are also Oxen with one horne and three horns, whole houed, and not clouen cleed.

The Vnicorne,

But the cruellest is the Vnicorne, a Monstar that belloweth horriblie, bodyed like a horse, footed like an Oliphant, tayled like a Swyne, and headed like a Stagge. His horne sticketh out of the midds of hys forehead, of a wonderfull brightnesse about foure foote long, so sharp, that whatsoeuer he pusheth at, he striketh it through easily. Hee is neuer caught aliue: kylled he may be, but taken he cannot bee.

Strange Eeles

The waters also breede no lesse wonders. Ganges breedeth Eeles of fortie foote long, and *Statius Sebosus* saith, that the same Ryuer (among the chiefest miracles) swarmeth with wormes bothe in name and colour gray. These haue as it were armes not vnder sixe cubits long a peece, so boysterous of strength, that with the hande thereof, they take holde of Olyphants that come thither to drinke, and hale them so rudelye, that they pull them vnder the water. The Indian Seas haue Fyshes called Thyrlpooles, aboue the byg nesse of foure Acres of grounde. There are also which they call * Physeters, which béeing huge beyonde the measure of great Pyllars, lift themselues aboue the sayleyards of Shyppes, and puffe out the water that they haue baled in at theyr venting pipes, in such wise that many times they sinke the vessels wyth the rage of water, that they let fall vppon the Marryners. Only Inde bréedeth the Poppiniey, of colour gréene, wyth a redde list about hys neck, whose byll is so hard, that when he is throwne from high vpon a stone, he saueth himselfe vppon his byll, vsing it as an extraordinary defence of hys infirmitie. And his heade is so stronge that if at any time he haue néede of stripes to put him in mind of hys lesson, (for he learneth to speake like a man) he must be knockt on the pate wyth a wande of yron. While he is a Chicken, and as yet vnder two yeeres old, he learneth the things that are taught him more spéedilie, and beareth them more stedfastly in remembraunce. Aboue that age hee is somewhat more slow of taking, forgetfull, and vnapt to be taught. The number of toes maketh the difference betwéene the nobler and the rascaller sorte. The better haue fiue toes on a foote, the worse haue thrée. Hys tongue is broade, and much broader then the tongues of other byrds: and that is the cause of his perfection in vttering words so distinctly. This nature of his made the Romaines to haue so great pleasure and delight in him, that the barbarous people made a merchandise of their Poppinieyes. The trées of Inde grow vp in such an excessiue height, that they cannot shoote an arrowe ouer them. The Orchyards haue Fig trées, the bodies whereof are thréescore paces about, and theyr boughes shadow two furlongs euerie way, the largenesse of theyr

*Spowters

Popinieyes and Parrets.

Of Figtrees

their leaues is compared to the shielde of the Amazons, and the fruit is of verie singuler swéetnes. The Fenny grounds bring forth a Réede of such grosenes, that betwéene knot and knot they make boates of thē to rowe in. Out of the rootes whereof, is pressed a swéete iuyce, as pleasant as honny. There is an Iland of Inde called Tylos, which beareth Date trées, bringeth forth Olyues, and aboundeth in Wynes. It surmounteth all landes in this one wonder, that what tree soeuer groweth therein, is neuer without leaues. Reedes. The prerogatiue of the Iland Tylos.

There beginneth Mount Caucasus, which wyth his continuall ridge, peirceth through the most part of the worlde. The same hyll on hys front that faceth the Sunne, beareth Pepper Trées: which men affyrme to be like the Iuniper Trée, and to bring forth sundrie fruits. That fruite that commeth forth first, is like the agglets of Hasles, and is called long Pepper. That which is vncorrupted, is called white Pepper. That which hath the skynne wrinckled and scorched wyth the heate, is called black Pepper. Lastly, that which falleth downe and is parched with the burning Sun, taketh hys name of hys colour. But that which is stripped of the Trée as it is, is called white Pepper. And as onely Inde yéeldeth Pepper, so alonely yéeldeth it Ebonye: & yet not in all places but in a verie little part of the Countrey doth it yéelde thys kynd of woode. Of Pepper and of the Pepper-tree, Ebony,

The Trée for the most part is slender, and growing manie together, thin branched, swelling to the bignes of the stock, with a houen rinde, and very full of holes with open veines, insomuch that for all the vttermost barke, the very wood is scarce couered with a thynne rynde. All the wóode of it is medicinable, & it is, almost of the same fashion & colour that is in the Peat stone.

The Kinges of Inde haue theyr Scepters heereof,

and they make the Images of their Gods of none other wood then Ebonye. They report also that no noysome liquor can be contained in this kind of stuffe, and that whatsoeuer is hurtfull, is disapointed by the touching thereof. And for this pleasure they make Cups of Ebonye, wherefore it is no maruell though it be had in great price in forraine Realmes, considering it is so much honoured in the place it comes from, and where it growes. The great *Pompey* brought Ebonye first out of Inde and shewed it in Rome, when he tryumphed for vanquishing *Methridates*. Inde yeeldeth also *Calamus odoratus*, a special remedy against greefes in the bowels. It giueth many other sweete Odours, acceptable for the pleasantnesse of their wonderfull flauor.

Calamus odoratus.

Of the Iewels of Inde, the chiefe preheminence is in the Diamond, as which driueth away franticknes, resisteth venims, and expulseth vaine feares from such as haue qualmes comming ouer their harts. Thys I thought was to bee spoken first, of those thinges that haue respect to profit. Now will I shewe howe many and what sortes of Diamonds there be, and what colour is best to be liked in eche of them. In a certayne kinde of Crystall, there is founde this kinde of stuffe: which groweth after the likenes of most sheere water gently gathering sharpe at both endes to a sixcornered poynt, and it is neuer found aboue the bygnesse of a Filberd kernell. The next vnto this is founde in the excellentest golde, somewhat paler, and shyning more toward the colour of siluer. The thyrd is found in the veynes of Copper, drawing towarde the coloure of brasse: which is very effectuall in medicine, and is called Siderites. The fourth is gathered in yron mines, of weightier substance then the rest, but not like them in vertue. For bothe this and that which is founde in

The Diamond and the sundry sorts and natures of them.

The Syderite

Copper

Copper may be broken, and for the most part they are peirced through with another Diamond. But those that we spake of first, can neyther bee broken wyth yron nor hurt with fire. Notwithstanding, if they bee stéeped long in Goats blood, (so it be warme & freshe bléeding from the beast,) at length (with the breaking of some Hammers, and styths before) they yéelde and shyuer in péeces: which sparks are greatly sought for of engrauers to drawe in any precious stone withall. Betwéene the Diamonde and the Lodestone is a certaine priuie dissention of nature, in so much as if they bée layd néere together, the Diamonde will not suffer the Lodestone to drawe yron vnto him: or if ẏ Lodestone haue alreadie drawne a péece of yron to it, the Diamond snatcheth and pulleth away as hys bootye whatsoeuer the Lodestone hath taken hold of. Moreouer, Inde bringeth forth the Lychnite, the freshnes of whose light is furthered by the brightnes of burning candles: and therfore the Greeks haue called it Lychnits. There are of two sorts: for either it is of an orient purple colour, or els it is shadowed somewhat with a shéere scarlett. If it bee pure, it admitteth an vnstayned cléerenesse through all the inward parte of it. Also if it be heat wyth the Sunne beames, or catch warmth by chafing betwéene ones fingers, it draweth harde to it eyther the husks of chaffe, or the shreds of paper, and it resisteth stoutly against engrauing. And if at anie time it be engrauen, when a manne sealeth therewith, it holdeth part of the wax still, as it were some liuelie thing shold byte it. The Indians do grind their Beryll in peeces sixe square, to the intent by reflexion of the corners, to chéere vp the dulnesse of hys weake colour. Of Beryll are sundry sorts. The excellentest do with a certaine equall mixture of ruddines and déepe blew, ouershadowed with a gréene, resemble

The Lodestone

The Lychnite or Lampstone.

The Beryll

The Chrysoberill, or goldberill
The Chrysoprase or goldenleeke
The bastarde Iacints,

ble the grace of the pure Sea. A degrée beneath these are the Chrysoberyts, which hauing a fainter glosse, are shadowed about wyth a golden clowde. The Chrysoprases also (whose glosse is of golde and Léekgréene mixed together) are iudged to the kinde of Beryll as well as the other. The bastard Iacints, that is to say, those which in manner resemble the Iacints, are also allowed for Beryls. But as for those that are like Crystall, and are stayned with little hayres running in and out, (for that is the name of theyr fault) the skilfullest Lapidaries haue accounted for ẏ meanest sorte. The Kinges of Inde loue to fashion this kind of Iewels into very long rols: & making holes through them they hang them at the brystles of their Olyphants in stedde of poytrels and trappers, or els at theyr eares, on both sides of theyr heads, sette in bosses of golde, to the intent to florish their withered colour with a more fulsome brightnesse, by meanes of the mettall cunningly wrought about them, (which as a foyle) may cause them to gather a more glystring light.

CAP. LXV.

Of the Ile Taprobane, *and by what meanes it came first to knowledge: what manner of sayling is there: what is the custome of that Countrey in choosing theyr King, also of the shelfishes Margarits, and perles.*

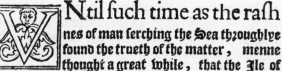

The first discouerers of the Ile of Taprobane now called Zeilan,

VNtil such time as the rashnes of man serching the Sea throughlye found the trueth of the matter, menne thought a great while, that the Ile of Taprobane had béene another world, and ẏ very same which

which the Anticthones were beléeued to inhabit. But the valiantnes of great *Alexander*, suffered not the ignoraunce of the common error to continue any longar: but he spred the renowne of his name euen into these vnknowne places. For *Onesicritus* Admirall of the fléete of Macedonie serching out this land, brought vnto our knowledge howe bigge it is, what it bréedeth and in what case it stood. It extendeth seauen thousand furlongs in length, and fiue thousande in bredth. It is deuided into two parts with a Riuer. For part thereof is replenished with beastes and Olyphants, greater than Inde beareth, and the rest of it is possessed by men. It is aboundantly stored with moother Perles and all precious stones. It is situate betwéene the Easte and the West. It beginneth at ẏ Easterne Sea, and lyeth full before Inde. From the Parsians a nation of Inde it hath béene twenty dayes sayling thither. But forasmuch as they went in boates of Reede and shyps of Nyle, it is now abridged to seauen daies sayling of one of our shyps. Betwéene them and Inde lyeth a shallow Sea, not aboue sixe fathom déepe, and yet in certaine Channels of such an excéeding depth, that there was neuer Ancor yet that coulde come to the bottome thereof. There is no héede to bee taken of the starres in sayling there. For neither is Charles wayne séene there, neither do the seauen stars called * Vergiliæ at any time appeare there. They sée the Moone aboue the earth, only from the 8. day to the 16. There shineth Canopos a bright star, & of very great largnes. They haue the sun rising on their right side, and ẏ sun setting on their left. Wherefore as there is nothing for men to obserue whereby they may saile to arriue at ẏ appointed place: birds lead thē whose flight in making to ẏ landward, they vse as a lodestar to direct their course. Ther is no sailing thither but 4. moneths in

Margarits or moother perles.

A shalow Sea.

* They bee also called Pleiades and Athlantides.

Sayling by the flight of birds

monethes in all the yeere. Heere is all that we knewe of Taprobane vntill the raigne of the Emperor *Claudius*, at which time fortune opened a wyder gappe of knowledge. For one that late before was the seruant of *Annius Plocamus* (who then was customer of ye red Sea) as he was sayling toward Arabie, was dryuen by violence of the North wynde along the Coaste of * Carmanie, and the fifteenth day arriued at this shore and tooke harbrough in a Hauen called Hyppuros. There learning the language in sixe moneths, and being admitted to the Kinges speeche, hee brought worde againe, what he had found. That is to say, howe the king wondred at the mony that was taken with him, because the same beeing stamped with diuers faces, had neuerthelesse like weight. At the contemplation of which equalitie, when hee coueted more earnestlye the freendship of the people of Rome, he sent Ambassadours to vs, of whom the chiefe was Rachias, by whō all things were brought to our knowledge. Those men excelled all others in talenesse of personage, and making. They dye theyr hayre, they are gray eyed, grym of countenance, and haue a terrible reere in speaking.

* Now called Rasigut

A description of the personages and manners of the people of Taprobane.

Such of them as are short liued, continue to the age of a hundred yeeres: all others liue much longer, and farre beyonde the reache of mans frailtie. They sleepe not from before the day breake till the night be shutte in, for they euer ryse before day. They make theyr houses but a little height aboue the grounde. Corne holds alwayes at one stay. They knowe not what Vynes meane. They haue aboundaunce of Apples, and such other kind of fruites. They worshyp *Hercules* for theyr God. In choosing theyr King, nobilitie auaileth not, but the generall consent of the Country. For the people chooseth such a one, as is of approoued

The choosing of theyr king

good

good behauiour, and rooted in gentlenesse from hys cradle, and at that time an olde man. And this is chiefly requisite in him, that he haue no children. For hée that is a Father, though his life be neuer so vertuous he is not admitted to the kingdome. And if perchance in the time of his raigne he beget a childe, hee is deposed. For aboue all thinges this is most straightly obserued, that the kingdome goe not by inheritance. Furthermore, although the King séeme to be neuer so good a Iusticer, yet they will not let him haue the Law in his owne hande. And therefore hee admitteth fortye Moderators, because he shall not sitt alone vpon matmatters of life and death. Yea and if the iudgment shall then also be misliked: appeale is made to ye people, who appoint thréescore and ten Iudges, to whose determinatiō there is no remedy but they must nedes stand. The King is apparelled in rayment vnlike the common fashion, called Syrma, a robe wherewyth we sée *Liber Pater* was wont to be clad. If it happen that the King himselfe be taken tardie in any offence, and thereof conuicted, he is punished with death: howbe it, not so that any man layeth handes vppon him. But by the common consent of the whole Realme, hée is vtterly forbidden the vse of all thinges: yea euen communication wyth any manne is denyed him after he is cast. They giue themselues to good nurture vniuersallie. Sometime they spende the time in hunting, and that of no rascall game, for they séeke onely for Tygers or Oliphants. Moreouer they ransacke the Seas in fishing, for delight to catch the Sea Tortoyses: the hugenesse of whom is such, that the shell of one of them wyll make a house able to receiue a great housholde of many persons wythout pestring. The greater part of this Ile is parched with heate, and endeth in waste wyldernesse.

The executing of Iustice

The King is subiect to the Lawes,

Theyr pastymes

Monstrous Sea Tortoyses

The Sea that beateth vppon the one side thereof, groweth so full of shrubs (and those of very gréene colour) that sometime the tops of the trées are brushed away with the sternes of shyps. From the toppes of their Mountaines they beholde the Sea coast of ẏ Seres. They delight greatlie in golde : and to garnishe their Cups withall, they set them full of all kynde of Jewels. They hewe out Marble that is checkered, and gather great store of Moother perles, and those of the greatest sort. They be shelfishes in whome thys kinde of stones is sought, which at a certaine time of the yéere when desire of conception pricketh them forward, doo thirst after the deawe as after their milter: for desire whereof they gape , and when the Moone sheadeth most aboundance of moisture, they draw the desired humour by a certaine sucking, whereby they conceiue and are great with yong , and according to the qualitie of the thing they haue glutted in, such is the disposition of the perles that they bréede. For if it bee pure that they haue taken in, their little rounde stones are white: if it were troubled, either they haue a faint pale colour, or els are stained with a red. Thus haue they their séede rather of the ayre then of ẏ Sea. Finally, as often as they receiue in the morning dew the pearle becommeth cléerer : and when they suck in the euening dewe, they become dimmer, and the more they haue haled in, so much the stone groweth greater If it chaunce to lighten vpon the suddaine, they shutte for feare, and closing fast for suddaine fearefulnes, they take in that which they lose againe ere it be ripe : for then they haue very small stones , or els none at all. And the shelfishes themselues haue a kinde of vnderstanding, for they are afraide to haue their issue stayned : insomuch as when the day is at ẏ hotest, because their stones shoulde not bee dimmed with the heate, they

Of the Margarite or Moother perle,
Of Perles,

they ducke vnder the water, and diue into the déepes to saue them from the heate. Neuerthelesse, age fore-standeth this foresight of theirs. For the whitnes decayeth by age, and as the shelfishes were greater, the perles were more yellowe. While the perle is in the water it is soft, and as soone as it is taken out of the shell it becommeth harde. There are neuer founde aboue one in a shell, and therefore the Latins call them *Vnions*. They say they be neuer found aboue halfe an inche big. The shelfishes are afraide to be layde for by the Fyshers: and thereon it comes to passe, that they hide themselues for the most part, eyther among the Rocks or els among the Dogfishes. They swymme in scoles. Some one is Captaine of the whole scole. If he be taken, euen those that escaped returne into the nett againe. Inde yéeldeth perles, and so doth the Seacoast of Brytaine, as *Iulius Cæsar* (by the inscription ẏ was written vpon it) witnesseth, that the brestplate which he dedicated to his mother *Venus* in her Temple, was made of British perles. It is a thing cōmonly knowne that *Lollia Paulina*, the wyfe of the Emperour *Caius*, had a gowne of perles valued then at foure hundred thousande Sestertius: through couetousnes in getting wherof, her father *Marcus Lollius* for spoyling the Kinges of the East, offended *Caius Cæsar* the sonne of *Augustus*, and was put out of the Princes fauor, for sorrow whereof he poysoned himselfe. This is also registred by the diligence of olde men, that perles were first brought to Rome in the time of *Sylla*.

Vnions

Perles

Iulius Solinus Polyhistor.

CAP. LXVI.

The Iournall of Inde.

FRom the Ilande *Ausea there is a directe cut to the firme land. Therfore from the Iland Taprobane let vs returne back to Inde: for the thinges of Inde are worth the seing. But if I shoulde make tariance about the Citties & nations of Inde, I should passe the bounds of my prepurposed abridgment. Next vnto the Ryuer Indus, they had a Cittie named Capissa, which *Cyrus* rased. Arachosia standing vppon the Ryuer Arachota was builded by Semyramis. *Alexander* the great builded the Towne of Cadrusia by Mount Caucasus, wheras also is Alexandria which is thirty furlongs wyde. There are manie other also, but these are of the most renowmed. After the Indians the *Icthyophags possesse the Hill Countryes: whom great *Alexander* subduing, forbad them to eate fish, for they liued thereby before. Beyond these are the deserts of Carmania, then Persia, and so a iourney by Sea, wherein is the Iland of the Sunne which is alwayes red, and not able to be come vnto by any liuing creature: for it killeth all lyuing things that are brought into it. As men returne out of Inde, the first sight that they haue of Charlsis waine is at Hytanis a Ryuer of Carmania. They say that the dwelling of Achæmenides was in this Coaste. Betweene the Promontorie of Carmania and Arabie, is fifty

* In stedde of Ausea it shoulde be Taprobane

Arachosia

* Fisheaters

The Iland of the Sunne

* Rasigut

fifty miles. Then are there thrée Iles : about which there come forth salt water Snakes of twenty cubits long. Hére it is to be declared, howe the way lyeth from Alexandria in Egypt vnto Inde.

The way from Alexandria in Egypt vnto Inde

Fyrst yée must goe by water vppe the Nyle wyth a Northeast wynde vnto Copton. Then by lande vnto Hydreum. From thence passing ouer certaine mansions, ye come to Berenice wheras is a Hauē of the red Sea. After that, ye must arriue at a Hauen of Arabie called Ocelis. The next arriuall vnto that is Muzirū, a Marte Towne of Inde, diffamed for Sea Rouers. Afterward by diuers Hauens yée come to Cottonare, to which Towne they conuey theyr pepper in boates made of one whole Trunke. Those that goe to Inde take water eyther before the beginning of the dogge dayes, or immediatly after the beginning of them, in the mids of Summer. And when they come backe againe they saile in December. The spéediest wynd out of Inde, warde is the Northeast. But when they come to the Red sea, then must eyther a Southeast or a full South winde serue. The largenesse of Inde is reported to be seauen thousand and fifty myles. The space of Carmania is a hundred myles, a part wherof is not wythout Vynes. Moreouer, they haue a kind of men that liue by nothing els but by the flesh of Tortoyses, rugged and hayrie all sauing the face, which alonelie hath a thynne skinne, and they be clad in skynnes of fishes. They are named * Chelonophages.

Tortoyseaters

Iulius Solinus Polyhistor.

CAP. LXVII.

Of the Gulfe of Persia, *and the Gulfe of* Arabic, *and of the* Azanian *Sea.*

The Gulfe of Persia,

The Gulfe of Arabic

Persia,

Susa,

The vncertaintie of measuring in Persia,

THe red sea breaketh into these Coasts, and is deuided into two Gulfs. Whereof, that which is toward the East, is called the Gulfe of Persia, because the Persians inhabit that coast. It is in compasse fiue thousande and twenty myles about. The other Gulfe ouer against which lyeth Arabic) is called the Arabick Gulfe, and the Ocean that floweth in there, is called the Azanian Sea. Uppon Carmania ioyneth Persia, which beginneth at the Ilande Aphrodisia, welthy of sundry sortes of ryches, translated sometime into ŷ name of Parthians, stretching fiftie myles along the sea coast, where it faceth the West. The noblest Towne of that Realme is Susa, in which is the temple of *Susia Diana*. A hundred and fiue and thirty myles from Susa, is the towne Babytace, all the inhabiters whereof (for the hatred they beare to golde,) doo bye vp this kynde of metall, and delue it deepe in the ground, to the intent they shoulde not be defiled with the vse thereof, and so worke vnrighteously for couetousnesse sake. Heereabouts is most vncertaine measuring of grounds, and not wyth out cause, inasmuch as some nations about Persis meet theyr lands by Schænes, some by Parasanges, and othersome

thersome after an unknowne manner, so that theyr uncertaine order in méeting, maketh that a man cannot tell what measure to trust unto.

CAP. LXVIII.

Of Parthia, *and of King* Cyrus *tombe.*

PArthia is so large a Country, that on yͤ southside it encloseth the red sea, and on the North side the Hyrcanian Sea. In it are eightéene Kingdoms which are devided into two parts. Eleuen of them which are called the upper kingdoms, beginne at the borders of Armenie, and passe along the Caspian sea coast, to the land of the Scithians, with whom they liue like good peaceable neighbors. The other seauen nether kingdoms (for so they terme thē) haue on the East the Aries and Arians, on the South Carmania, on the West the Medes, and on the North the Hyrcanians. And Media it selfe, running overthwart on the west side, encloseth both the kingdoms of Parthia. On the North it is bounded with Armenia, on the East it beholdeth the Caspians, on yͤ South Persis, and from thence this Coast passeth forth to a Castle which the Wysemen call Passargada, and here is the Tombe of King *Cyrus*. Media,

CAP. LXIX.

Of Babylon, *of the* Athlantish *Ocean, of the Ilands of the* Gorgons, *and of the fortunate Iles.*

The heade of the Countrey Chaldea is Babylon, builded by *Semyramis*, so renowmed that for the noblenesse thereof, both the Assyrians and Mesopotamians yéelded into the name of Babilon. The Cittie is in compasse thréescore myles, enuironed wyth walles two hundred foote hygh and fiftie foote broade, euery foote béeing longer then the foote which we measure wyth, by the bredth of thrée of our longest fingers. The Ryuer Euphrates runneth through it. There is the Temple of *Belus Iupiter* whom euen the religion it selfe that beléeueth there is a God, reporteth to haue béene the founder of that heauenly discipline. In spyght of thys Citty, the Parthyans builded Ctesiphon. But nowe it is time to retyre to the Coasts of the Ocean, and to call backe my penne into Aethyop. For as wee haue alreadye tolde howe the Athlantish Sea taketh his beginning at the west and at Spayne: so it is also conuenient to be declared, from whence hee beginneth first to beare the name of Atlas in these partes of the worlde also. The Azanian Sea holdeth on vnto the Coaste of Aethyop. The Aethiopian Sea continueth from thence

Babylon,

Ctesiphon

to

to the Promontorie Mossylicum, and from thence forth it taketh againe the name of the Athlantish Ocean. Therefore, whereas many haue helde opinion, that all that part is not possible to bee sayled by reason of the exceeding heate: *Iuba* auoucheth the contrarye. And for assured proofe that the matter is so indeede, hee maketh a rehearsall of the Nations & Ilandes by the way: giuing vs to vnderstande, that all that Sea is saylable from Inde vnto the straights of Marrock: so as it be when the wynde lyeth Southwest & by west, the blast whereof is able to driue anie Nauie by Arabie, Egypt, and Mauritanie, so they direct theyr course from that Promontory of Inde which some call Lepten acran, and othersome name Drepanum. Moreouer, he added the places of harbrough and the distance of them one from another. For from the promontorie of Inde to the Ilande Malachus, they affyrme to bee fifteene hundred myles. From Malachus to Scæneon two hundred twenty fiue miles. From thence to the Ilande Sadanus a hundred and fiftie myles: and so is made to the open Sea, eyght hundred threescore and fifteene myles.

The nauigation from Inde to Spayne

The same *Iuba* so striueth against the opinion of manie which saie that most parte of this Coast is vninhabitable of mankind by reason of the heate of the Sunne, that he affyrmeth the Merchantmen to bee troubled in their passage out of the Iles of Arabie, which the Arabians called Ascitæ possesse, who haue that name of their doings. For they ioyne borders together, and couer them ouer with Leather, and sayling forth in this kinde of Shyppe, assaile the passengers with venomed Darts.

For Askos in Greeke signifieth a bottle or a Tubbe.

And hee affyrmeth also that the scorched Countries of Aethiop are inhabited by the nations of the Icthyophages and Troglodits, of whom the Troglodits are

The Troglodits

ſo ſwift a foote, that they ouertake the wilde Beaſtes whom they chace. The Icthyophags are able to ſwim in the ſalt water as well as the verye Beaſtes of the Sea.

In ſerching the Athlantiſh Sea euen to the weſt hee maketh mention of the Iles of the Gorgons alſo. The Gorgon Iles (as we vnderſtand) are oueragainſt the Promontorie which wee call * Heſperionkeras. These are inhabited by the Monſtars called Gorgons: and ſurelie a monſtrous nation poſſeſſeth them yet. They are diſtant from the maine land two dayes ſayling. *Xenophon Lampſacenus* hath reported that *Hanno* King of the Afers waſted ouer into them, and founde women there as ſwyft as byrds, and that of all the number that were ſeene, but two could bee taken, which were ſo rough and rugged of bodye, that for a remembraunce of the ſtrange ſight, hee hung vp theyr two ſkinnes for a wonder among other gyfts in the Temple of *Iuno*, which continued there vnto the deſtruction of Carthage.

The Gorgon Iles.

* The weſterne horne.

Beyond the Gorgons are the Iles of the Heſperides, which (as *Seboſus* affyrmeth) are withdrawn fortie dayes ſayling into the innermoſt hart of the Sea. They report that the fortunate Iles lye againſt the left ſide of Mauritanie, which *Iuba* ſayth are ſituate vnder the South, but next vnto the Weſt. By reaſon of the names of theſe, I ſuppoſe a great wonder is looked for: but the matter is not equall to the fame of the worde.

The Canaries

In the firſt of them which is called Ombrion, neither is nor hath beene anie houſes. The toppes of the Hyls are watry with Pooles. Reedes growe vp to the bygnes of Trees. Thoſe of them that be blacke, when they be preſſed yeelde a moſt bitter liquor, but thoſe that bee white, yeeld a iuyce good to make drinke of.

They

They say that another of those Iles is named Iunoma, wherein are a fewe cotages ilfauoredly pyked at the toppes. The third is nère vnto this and of ẏ same name, but all is bare and naked. The fourth is called * Capraria, which swarmeth beyond al measure with monstrous great Lucerts. *Goateland

Next followeth * Niuaria, where the ayre is thick and clowdie, and therefore euer snowing. And lastlie * Canaria replenished with Dogs of excèding hugenesse, whereof two were presented to King *Iuba*. In that Ile remain some foundations of buildings. Ther is great plenty of byrds, fieldes full of fruitful Trèes, places bearing Dates, great store of Pyneapples, abounndance of Honney, and Ryuers swarming wyth Fysshes called Silures. Also it is sayde that the wauing Sea casteth vppe monstrous beastes vppon the land, which lying styll there and rotting, infect all thinges wyth an horrible stinche, and therefore the qualitie of those Ilands agrèe not altogether to their name. *Snowland, *Dogland Much like a Sturgion

FINIS.